Elizabeth

VIRGIN QUEEN

Philippa Jones was an historian and read Egyptology
at Cambridge University. She lived in Bristol and
had worked at Bristol's Museum and University.
She published many books and articles, including
the critically acclaimed *The Other Tudors:
Henry VIII's Mistresses and Bastards*.

ॐ

By the same author

*The Other Tudors:
Henry VIII's Mistresses and Bastards*

Elizabeth
VIRGIN QUEEN

PHILIPPA JONES

METRO BOOKS
New York

METRO BOOKS
New York

An Imprint of Sterling Publishing
387 Park Avenue South
New York, NY 10016

This 2011 edition published by Metro Books by arrangement
with New Holland Publishers (UK) Ltd.

Publisher: Aruna Vasudevan
Editor: Elise Bradbury
Inside Design: Sarah Williams
Cover Design: Vanessa Green
Production: Melanie Dowland

ISBN: 978-1-4351-3292-4

For information about custom editions, special sales, and premium
and corporate purchases, please contact Sterling Special Sales at
800-805-5489 or specialsales@sterlingpublishing.com

2 4 6 8 10 9 7 5 3 1

www.sterlingpublishing.com

Contents

Illustrations

❧

Acknowledgements

Every author worthy of their salt has reason to thank their publishers, those largely unsung heroes who turn our thoughts and endeavours into the finished product we hope you will enjoy. However, I have particular cause to tender my thanks to Aruna Vasudevan, my Publisher, and Elise Bradbury, my Editor, as well as all the people at New Holland for their unflagging support and guidance, including some serious editing.

In mid-2009 I was diagnosed with cancer and have been undergoing some pretty aggressive chemotherapy for the last six months. Without their help, this book might not have seen the light of day. I won't bore you or put you off your lunch by giving a short discourse on the side effects of chemotherapy; suffice to say that it would take a large sum of cash in excess of that won by the couple from Cirencester [£56,000,000 on the Lottery] to persuade me to do it again.

I thoroughly enjoyed researching and writing this book, and watched in awe as Aruna and Elise turned my initial text into this finished product. A poor 'thank you' hardly seems to do them justice, but I offer it anyway. *Thank you.*

As Elizabeth herself wrote to François, Duc d'Alençon in May 1581:

'It is time to finish those uneven lines which keep you from your affairs, praying the Creator to keep you in His holy keeping, having trusted myself very cordially in your hands.

Your very assured as well as obliged',

Philippa Jones

Introduction

❧

'... he [Robert Dudley] hath given her [Elizabeth] a child ...
if she hath not, he hath put one to the making.' [1]
—Ann Dove, 1560

'My Lord Robert [Dudley] hath had five children by the Queen,
and she never goeth in progress but to be delivered.' [2]
—Henry Hawkins, 1581

Elizabeth I (1533–1603; Queen of England and Ireland 1558–1603), the last of the Tudor monarchs, reigned over a golden age in English history. The Elizabethan age is known for a flowering of literature and poetry – the time of Shakespeare, Spenser and Marlowe – as well as for establishing England as a seafaring power, whose explorers sailed to distant lands to establish colonies and trade. Regal, beautiful and independent, this indomitable Queen presided over a domestic and European political landscape of intrigue, where courtiers and officials vied for attention and favour, and Catholics and Protestants struggled for dominance. As a woman of great intellect, born to Henry VIII, a man known for his significant achievements, as well as an extremely complicated love life, Elizabeth had a multitude of reasons to choose a path of independence.

As a girl, Elizabeth had witnessed the ruthless banishment and execution of her mother, Anne Boleyn, when she no longer served the King's purpose. As a young princess, Elizabeth was herself in and out of favour, observing at firsthand the machinations of political ambition and how family could turn against one in an instant, leading to betrayal and even death in some circumstances. A cautious reaction to marriage would, therefore, be an understandable reaction for any young girl in her position.

For Elizabeth, growing up at a time when marriages, particularly those of royalty, were largely arranged to forge alliances that could potentially lead a kingdom into war, it might have seemed a wise course of action to remain unmarried. In reality, however, probably a mixture of factors led Elizabeth to choose this path, including her own desire for independence, free from the influence of a man behind her throne, fears for her own future and that of her country's and an innate distrust of men, resulting from her own early experiences with her father, Henry VIII, and later with such men as Thomas Seymour, her guardian's husband. Perhaps it was simply that Elizabeth fell in love with a man that she could not have – for whatever reason, Elizabeth would never choose to marry.

This decision proved to be a major headache for her government, who tirelessly sought to find a husband for Elizabeth. Her decision would later be used to show how much the popular Queen was devoted to her people. She would be called 'Good Queen Bess', 'Gloriana' (following the 1588 victory against the Spanish Armada) and, of course, the 'Virgin Queen'. A highly intelligent woman and an articulate and talented public speaker, Elizabeth made a virtue out of her reported virginity and promoted it as a pious ideal, with considerable success.

Elizabeth clearly enjoyed the company of men, however. She was attractive and valued the attentions of handsome young admirers. As Queen, she had several 'favourites', men who enjoyed her attentions, while benefiting from such powerful patronage. Rumours abounded about Elizabeth's lovers, who included her closest minister, Robert Dudley, 1st Earl of Leicester. There was even some talk of the existance of an illegitimate child or children resulting from at least one of these relationships – but were these just rumours, unpleasant gossip put about to discredit the Queen or the men she associated with at the time? Or, is it at all possible that Elizabeth was the mother of one or more illegitimate children? This book seeks to examine the possibility that the Virgin Queen was a myth and that Elizabeth not only enjoyed physical relationships with some of her favourites, but also may have had children as a result, who were secreted away to be brought up by other people.

This, of course, raises several issues, most important of which is the question of whether Elizabeth could actually have children. Was it a physical possibility? The matter of Elizabeth's health was one that concerned and fascinated foreign ambassadors at the time, who faithfully reported every detail of ill health or any evidence of her menstrual cycle to their masters. Elizabeth's ability to bear children was, after all, of supreme importance to any foreign king, prince or noble who might consider making an offer of marriage, as the birth of a child as heir to the English throne was politically important. Evidence from her physicians seems to suggest that Elizabeth was fully capable of giving birth to a healthy child. The second question must, therefore, be – were there really any men with whom she might have been tempted into a sexual relationship, bearing in mind the risk and the logistical difficulties involved? Two immediately spring to mind – Thomas Seymour and Robert Dudley, 1st Earl of Leicester. Seymour was the brother of Jane Seymour, Henry VIII's third wife; he courted Elizabeth when she was a vulnerable teenager, while he was married to Catherine Parr, her guardian and the sixth wife of the late King. Robert Dudley was the man whom Elizabeth teased, fought with, punished, forgave and adored for nigh on 30 years.

In addition to Seymour and Dudley, there were other possible candidates, men with whom Elizabeth might have indulged in intimate relationships, including Thomas Heneage, Christopher Hatton, Walter Raleigh and Robert Devereux, 2nd Earl of Essex – men with whom she exchanged flirtations, at the least. If rumours are to be believed, Hatton was certainly a possible father of the Queen's child.

Elizabeth's relationships with her various suitors were never simple, though. For most men the separation of Elizabeth *the woman*, and Elizabeth *the monarch*, Queen of one of the most important and powerful European nations at the time, was clearly impossible. For the latter reason, it is even less likely that if Elizabeth did give birth to an illegitimate child either before or during her reign that its father was of foreign origin, as this would have threatened the delicate balance of power in Europe.

Elizabeth's wooing by François, Duc d'Alençon, the brother of Henri III, King of France, is a case in point. This courtship dragged on for more than a decade throughout the 1570s, with fluctuating intensity as the Duke fell in and out of favour with the Queen's Council. In 1581, when Elizabeth was nearly 50 years of age, she stated to the French Ambassador that she would marry the Duke, although she later reneged on this decision. Despite the heat of the ardour expressed in the Duke's letters to Elizabeth, and the possibility that they had been physically intimate, it was never suggested that the Queen had borne a bastard to the heir to the French throne, someone whom she could have married at any time she chose.

Another issue that arises when considering Elizabeth's intimate relationships and possible children is a logistical one: how could she have kept the birth of a child or children a secret while inhabiting such a public position in English society? Before Elizabeth ascended the throne, it might just about have been possible. After the death of Henry VIII in 1547, when Elizabeth was 13 years old, her 9-year-old half-brother, Edward, who had succeeded to the throne, became the focus of attention for the continuation of the royal line. Even if

Edward died before he could bear any heirs, his half-sister Mary, the eldest daughter of Henry VIII and Catherine of Aragon, was next in line to the throne and might hopefully mother a future King or Queen. Elizabeth, at this time was viewed as illegitimate following the execution of her mother for treason. She was, therefore, outside of the real seat of power.

Elizabeth's household was small and she was surrounded by a small group of attendants who would go to any lengths to serve and protect her. Chief among them were Katherine Champernowne (who married a kinsman of Elizabeth's and became her beloved 'Kat Ashley') and Blanche Parry. Both women were extremely loyal – Kat Ashley was actually imprisoned twice in the Tower of London rather than betray Elizabeth, while Blanche Parry joined the household when Elizabeth was an infant and was still in her service when Blanche died, aged 82. Those who truly loved Elizabeth formed a veritable human wall around her and any of them could have easily conspired to hide a pregnancy, and help place a baby safely and secretly with a suitable family.

The first rumour of Elizabeth's pregnancy arose when she was 14, living in Whitehall and Chelsea under the protection of her stepmother, the Queen Dowager Catherine Parr, Henry VIII's last wife from 1543 to 1547. Four months after the King's death, Catherine married her fourth husband, Thomas Seymour, the Lord High Admiral of England. Seymour had great political ambitions and wanted to displace his brother Edward as the guardian of the young King, Edward VI. By marrying Catherine in secret, he risked both the King's and his own brother's displeasure, but he was forgiven as Edward VI found him entertaining.

Seymour is arguably the first man with whom Elizabeth fell in love. In his thirties at the time, and handsome, flirtatious and clever, Seymour quickly won over the young Elizabeth. Rumours

13

began to circulate about the morning visits that he paid to Elizabeth's bedchamber and although she denied any impropriety she left the household in 1548 – possibly for her own protection, possibly because Catherine was now pregnant and wanted rid of a young, attractive girl from her household. There could have been another more sinister reason, however, such as Elizabeth's unexpected pregnancy. Certainly, there were rumours at the time, and the nature of their relationship came under question after Catherine Parr's tragic death in childbirth when Seymour made an unsuccessful application to the Privy Council to become Elizabeth's suitor. Whether his suit was motivated by genuine love or his own political ambitions, when Seymour was arrested for treason, Elizabeth was implicated in the plot as it was widely suspected that she had enjoyed a sexual relationship with Seymour; some even claimed that she had fallen pregnant. Although Elizabeth denied this vehemently, she became more wary in her dealings with men after this time. Seymour was eventually executed in 1549.

Another period during which Elizabeth may have given birth to a child was between 1560 and 1580, when Elizabeth was Queen and was aged between 27 and 47. The most likely candidate as father of the Queen's child was Robert Dudley. This extraordinarily handsome man, who the Queen called 'Dear Robin', was most probably the great love of Elizabeth's life from 1559 until the day that he died in 1588. Rumours of a child from their union began to surface around 1560, two years after Elizabeth ascended to the English throne. The stories continued well into the 1580s, when the Queen was actually no longer physically capable of bearing children.

In 1560, however, it seemed likely to some of the ambassadors at Elizabeth's Court that the Queen might actually marry Robert Dudley – if it were possible. The obstacle to their union lay in the existence of Amy Robsart, Robert Dudley's wife. Amy lived quietly in the country, away from Court, and suffered from a long-term illness and depression. Reports at the time suggest that Elizabeth and Dudley were waiting for Amy to die naturally before they married, but, in 1560, Amy was found dead at the foot of her staircase, her neck broken. Despite the verdict of accidental death reached by the court, many believed that Dudley had ordered his wife's murder, unwilling to wait and afraid that Elizabeth's interest might stray elsewhere. Other theories indicate that Amy may have committed suicide. However, if Amy was murdered, available evidence suggests that it was not at the Earl of Leicester's hands.

Even so, if the Queen had a secret child with Robert Dudley, how would she have managed it? By that time, Elizabeth I headed a household of more than 1,000 people and rarely had any time to herself. She was constantly observed by the officials of her Court, who were desperate to stay abreast of events, as well as by the spies and representatives of various foreign powers. Logistically, how viable was it for the Queen to find sufficient time alone with a lover, hide any signs of a pregnancy for a long nine months and then have a secret labour and birth? In actual fact, although it would have been difficult, it was not impossible. As a contemporary, Henry Hawkins, reported, in 1581, the Queen often went on summer progresses (royal visits to towns or aristocratic homes). In a host's house, Elizabeth might retire alone to the library to read her dispatches or write letters in peace. The Queen's rooms might be too small to allow even a small number of people to congregate, enabling her to be alone, even if briefly, and doors that should have been kept locked could be left unlocked by a loyal servant or with the right motivation to the recipient. When Elizabeth believed she was dying, she made a substantial bequest to Robert Dudley's valet – a man who could have guided his master to various assignations with the Queen and stood watch to prevent them being discovered.

If this did happen and the Queen fell pregnant and was able to give birth in secret, there remains the question of the identity of her child or children. Several candidates have been put forward by historians over the years. Three – Sir Francis Bacon, Edward de Vere, 17th Earl of Oxford, and Robert Devereux, 2nd Earl of Essex – were prominent members of the Elizabethan Court, men whom the Queen admired or favoured. But would Elizabeth have really publicly favoured a son whose existence she had gone to such trouble to hide in the first place?

Perhaps a slightly more plausible candidate might be Arthur Dudley, a man who claimed to be the illegitimate son of Elizabeth and Robert Dudley? Another possibility was John Harington, Elizabeth's godson. Born in 1560, he grew up in the household of Isabella Markham, Elizabeth's loyal maid of honour before she became Queen, and John Harington, Senior, who had served under Sir Thomas Seymour. When Seymour was accused of treason, Harington had suffered imprisonment in the Tower rather than betray his commander. John Harington, the younger, earned himself a place at Court and he also became a great favourite of the Queen. He is believed to have been one of the last people to speak to Elizabeth before she died.

In the following chapters, I examine Elizabeth's life both before and after she ascended the English throne, exploring how possible it is that the Virgin Queen enjoyed intimate relationships with one or more of her favourites and bore at least one illegitimate child, as a result.

Elizabeth

the early years

1

The Young Elizabeth

'As goodly a child as hath been seen.'
—William Kingston to Lord Lisle, April 1534

❧

In 1527, at the age of 36, Henry VIII (1491–1547; King of England 1509–47) started on a tortuous path that eventually resulted in a break with the Roman Catholic Church, the English Reformation and the founding of the Protestant Church of England. It also led to the King's 'Great Matter' – Henry's divorce from Catherine of Aragon (1485–1536) and his claim that Princess Mary, his daughter from that marriage, was illegitimate. Arguably, the cause of these momentous ruptures was that the King was facing middle age, married to an aging Queen who had thus far failed to give him a male heir.

By 1528, when Cardinal Thomas Wolsey was considering the matter of a possible divorce, Henry VIII was already infatuated by Anne Boleyn, the sister of one of his alleged mistresses. But Anne had her eye on being more than just the King's next lady love; from 1526 to the early 1530s, while Anne regularly proclaimed her love for the King, she also withheld her sexual favours from him. She played her hand with consummate skill, as in Henry's early love letters to Anne it is clear that marriage was not on his mind: 'I promise you … that also I will take you for my only mistress, rejecting from thought and affection all others save yourself to serve you only."[1] In turn, Anne frequently commented in her letters to the King that although her heart and soul were his to enjoy, her body would never be. By refusing to become Henry's mistress, Anne caught and retained his interest. Henry might find casual sexual gratification with others, but it was Anne that he truly wanted; Anne who became his grand passion.

As the years passed and the prospect of Henry's divorce from Catherine of Aragon became more real, Anne began to hint that she might be persuaded to take that 'final step' and give Henry the physical relationship that he craved above all else. In mid-1531 Henry separated from Catherine, and Anne began to take a more open role in the King's life and at Court functions.

In September 1532, Anne was made Marquis of Pembroke, a title not previously held by a woman, and one that brought with it an annual income of £1,000. The title documents stated that the marquisate would pass to Anne's male heirs born 'of her body', breaking with the usually worded 'of her body lawfully begotten', which meant heirs begotten from a married lady.[2] In the following month, Henry went to meet François I, the King of France, at Calais, this time taking Anne with him as his consort. By November, Henry and Anne had adjoining rooms in the Calais Exchequer and their relationship appears to have become a sexual one. Certainly by January 1533, Anne believed that she was pregnant.

On 25 January, Henry and Anne were married in a small secret ceremony, although the divorce from Catherine had not yet been finalized. The union could be formally solemnized in church at a later date, ensuring that any child conceived at this time was 'lawfully begotten'. It was not until April of that year that the King sent a deputation to Catherine of Aragon to tell her officially that she was no longer his wife and would be referred to henceforth as the Dowager Princess of Wales, Catherine's title when her first husband, Arthur, Henry's older brother, died. Perhaps unsurprisingly, Catherine refused to accept Henry's decision, but, in May, Thomas Cranmer, Archbishop of Canterbury, declared their marriage annulled on the grounds that Catherine had consummated her marriage with Prince Arthur. This was an unlikely event given Catherine and Arthur's ages and the state of Arthur's health at the time of their union. Five days later, the Archbishop publicly declared Henry's marriage to Anne valid and she officially became Queen of England – at least to those who recognized the marriage. Anne was six months pregnant at the time.

Finally, Henry's dream of a son seemed to be within his grasp. Anne's pregnancy was difficult, it was true, but the labour itself proved far easier than anticipated. In the end, however, the King was to be bitterly disappointed. On Sunday, 7 September 1533, between 3 p.m. and 4 p.m., Anne Boleyn gave birth to a baby girl. Eustace Chapuys, the Ambassador for Charles V (Holy Roman Emperor 1519–58; King of Spain 1506–56), reported gleefully: 'The king's mistress was delivered of a girl, to the great disappointment and sorrow of the king, of the lady herself, and of others of her party, and to the great shame and confusion of physicians, astrologers, wizards and witches, all of whom affirmed it would be a boy.'[3]

Henry's daughter was christened Elizabeth after his mother – although the King was conspicuously absent from the occasion. Despite the King's obvious disappointment in the sex of his new child, a splendid household was set up for the princess when she was just three months old, in accordance with the custom for babies of royal blood. The nursery was based at Hatfield in Hertfordshire, but Elizabeth was subsequently moved between several sites as each was 'sweetened' (cleaned and aired), including Ashridge House, Hertfordshire; Eltham Palace, London; Hunsdon House and Hertford Castle, both in Hertfordshire; the More near

21

Rickmansworth; Richmond Palace in Surrey and Greenwich Palace in South London.

Although Anne Boleyn visited her daughter, for the most part she was cared for by a large staff. Lady Margaret Bryan was Lady Mistress, the governess with day-to-day control of the nursery. Anne Boleyn would have approved Lady Margaret's appointment, but it was Henry VIII himself who chose Margaret to care for his children. Henry held Margaret in great esteem: she was a distant relative and both Henry and Margaret were descended from Edward III through different sons. Lady Margaret had also been lady-in-waiting to Catherine of Aragon, as well as Lady Mistress to the young Princess Mary, Elizabeth's elder half-sister. Lady Margaret was now made responsible for all the important matters relating to the young Elizabeth, and her parents only saw the child on special occasions.

Blanche Herbert was another key member of Elizabeth's staff. Blanche was Lady Troy, the wife of William Herbert, the illegitimate son of the 1st Earl of Pembroke, and was a governess in Princess Elizabeth's household. She offered a place to her 26-year-old niece, Blanche Parry (her surname was an anglicization of 'ap Harry', a derivation of her father's Christian name, according to Welsh tradition). Blanche became one of Elizabeth's closest and most trusted servants and friends and must have been present at Hatfield in the early months of Elizabeth's life, as she recorded in her epitaph that she saw the baby princess rocked in her cradle. Blanche was well-educated and could read and write in English, Welsh and Latin, as well as run a household, play music, sing, sew and embroider.

While Elizabeth was being established in a fitting manner as Henry VIII's only legally recognized daughter, Mary, his elder daughter by Catherine of Aragon, was declared illegitimate, lost her rank and status as a princess and was exiled from Court. Now called 'Lady Mary', she was forbidden to see her parents and would never see her mother, Catherine, alive again. For the first months Mary lived quietly at Beaulieu in Newhall Boreham, Sussex, with her Lady Governess, Margaret Pole, Countess of Salisbury, but in October of that year, Beaulieu was given to Anne Boleyn's brother.

In December 1533, Mary was sent to Hatfield, where she was forced to act as lady-in-waiting to her half-sister, Elizabeth. She found herself under the authority of Anne Boleyn's uncle and aunt, Sir John Shelton, the Master of the Household, and his wife, Lady Anne; Lady Alice Clere (another Boleyn aunt) ran the household. Refusing to surrender her dignity or her rank, when Mary was asked if she wanted to see the princess, she replied that she 'knew of no other princess in England but herself', adding that the daughter of 'Madame of Pembroke' was 'no princess at all'. Mary commented that as Henry VIII was her father, she would call the infant Elizabeth 'sister', just as she called her father's illegitimate son, Henry Fitzroy, 1st Duke of Richmond, 'brother'.[4]

Mary's position was a difficult one. She was denied permission to attend Catholic Mass (her mother, Catherine of Aragon, was Roman Catholic), and when Henry VIII visited Hatfield, she was deliberately kept out of his way. This treatment continued for the first two-and-a-half years of her half-sister Elizabeth's life, during which time Mary was bullied unmercifully by the Sheltons, humiliated, and was constantly afraid that she would be imprisoned or executed. Historian Alison Plowden has concluded that the treatment Mary received 'turned a gentle, affectionate child into a bigoted, neurotic and bitterly unhappy woman.'[5]

23

Even though Elizabeth was a girl, the birth of a healthy and bonny child was an excellent omen for Henry and suggested that a second, successful pregnancy might result in the birth of a healthy boy. However, in June 1534, Anne miscarried and in July her belief that she might be pregnant again turned out to be false.

By Christmas 1535, Anne was pregnant again, and on 7 January 1536, Catherine of Aragon died. The King and Queen Anne celebrated with festivities; however, on 29 January, the day on which Catherine was buried, Anne miscarried, and this time it was a baby boy. Anne later claimed that she had miscarried after hearing the news that Henry had been seriously injured at a joust, but the King, it seemed, had had enough. He saw the hand of God in his misfortune, reportedly stating, 'God will not give me male children.'[6] At about the same time, Henry's interest in Anne began to wane, and his straying eyes were captured by Jane Seymour, a maid-of-honour at the Court.

It was obvious that the King was tiring of his second wife and was looking for a way out of his marriage. This time it was up to Thomas Cromwell, an adviser to Henry VIII, to find a way out, but divorce seemed an unlikely solution to Henry's predicament. Unlike the Spanish-born Catherine of Aragon, who had been brought to live in a strange land, far from her family and native country, Anne Boleyn was English and, moreover, had connections to a large number of prominent noble families. Furthermore, she had lawfully given birth to the King's child, a daughter who might make a bid for the throne in the future. This time, Thomas Cromwell built up a case against Anne Boleyn, accusing her of sexual affairs with several men, including Mark Smeaton, one of the Court musicians, Henry Norris, Francis Weston and William Brereton. But more lay in store for Anne – part of the formal charges read that, while married to the King, Anne had had relations with her own brother, George, Lord Rochford, Gentleman of the Privy Chamber. Anne was alleged to have 'procured and incited [George] … to violate and carnally know her, with her tongue in the said George's mouth, and the said George's tongue in hers, and also with open-mouthed kisses, gifts and jewels.'[7]

Cromwell was careful that the charge should stipulate that Anne Boleyn had only been unfaithful to the King *after* the Princess Elizabeth's birth in 1533. Henry wanted Elizabeth to be acknowledged as his daughter, but at the same time he wanted her removed from any future claim to the succession.

As well as the adultery charges, Anne was accused of planning to poison Lady Mary and Henry Fitzroy, possible rivals to the throne. Anne and her reported lovers were also alleged to have openly discussed Henry VIII's death. Found guilty of these charges, Anne was arrested on 2 May 1536 and moved to the Tower of London to await the King's justice. The five men accused of being her lovers, including her brother, George, were also arrested. On 17 May, they were executed. On the same day, Henry divorced Anne, making their marriage null and void, and thus Elizabeth illegitimate. Two days later, on 19 May at 8 a.m, Anne Boleyn was beheaded on Tower Green in London.

While Anne Boleyn was being buried in haste within the confines of the Tower of London, Henry VIII visited Jane Seymour at her lodgings at Whitehall Palace.

⌒♨

Elizabeth and her half-sister Mary were at Hunsdon House while events unfolded with dizzying swiftness in London. When Anne Boleyn was executed, Elizabeth was just two years and eight months old.

On 20 May, the day after Anne's execution, Henry VIII and Jane Seymour were formally betrothed. Even those who had previously disapproved of Henry's marriage to Anne found the timing distasteful.

25
♨

Ten days later, on 30 May, the couple were married in the chapel at York Place. This time Henry took no chances. A new law was passed making Jane's children his only lawful offspring, but should she fail to have children, Henry was free to nominate his successor. If Henry Fitzroy, his illegitimate son, was his choice, the King was unlucky, as the young man died on 22 July.

In June 1536, Elizabeth was formally proclaimed illegitimate. With this turn of events, it seemed possible that the Lady Mary and her father might become reconciled. Instead, Mary found herself under more pressure than ever, first to acknowledge the King as Head of the Protestant Church in England when she was herself staunchly Catholic, and also to accept that his marriage to her mother, Catherine of Aragon, had been unlawful, thereby making Mary illegitimate. Heartsick and disillusioned, in July of that year Mary finally agreed to these demands, although she begged Spanish Ambassador Chapuys to tell the Pope that she had only agreed under duress and remained a true Catholic at heart and the lawful child of her father and mother in the eyes of God.

Mary's outward show of obedience was enough to satisfy Henry. Accompanied by the new Queen, he visited Mary at Hunsdon, where Jane presented her stepdaughter with a diamond ring and the King gave her an order for 1,000 crowns. As long as Mary remained dutiful, the days of poverty and neglect were over, it seemed. Chapuys, happy to see Mary back in the King's graces, wrote: 'It is impossible to describe the King's kind and affectionate behaviour towards the Princess [Mary], his daughter, and the deep regret he said he felt at his having kept her so long away from him ... There was nothing but ... such brilliant promises for the future, that no father could have behaved better towards his daughter.'8

Mary was permitted to return to Court and given a household suitable to her standing as the King's daugher, albeit an illegitimate one. Elizabeth, stripped of the title of princess, still shared an establishment with Mary, who was now the principal mistress of the household. Mary's servants, driven away during her days of torment, were allowed back. Queen Jane treated Mary well, befriending her husband's oldest child, and returning some of the signs of rank that Mary had been denied while Anne Boleyn had been alive. Jane had been a lady-in-waiting to Catherine of Aragon and had much admired her.

One of Jane's first requests of the King was that Mary be allowed to attend her, which Henry was pleased to allow. Mary was chosen to sit at the table opposite the King and Queen and to hand Jane her napkin at meals when she washed her hands. For one who had been banished to sit with the servants at Hatfield, this was an obvious sign of her restoration to the King's good graces. Jane was often seen walking hand-in-hand with Mary, making sure that they passed through the door together, a public acknowledgement that Mary was back in favour. In August, Chapuys wrote, 'the treatment of the princess [Mary] is every day improving. She never did enjoy such liberty as she does now ...'[9] Meanwhile, Henry, wary of relying on Jane to give him a son, raised the question of the 20-year-old Mary's marriage – the next best thing to a son, after all, would be a healthy grandson.

In October 1536, an anonymous letter to the Cardinal de Bellay, Bishop of Paris, described Mary and Elizabeth's situation at Court: 'Madame Marie is now the first after the Queen, and sits at table opposite her, a little lower down ... Madame Isabeau [Elizabeth] is not at that table, though the King is very affectionate to her. It is said he loves her very much.'[10]

Mary appeared to show great affection towards her little sister Elizabeth during this time, giving her small gifts from her own privy purse. Mary wrote to her father, who was now in the happy

27

position of being able to be gracious to both his daughters, 'My sister Elizabeth is in good health, thanks be to our Lord, and such a child toward, as I doubt not but your Highness shall have cause to rejoice of in time coming.'[11]

For Elizabeth, although bereft of her mother, there was a happy occurrence in June 1536. Katherine Champernowne joined the household as a Waiting Gentlewoman. Katherine, whom the little Elizabeth would come to call 'Kat', was the daughter of Sir Philip Champernowne of Bere and Modbury, in Devonshire. She was appointed on the recommendation of Thomas Cromwell. The Champernownes were a very well-connected West Country family. Kat's cousin, another Katherine, married twice, becoming the mother of the notable Elizabethan explorers and colonizers, Sir Humphrey Gilbert and Sir Walter Raleigh.

Kat became Elizabeth's Governess in 1537; she married Sir John Ashley, a distant cousin of Anne Boleyn, in 1545, and stayed in Elizabeth's service until her death. She was a well-educated woman and taught the three-year-old girl her letters and numbers. Kat joined a household in turmoil, however. In August, Kat's superior and Elizabeth's Governess at the time, Lady Margaret Bryan, wrote to Thomas Cromwell of her concerns about Elizabeth's rich diet, lack of appropriate clothing and the confusion in her status under the stewardship of Sir John Shelton (the Governor of the household at Hunsdon). The letter sums up all the anguish, frustration and confusion that resulted from the death and disgrace of Elizabeth's mother:

> … Now it is so, my Lady Elizabeth is put from that degree she was afore, and what degree she is of now, I know not but by hearsay. Therefore I know not how to order her, nor myself, nor none of hers that I have the rule of – that is her

women and grooms, beseeching you to be good lord to my lady, and to all hers; that she may have some raiment; for she hath neither gown, nor kirtle, nor petticoat, nor no manner of linen nor smocks ...

My lord, Mr Shelton would have my Lady Elizabeth to dine and sup every day at the board of estate. Alas! My lord, it is not meet for a child of her age to keep such rule yet. I promise you, my lord, I dare not take it upon me to keep her grace in health an' she keep that rule. For there she shall see divers meats, and fruits, and wine, which it would be hard for me to restrain her grace from ... She is yet too young to correct greatly ... Wherefore I show your lordship this my desire, beseeching you, my lord, that my lady have a mess [meal] of meat at her own lodging ... according as my Lady Mary's grace had afore, and to be ordered in all things as her grace was afore.[12]

There is no confirmation that the new clothes, or cloth to make them, ever arrived, but Lady Margaret's plea for a simple diet for the child, to be served in her private quarters, was addressed. On 16 August, Sir John Shelton wrote to Cromwell, 'I perceive by your letter the King's pleasure that my lady Elizabeth shall keep her chamber and not come abroad.' Shelton also requested money to buy food for the household; the King's warrant had not arrived on time.[13]

It is impossible to know the extent to which Elizabeth may have been affected by her parents' divorce and her mother's death. Two particular events possibly made some impression on the young child, though. The first occurred in January 1536, when Catherine of Aragon died at Kimbolton. As Ambassador Chapuys reported to Charles V:

The King dressed entirely in yellow from head to foot, with the single exception of a white feather in his cap. His bastard daughter Elizabeth was triumphantly taken to church to the sounds of trumpets and with great display. Then, after dinner, the King went to the Hall where the Ladies were dancing, and there made great demonstrations of joy, and at last went to his own apartments, took the little bastard in his arms, and began to show her first to one, then to another, and did the same on the following days.[14]

A second event occurred only a few months later, when, just days before her arrest, Henry VIII was angry at Anne Boleyn. Whether Elizabeth was old enough to recall it is unclear, but after she came to power in 1558, it was brought to her attention by Alexander Ales, a member of an embassy to the German Princes, who wrote to Elizabeth claiming: '… I saw the sainted Queen your mother, carrying you, still a little baby, in her arms, and entreating the most serene King your father … The faces and gestures of the speakers plainly showed the King was angry …'[15]

Elizabeth was certainly aware of a change in attitude towards her. She is credited with saying to Sir John Shelton, who had been deputed to explain to her the changes in her lifestyle following her mother's death, 'How haps it, Governor, yesterday my Lady Princess, and today but my lady Elizabeth?'[16]

Margaret Bryan, Kate Champernowne, Blanche Parry and others, still remained part of her immediate circle, but Elizabeth would never set eyes on her mother again, and she would see her father far less frequently. Her sister, Mary, was more kind to her, it was true, now that they were both victims of Court intrigue. And though both would have to cope with a string of further stepmothers, Jane Seymour was certainly considerate towards both Mary and Elizabeth.

There were to be futher changes in the Royal Court. In March 1537, Jane announced that she was pregnant, to Henry's great pleasure. On 16 September, the Queen retired to Hampton Court, and on 9 October she went into labour, giving birth to a baby son, Edward, the new heir to the throne, at 2 a.m. on 12 October 1537.

The Court and the city of London immediately burst into celebration. People poured into the streets to celebrate the news. Pork, supplied by the Court, was roasted over open fires and the water conduits ran with ale and wine. A special song was written and printed that soon flooded the city:

> *'God save King Henry with all his power,*
> *And Prince Edward, that goodly flower,*
> *With all his lords of great honour ...'*[17]

On 15 October, the christening of the new prince took place in the chapel at Hampton Court. Henry and Jane remained in their apartments while the splendid procession wound its way down to the chapel. Among all the magnificence, the young Elizabeth played her part, carrying the christening robe. As she was barely four, Edward Seymour, Jane's brother, carried her. On the way out, as the christened Prince Edward was carried back to his parents, little Elizabeth walked hand-in-hand with her sister Mary, also the baby's godmother, helped by Blanche Herbert, who supported the train of her elaborate robes.

This was another event that Elizabeth would remember: the kindness of her sister, the emotional tears of her father, the frailty of her stepmother, not yet recovered from the ordeal of childbirth, obliged to watch the procession from her rooms while wrapped in velvet and furs. A week later it was all over: on 24 October, the 29-year-old Jane Seymour died of puerperal fever – a form of septicaemia that often resulted after childbirth in those times. On

12 November, Henry VIII's third wife and the mother of his only legitimate son was given a magnificent funeral, attended by the whole of the Tudor Court. It may be safely assumed that Elizabeth was there: her sister, Mary, headed the cortege as Chief Mourner.

❦

Henry VIII was not in a hurry to choose his next Queen: he now had a legitimate male heir. He lavished love and care on his son, and also took time to consider how his daughters, illegitimate or not, could be used as political assets in terms of future alliances through marriage. Henry's priority was to prevent an alliance between the great Catholic powers of France and Spain. With this in mind, he offered himself in marriage to various French princesses, and then tried to negotiate a marriage with the niece of Charles V.

As for his daughters, in 1538, there was a suggestion that Elizabeth, now aged five, might marry one of Charles V's nephews, either Maximilian, heir to the Holy Roman Empire, Ferdinand, Archduke of Austria, or Charles, Archduke of Austria. This political manoeuvring was not taken too seriously despite a report by Chapuys in March 1538 that he had seen Elizabeth and she was 'certainly very pretty'.[18] Charles V might have wanted an alliance with England, but not in this way.

Meanwhile, Elizabeth's childhood seemed to be progressing well. In December 1539, Sir Thomas Wriothesley was sent to see the six-year-old Elizabeth at Hertford Castle, where she was spending Christmas. He brought messages from her father, who wished her and her household a happy Christmas. Sir Thomas reported back favourably:

> When I had done with her Grace [Mary], I went then to my Lady Elizabeth's Grace, and to the same made the

King's Majesty's most hearty commendations, declaring that his Highness desired to hear of her health and sent her his blessing. She gave humble thanks, enquiring again of his Majesty's welfare, and that with as great a gravity as she had been forty years old. If she be no worse educated than she now appeareth to me, she will prove of no less honour to womanhood than shall beseem her father's daughter.[19]

With Prince Edward's birth, several changes had been made to Elizabeth's daily routine. Lady Margaret Bryan had left to become Edward's Governess. Blanche Herbert was now head of the household and Kat Champernowne became Elizabeth's Governess. These two women, in particular, provided stability and emotional support for the child. Blanche only left Elizabeth some 10 years later, when she retired, while Kat would remain a loyal companion for life.

Elizabeth was to have three more stepmothers, but there is no evidence that she was ever ill-treated by any of them. Anne of Cleves, a German noblewoman who became Henry VIII's fourth wife in January 1540, went out of her way to befriend her stepdaughters and remained on friendly terms with Mary and Elizabeth even after her brief seven-month marriage to the King had been annulled.

Henry's fifth wife, Catherine Howard, who he wedded immediately after the annulment of his marriage to Anne of Cleves, was said to be poorly educated, selfish and foolish. It appears that she got on badly with Mary who, she said, failed to treat her with 'the same respect as her two predecessors' (Jane Seymour and Anne of Cleves).[20] Catherine tried to have two of Mary's maids, who presumably offended her, sent away from Court. It also cannot have helped that Mary was three years older than her stepmother, and that she was well-educated, beautifully mannered and the daughter of Spanish royalty. She had very little in common with a poor relation from a nouveau-noble family who was barely able to read or write.

Catherine Howard, however, was a close relation of young Elizabeth. Catherine and Anne Boleyn had been first cousins. Some accounts suggest that Queen Catherine made a gift of some small items of inexpensive jewellery to Elizabeth and also invited the girl to sit opposite her at table, just as Queen Jane had done for Mary. However, as Catherine was only Queen of England for 16 months and spent a large proportion of that time away from London under arrest, it is hard to gauge exactly what relationship the two had, if they had one at all.

It is clear, however, that Catherine Howard's beheading for infidelity in 1542 had a lasting impression on the eight-year-old Elizabeth. Many years later, Robert Dudley, who was the same age as Elizabeth and a page to the King at the time, told the French Ambassador that Elizabeth had announced, 'I will never marry.'[21] He sighed as he recalled her words.

The arrest, trial and execution of Catherine Howard, her mother's cousin, must have prompted Elizabeth to recall the circumstances of Anne Boleyn's death. Kat Champernowne may have used the occasion to tell Elizabeth about her mother's death, explaining the political context to ease the horror of Anne Boleyn's condemnation. Although she rarely mentioned her mother, Elizabeth took one of her emblems as her own: a crowned white falcon perched on a tree stump from which grew red and white roses. The Chequers Ring, which is supposed to have belonged to Elizabeth, also still exists; it is hinged and opens to show tiny portraits of Elizabeth and a second lady who looks very similar to Anne Boleyn.

Elizabeth's childhood experiences may explain why she never took the final step to marriage: refusing to put herself wholly in the power of another. Even at her tender age, Elizabeth's vision of married life must have been tainted by her father's treatment of his various wives: Catherine of Aragon had come to a strange land to be pushed aside and left to die in poverty because she failed to have a son. Elizabeth's mother, Anne Boleyn, had been beheaded for treason, while Jane Seymour, her dear stepmother, had died in childbirth. Anne of Cleves had been abandoned by Henry, seemingly on a whim, and now history was repeating itself with Catherine Howard's imprisonment and execution.

Meanwhile, Henry continued his political manoeuvring in planning alliances for his son, Edward, and his daughters. After the Scottish King James V died a week after his daughter Mary's birth in 1542, leaving the baby Queen (Mary, Queen of Scots, 1542–67), Henry had taken an interest in the young girl, thinking to unite Scotland and England through marriage. He immediately entered into negotiations with Mary's Regent, James Hamilton, 2nd Earl of Arran, pressing for the marriage of Mary to his five-year-old son, Prince Edward.

To sweeten the negotiations, Henry suggested that the Regent's son, James Hamilton, might marry the young Elizabeth. As Regent, Hamilton Senior, was the next heir to the Scottish throne should Mary die, thus if both marriages took place, whatever occurred, Scotland and England would eventually unite. The negotiations later faltered when Hamilton Senior attempted to marry Mary, Queen of Scots to his son James, and in 1548, they failed completely when Marie of Guise, the Dowager Queen, took her five-year-old daughter to France and arranged for her betrothal to the three-year-old French Dauphin, François.

Although busy plotting marriages for his children, Henry did not give up on his own needs. In July 1543, he married for the last time, making Catherine Parr, his sixth wife. Elizabeth was nearly 10 years of age at the time of their marriage, and Catherine, of all Henry's wives, had the greatest impact on her. She was a well-educated and intelligent woman, and she formed an immediate bond with both of her stepdaughters. She knew Mary already: as children they had had lessons together, as her mother had been an attendant of Catherine of Aragon.

A contemporary Spanish writer described Catherine Parr as 'quieter than any of the young wives the King had had, and as she knew more of the world she always got on pleasantly with the King, and had no caprices, and paid much honour to Madam Mary and the wives of the nobles.'[22] Catherine and Mary often wrote to each other, exchanging gifts and even lending one another servants. Their friendship surmounted their religious beliefs: Mary was an uncompromising Catholic, as her later reign would illustrate quite bloodily, and Catherine, a dedicated Protestant.

Not only did Catherine do much to reconcile Henry with his daughers, but she likely influenced the Act of Succession passed by Parliament in 1543 to restore Mary and Elizabeth's succession to the throne, behind their brother, Edward. Catherine also acted as Regent when Henry went on campaign to France from July to September 1544 to attack the French city of Boulogne.

Catherine was responsible for the family while the King was away. In late summer, she took the children to Hampton Court, where their education continued in earnest, particularly that of Elizabeth. Nicholas Udall, master of Eton and an editor of Greek and Latin translations, noted the increase in classical education for girls.[23]

Before she joined her stepmother at Hampton Court, Elizabeth had written to her on 31 July 1544, bemoaning the fact that she had not seen Catherine or her father for some time, due to severe ill health. She asked the Queen to mention her to her father, the

King, wished them both well and hoped that she would see them again as soon as possible:

> Inimical fortune, envious of all good and ever revolving human affairs, has deprived me for a whole year of your most illustrious presence, and, not thus content, has yet again robbed me of the same good; which thing would be intolerable to me, did I not hope to enjoy it very soon. And in this my exile I well know that the clemency of your Highness has had as much care and solicitude for my health as the King's Majesty himself. By which thing I am not only bound to serve you, but also to revere you with filial love, since I understand that your most illustrious Highness has not forgotten me every time you have written to the King's Majesty, which, indeed, it was my duty to have requested from you. For heretofore I have not dared to write to him. Wherefore I now humbly pray your most excellent Highness, that, when you write to his Majesty, you will condescend to recommend me to him, praying ever for his sweet benediction, and similarly entreating our Lord God to send him best success, and the obtaining of victory over his enemies, so that your Highness and I may, as soon as possible, rejoice together with him on his happy return. No less pray I God that he would preserve your most illustrious Highness; to whose grace, humbly kissing your hands, I offer and recommend myself ...
>
> Your most obedient daughter, and most faithful servant, Elizabeth.[24]

Elizabeth's letter mixes affection and diplomacy remarkably well for one so young – she was 11 years old.

37

The political situation at the time, particularly Henry VIII's alliance with Charles V, raised the question of other possible dynastic marriages for Henry's heirs. In 1545, a treaty between the two Kings included the proposal that Prince Edward marry Charles V's daughter, Maria, and that Mary would marry Charles V himself (at 29 years of age, she was 16 years younger than Charles).[25] It also mooted the idea of Elizabeth's marriage to Charles V's son and heir, Philip of Spain, although that failed to go beyond the initial stages of negotiation. Charles was polite, but not encouraging. Nine years later, Philip would come to make a far better match with the Tudors by wedding Mary, who had then become Queen of England (1553–58), and who also shared his Catholic faith.

38

Queen Catherine had every reason to be proud of her stepchildren. Little Edward, around seven at the time, was developing well and was happy to call her 'mother', Mary was friendly and much happier now that Henry had married Catherine, and Elizabeth was already a notable scholar and shared Edward's classes with Dr Richard Cox and Sir John Cheke. In 1544, Elizabeth was given her own tutor, William Grindall, and showed particular skill as a linguist; she was now fluent in Latin and Greek, in French and Italian, and was conversant in Spanish.

In 1545, Elizabeth sent Catherine a book that she had handwritten herself, a translation from the French of *The Glass or Mirror of the Sinful Soul* by the French princess Margaret of Angoulême, with a cover she had herself embroidered. The following year, she presented Catherine with another personally embroidered and translated volume, *How We Ought to Know God* by Jean Calvin, and she gave her father a selection of his wife's favourite prayers translated from English into Latin, French and Italian.

These gifts were labours of love for Elizabeth, and an attempt to win the admiration and praise of the two people who mattered most to her personal well-being. The letter Elizabeth wrote to accompany the book to Henry VIII illustrates her reverence for him:

To the most illustrious and most mighty King Henry the Eighth, King of England, France, and Ireland, Defender of the Faith, and second to Christ, supreme head of the English and Irish Church, Elizabeth, his majesty's most humble daughter, wishes all happiness, and begs his blessing. As an immortal soul is superior to a mortal body, so whoever is wise judges things done by the soul more to be esteemed and worthy of greater praise than any act of the body. And thus, as your majesty is of such excellence that none or few are to be compared with you in royal and ample marks of honour, and I am bound unto you as lord by the law of royal authority, as lord and father by the law of nature, and as greatest lord and matchless and most benevolent father by the divine law, and by all laws and duties I am bound unto your majesty in various and manifold ways, so I gladly asked, which it was my duty to do, by what means I might offer to your greatness the most excellent tribute that my capacity and diligence could discover. In the which, I only fear lest slight and unfinished studies and childish ripeness of mind diminish the praise of this undertaking and the commendation which accomplished talents draw from a most divine subject. For nothing ought to be more acceptable to a king, whom philosophers regard as a god on earth, than this labour of the soul, which raises us up to heaven and on

39

earth makes us heavenly and divine in the flesh; and while we may be enveloped by continual and infinite miseries, even then it renders us blessed and happy.

Which work, since it is so pious, and by the pious exertion and great diligence of a most illustrious queen [Catherine] has been composed in English, and on that account may be more desirable to all and held in greater value by your majesty, it was thought by me a most suitable thing that this work, which is more worthy because it was indeed a composition by a queen as a subject for her king, be translated into other languages by me, your daughter ... May He who is King of kings, in whose hand are the hearts of kings, so govern your soul and protect your life that in true piety and religion we may live long under your majesty's dominion.[26]

Elizabeth's feelings for her stepmother were perhaps less reverent, but still very fond. In 1546, Mary and Elizabeth were invited to Court to live with the Queen as ladies-in-waiting and act as her companions. Settled and secure, Elizabeth developed a real affection for Catherine Parr and many of the Queen's ladies would play a significant part in Elizabeth's life. They included Anne Parr (Catherine's sister), wife of William Herbert, 1st Earl of Pembroke; Maud Parr (Catherine's cousin), widow of Sir Ralph Lane; Elizabeth Borough (Catherine's stepdaughter), wife of Sir Robert Tyrwhitt; Joan Champernowne (Kat's sister), wife of Sir Anthony Denny; Katherine Willoughby d'Eresby, widow of Charles Brandon, 1st Duke of Suffolk; Margaret Stanley, wife of Robert Radcliffe, 1st Earl of Sussex; Anne Shapcote, wife of Sir William Fitzwilliam (his aunt was married to Sir Anthony Cooke, whose daughters married William Cecil, Sir Nicholas Bacon and Sir Thomas Hoby); Jane Guildford, wife of Sir John Dudley,

Viscount Lisle (later 1st Duke of Northumberland), and Anne Stanhope, wife of Sir Edward Seymour, 1st Earl of Hertford (later 1st Duke of Somerset).

The Act of Succession that Henry VIII had recently passed stated that in the case of his death the throne would pass to his son Edward and his heirs, but, if Edward died without children, Princess Mary would succeed to the throne. If she, too, died without heirs, the throne would pass to Princess Elizabeth, and after her to Frances Brandon (Lady Grey, Duchess of Suffolk) and then to Eleanor Brandon, the surviving children of Henry VIII's younger sister, Mary Tudor, and her husband, Charles Brandon, 1st Duke of Suffolk. He excluded his elder sister, Margaret Tudor's heirs (she had died in 1541), who were the royal family of Scotland. Margaret had married James IV (King of Scotland 1488–1513); Archibald Douglas, 6th Earl of Angus; and then Henry Stewart, and was survived by a daughter, Lady Margaret Douglas, and a granddaughter, the infant Mary, Queen of Scots.

By November 1546, the King's health was seriously failing, although it was treason to say so. Although historians do not know the exact cause of Henry's health problems, he was obese and it is possible he had diabetes. In his last weeks, Elizabeth was devastated by the knowledge of her father's forthcoming death, but comforted herself with her close relationship to her little brother, Edward, the future king, but their households were separated, with Edward moving to Hertford Castle and Elizabeth to Enfield Palace. Edward wrote to her in 1546: 'The change of place, in fact, did not vex me so much, dearest sister, as your going from me ... this is some comfort to my grief, that I hope to visit you shortly ...'[27]

After Henry VIII, died on 28 January 1547, Edward Seymour arranged for 9-year-old Edward to join his half-sister, 13-year-old Elizabeth, at Enfield. Once together, they were told of

41

their father's death and were able to cry in each other's arms and comfort each other.[28]

Apart from their place in the succession, Henry VIII left each of his daughters the sum of £3,000 per year. If either Mary or Elizabeth married, they would receive a one-off payment of £10,000 and the annuity would cease. This was not considered particularly generous at the time. Both princesses had to have the Privy Council's consent to marry, and Henry VIII's will specifically said that if Elizabeth failed to get this consent, she was to be struck out of the succession altogether.

2

The Seymour Affair,
1547–49

❧

ollowing the death of Henry VIII, Elizabeth's life initially
changed remarkably little. Her younger brother was now King
Edward VI and Elizabeth wrote to him with all the humility
and reverence she had previously used when addressing their father.
She maintained her household and ladies-in-waiting, including
Blanche Herbert, Kat Champernowne and Blanche Parry. Now aged
14, Elizabeth was an attractive girl of a suitable age for marriage.
According to the terms of Henry VIII's will, she could only marry if
she had the approval of the King and his Council. Catherine Parr,
now Queen Dowager, asked the Council if Elizabeth could join her
in her home in Chelsea.

As his son was only nine years old, Henry VIII had nominated
a Council of Regency, made up of 16 nobles and churchmen, to
assist Edward VI in governing his new realm. It was composed of
the most important men of the time: Thomas Cranmer, Archbishop
of Canterbury; Edward Seymour, 1st Earl of Hertford and later 1st
Duke of Somerset; John Russell, Baron Russell and later 1st Earl of
Bedford; John Dudley, Viscount Lisle, later 2nd Earl of Warwick
and 1st Duke of Northumberland; Sir Anthony Denny; Sir
William Herbert, 1st Earl of Pembroke; Thomas Wriothesley, 1st
Earl of Southampton; Cuthbert Tunstall, Bishop of Durham; Sir
Anthony Browne; Sir Edward Wotton; Dr Nicholas Wotton,

Dean of Canterbury and York; William Paulet, Baron St John of Basing, later Earl of Wiltshire and 1st Marquis of Winchester; Sir William Paget, Baron Paget; Sir Edward North; Sir Edward Montague, Chief Justice of the Common Pleas and Sir Thomas Bromley, Chief Justice of the King's Bench. Even though Catherine Parr, now the Dowager Queen, had hoped to be Edward's guardian, with a minimum of opposition, Edward Seymour (Jane and Thomas Seymour's brother) was proclaimed Protector of the Realm and Governor of the King. Catherine made a request to the Council concerning Elizabeth's future domicile and the princess moved with her servants to Chelsea in London.

Before Catherine had even a chance to settle down in her new home, a suitor had appeared on the horizon – Thomas Seymour, an old friend who had pursued her before the King had himself expressed his interest in her. To ensure that Thomas did not interfere in his new marriage, Henry VIII had arranged for him to be sent on a diplomatic mission to Vienna, after which Thomas was appointed Ambassador to Flanders.

Now that Catherine was a widow, Thomas Seymour renewed his suit with perhaps undue haste. The widow of the King could not, under normal circumstances, remarry for several months after her husband's death simply because she might be pregnant with the future heir to the throne. However, Catherine welcomed Thomas's suit. She wrote to him in February 1547, just a few weeks after Henry's death:

> I would not have you think that this mine honest good will toward you to proceed from any sudden motion of passion; for, as truly as God is God, my mind was fully bent, the other time I was at liberty, to marry you before any man I know. Howbeit, God withstood my will therein most vehemently for a time,

and ... made that possible which seemed to me most impossible; that was, made me renounce utterly mine own will and to follow His will most willingly ... I can say nothing but as my lady of Suffolk saith, 'God is a marvellous man.'[1]

Thomas's desire to resume his relationship with Catherine was due, in part, to his previous affection for her, but it was also driven by ambition. His brother, Edward, was now arguably the most influential person in the land, and sadly for Thomas, his brother possessed all the qualities of leadership that he himself lacked. Henry VIII had recognized this and made Edward one of his close advisers, sending him abroad on key diplomatic missions. Edward VI's Council similarly recognized Edward's powers as a reliable, intelligent, capable soldier and administrator.

When the Council awarded titles to its various Councillors, Edward became the 1st Duke of Somerset. Thomas also received the title of 1st Baron Seymour of Sudeley and was appointed Lord High Admiral, but he was far from satisfied. Edward was still more important, and Thomas was furious that his brother had risen so far so fast. Thomas was not only ambitious: he genuinely believed that he was equal, if not superior, to his brother.

Thomas's subsequent behaviour both involving Catherine, and later, Elizabeth sought to level the playing field. Marriage to the Dowager Queen was just one step further towards reaching a particular goal. Until Edward VI married, which was some years off yet, Catherine was the First Lady in England and the beloved stepmother of the King. She was arguably the most important woman in the country and could be expected to use her influence to support her husband in gaining the King's favour, if he so required.

While he was wooing Catherine, Thomas was also in communication with some of the Councillors to see if they might match him with either of Edward VI's half-sisters, Mary or Elizabeth. He received a strong negative response, as sometime in April or May of 1547 he secretly married Catherine.

Edward VI noted Edward Seymour's reaction to the marriage in his journal: 'The Lord Seymour of Sudeley married the Queen, whose name was Catherine, with which marriage the Lord Protector was much offended.'[2] While Catherine had approached her stepson and asked for his approval for the union, which he gladly gave, neither Thomas nor Catherine had approached the Council, perhaps suspecting that the Lord Protector might prevent the marriage, not just on the grounds of timing, but also because it would give too much influence to Thomas. When Edward VI took the throne, Thomas had tried to persuade the young King to sign a Bill to allow him to share the role of Protector, which Edward had refused.

By June, the marriage was common knowledge at Court and Thomas was living openly at Chelsea with Catherine and her household, which now included Elizabeth, but soon grew to encompass 11-year-old Lady Jane Grey. As part of Thomas's plans to increase his power, he plotted to arrange a marriage between Edward VI and Jane, the granddaughter of Mary Tudor, Henry VIII's sister, and Edward's own cousin. Evidence for what happened next at Chelsea, and at Catherine and Thomas's houses at Hanworth and Seymour Place in London, came from statements given by witnesses in the 1548–49 enquiry into the treasonable actions of Thomas Seymour. The most prominent and damaging statements came from Kat Ashley and Sir Thomas Parry, Elizabeth's Cofferer (treasurer).

From the start Thomas's behaviour towards Elizabeth overstepped the mark of what was deemed appropriate for a stepfather and stepdaughter. Kat Ashley reported that he would 'come many mornings into the Lady Elizabeth's chamber, before she were ready, and sometimes before she did rise. And if she were up, he would bid her good morrow, and ask how she did, and strike her upon the back or on the buttocks familiarly, and so go forth through his lodgings; and sometime go through to the maidens and play with them, and so go forth.'[3]

If Elizabeth was in bed, he would 'make as though he would come at her. And she would go further into the bed, so that he could not come at her.'[4] One morning he tried to kiss her while she was in bed, but Kat Ashley 'bade him go away for shame'. At Hanworth he tried the same trick, but Elizabeth now tended to be up when he arrived. On a few occasions, Catherine accompanied Thomas to Elizabeth's bedchamber where they were observed tickling Elizabeth.[5] It was as if Thomas brought his wife with him to demonstrate the innocence of his actions.

One day, Kat found Elizabeth with her gown slashed to ribbons. In her subsequent testimony at Thomas's enquiry, she said that as 'my lady's grace walking with the Queen in the garden, my Lord Admiral did cut her gown in a hundred pieces, and I chid with her grace when she came up, that she was so trimmed. And she said the Queen held her while my lord did so dress it. "Well," said I, "I would my lord would show more reverence to you, although he be homely with the Queen."'[6]

Kat spoke to Thomas; he told her that it was all good fun. Similarly, when Kat mentioned the matter to Catherine, she made light of it.[7] Not only did Thomas continue with his attentions to Elizabeth, he became even more bold. He would come up every morning in his nightgown, 'barelegged in his slippers',[8] but Elizabeth had learned how to manage the situation; she was always up 'and at her book' by the hour he appeared, so he had to wish her good morrow from the doorway.

While they were at Hanworth, one day Catherine came to Kat with a strange tale. She reported that Thomas had told her that he had seen Elizabeth hugging a man. Kat immediately asked Elizabeth about this; she burst into tears and swore it was a lie. She was never alone, after all, and Kat only had to ask her ladies-in-waiting for verification. The only gentleman among Elizabeth's servants was William Grindal, her elderly tutor, an unlikely candidate for a passionate embrace. And why Catherine mentioned this at all remains a mystery. Possibly she knew or believed that Elizabeth was smitten with a young man, but did not know who it was and hoped to put a stop to any serious flirtation before it got out of hand and someone reported it to the Council. Possibly Thomas thought that someone had seen him embracing the young girl and he was acting to cover his tracks.[9]

While Thomas's actions with a younger child might have been seen as simple playfulness, Elizabeth was nearly 15, old enough to be a married mother by the standards of the day. Touching her in her nightdress, trying to get into her bed and kissing her were all wholly inappropriate actions, and while Catherine might have initially viewed them as innocent, evidence indicates she changed her mind. All the principal players in the events that unfolded seem to acknowledge that all was not well in the Seymour household.

Matters became more complicated when the 35-year-old Catherine announced that she was pregnant. Although Catherine was delighted with the news, she was undeniably concerned by the nature of the relationship between her husband and her ward, and this must have exacerbated the physical and psychological problems that came with a middle-aged woman's first pregnancy.

The pregnancy also put paid to any plans that Thomas had for Catherine to help him gain influence over the Council or the King, although she had shown a marked disinclination to become involved in his schemes. In any event, Catherine's own position and influence as Dowager Queen was also now in question. Anne Seymour, the Lord Protector's wife, resented Catherine's position as Dowager Queen, even though Anne was the wife of arguably the most powerful man in England. The resulting dispute between them led to some extremely petty behaviour, such as Edward's refusal, backed by Anne, to return some of Catherine's jewels – including her wedding ring – which he claimed belonged to the Crown. Catherine was no longer in a position of sufficient power to lobby for her husband, even if she wanted to.

In 1547, Elizabeth took a short break from the difficult situation at Chelsea, spending Christmas at Court with Edward and their half-sister, Mary. There, she behaved like a loyal and devoted subject, as well as a beloved sister of the King and the current heir to the throne. The Italian calligrapher and writer Petruccio Ubaldini, who was a visitor to the Court at the time, observed that he had seen, 'the princess Elizabeth drop on one knee five times before her brother, before she took her place.'[10] The half-siblings would have enjoyed a varied and exciting programme of religious ceremonies and entertainments over Christmas and New Year, all suitable for a young King who was still a child.

In January 1548, Elizabeth returned to Chelsea. In that same month, her tutor, William Grindal, died. Thomas and Catherine already had a suitable candidate to replace William, but Elizabeth had her own opinion on the subject. She chose Roger Ascham, who came recommended by Sir John Cheke, Edward VI's tutor.

As Catherine's pregnancy advanced, she spent more time resting. She no longer accompanied her husband when he visited Elizabeth, yet, one day in May or June 1548, Catherine made a discovery, according to Thomas Parry's evidence in the Seymour enquiry. Parry testified that Thomas loved Elizabeth and had done so for a long

49

time and that Catherine was jealous of that fact. On this particular occasion, Catherine 'came suddenly upon them, where they were all alone, he having her [Elizabeth] in his arms, wherefore the Queen fell out, both with the Lord Admiral and with her Grace also ... and as I remember, this was the cause why she was sent from the Queen, or else that her grace parted from the Queen.'[11]

Catherine was apparently devastated by this betrayal and is alleged to have ordered Elizabeth to be removed from her household.[12] Certainly, in May 1548, Elizabeth and her servants were sent away from Chelsea; they went to stay with Sir Anthony Denny and his wife, Lady Joan, at Cheshunt, Hertfordshire. Shortly after her arrival at the Dennys' home, Elizabeth wrote a letter to Catherine:

50

Although I could not be plentiful in giving thanks for the manifold kindness received at your highness' hand at my departure, yet I am something to be borne withal, for truly I was replete with sorrow to depart from your highness, especially leaving you undoubtful of health. And albeit I answered little, I weighed it more deeper when you said you would warn me of all evils that you should hear of me; for if your grace had not a good opinion of me, you would not have offered friendship to me that way that all men judge the contrary. But what may I more say than thank God for providing such friends to me, desiring God to enrich me with their long life, and me grace to be in heart no less thankful to receive it than I now am glad in writing to show it. And although I have plenty of matter, here I will stay for I know you are not quiet to read.

From Cheston [Cheshunt] this present Saturday,

Your highness' humble daughter, Elizabeth.[13]

This letter is perhaps remarkable in that it contains no explanation, apology or justification for whatever had happened before Elizabeth's departure from Catherine's household. If Catherine had sent Elizabeth away in anger, there is no reference to it in the letter rather, Elizabeth thanks her stepmother for her kindness and concern and also for her promise to let Elizabeth know if anyone is slandering her.

In sending Elizabeth away, Catherine could possibly have been punishing her ward for her bad behaviour, but equally, she could have been protecting the young girl. This letter seems to support the second explanation. Similarly, if Elizabeth were being punished, Catherine's decision to send her to the Dennys was an odd one. Sir Anthony Denny had been a Gentleman of the Privy Chamber and a friend to Henry VIII, and his wife, Joan, was a close friend of Catherine's and the sister of Elizabeth's beloved Governess, Kat Ashley. They were excellent guardians rather than strict jailers. Was Catherine protecting Elizabeth from Thomas's attentions? Or is there yet another explanation? Could Elizabeth have been sent away because she was already pregnant with Thomas's child?

Whatever the reason, Catherine now had other pressing matters to deal with. She left London on 13 June for Sudeley Castle in Gloucestershire, where she awaited her own baby's arrival. Lady Jane Grey was still in attendance and must have provided some distraction from her situation.

Elizabeth and Thomas were still in correspondence, as the following July letter from Elizabeth shows. It was sent in response to a missive from Thomas, stating that he could not fulfil a promise that he had made to her:

> My lord, you needed not to send an excuse to me, for I could not mistrust the not fulfilling of your promise to proceed for

51

want of goodwill, but only opportunity serveth not; wherefore I shall desire you to think that a greater matter than this could not make me impute any unkindness in you. For I am a friend not won by trifles, nor lost with the like. Thus I commit you and all your affairs in God's hand, who keep you from all evil. I pray you make my humble commendations to the queen's highness.

Your assured friend to my power, Elizabeth.[14]

Elizabeth also wrote a letter to Catherine around the same time, indicating that Catherine was aware of the contents of previous letters written by Thomas to her:

Although your Highness' letters be most joyful to me in absence, yet considering what pain it is to you to write, your Grace being so great with child and so sickly, your commendations were enough in my lord's letter. I much rejoice at your health with the well-liking of the country, with my humble thanks, that your Grace wished me with you, till I were weary of that country. Your Highness were like to be cumbered if I should not depart till I were weary of being with you; although it were the worst soil in the world, your presence would make it pleasant. I cannot reprove my lord for not doing your commendations in his letter, for he did it. And although he had not, yet I will not complain on him, for that he shall be diligent to give me knowledge from time to time how his busy child doth, and if I were at his birth no doubt I would see him beaten for the trouble he had put you to. Master Denny and my lady with humble thanks prayeth most entirely for your grace, praying the almighty God to send you a lucky deliverance.

And my mistress [Kat Ashley] wisheth no less, giving your highness most humble thanks for her commendations. Written with very little leisure this last day of July. Your humble daughter, Elizabeth.[15]

Such a light-hearted letter hardly seems to support the contention that Catherine and Elizabeth had parted acrimoniously.

Finally, on 30 August 1548, Catherine's child was born, a daughter named Mary. She was attended by her stepdaughter, Elizabeth Tyrwhitt, who recorded the event. After the birth, Catherine developed a fever, which was the beginning of puerperal sepsis. She became agitated and told the ladies attending her that she had not been well handled by Thomas, 'for those that be about me careth not for me, but standeth laughing at my grief; and the more good I will to them, the less good they will to me.'[16]

Thomas held her hand and replied, 'Why, sweetheart, I would do you no hurt,' but Catherine returned 'very sharply and earnestly', 'No, my Lord ... you have given me many shrewd taunts.'[17] Thomas is reported to have lain down beside her, but Catherine said she would give 1,000 marks to have a proper talk with the physician who attended her delivery, but dared not for fear of displeasing him.[18] This seems to indicate that Catherine believed Thomas no longer loved her and was, indeed, possibly working against her best interests. Whatever the truth of the matter, Catherine never recovered from the infection that had taken hold of her body.

Catherine Parr, the Queen Dowager and Elizabeth's stepmother, died on 5 September 1548. She was buried at Sudeley, where 12-year-old Lady Jane Grey took the position of Chief Mourner. News of Catherine's death was brought to Cheshunt, where Elizabeth was staying, and a servant told Kat Ashley that

53

Thomas was heavy-hearted at his wife's death.[19] Elizabeth did not attend the burial, an act that was strange in itself. Catherine had been enormously kind to Elizabeth, both as a stepmother and as her ward after Henry's death. Surely had she been able to, Elizabeth would have attended the funeral of a woman who, as her letters indicate, she held in such esteem? What happened to prevent this? Illness, perhaps, or something more?

It does appear that in the autumn of 1548, Elizabeth began to suffer from bouts of poor health, something that was common knowledge at the time. Elizabeth herself wrote to Edward Seymour in September, stating that she was bound to him in her time of sickness: '... you have been careful for my health, and sending unto me not only your comfortable letters but also physicians as Doctor Bill [Dr Thomas Bill, physician to Henry VIII and Edward VI], whose diligence and pain has been a great part of my recovery.'[20]

Similarly, in a letter to her brother, Edward VI, Elizabeth referred to an affliction of her 'head and eyes' which made it difficult to write to him.[21] And, perhaps, more tellingly, Kat Ashley in her February 1549 testimony at Thomas's enquiry, stated that immediately after Catherine's death, Elizabeth was bedridden for part of the time and unable to go more than a mile from the house throughout the second half of 1548.[22] Rumours began to circulate that the Lady Elizabeth was pregnant, and that those around her were protecting her by alluding to her 'illness'.

Without the influence of the more sensible Catherine Parr, Thomas began to pursue his plans to overset his brother, Edward, in earnest. His plans were largely unrealistic, extravagant and unworkable. Put simply, in Thomas's bid to oust his brother from power, he was intemperate. He had already suggested that Edward and he should share the protectorate and control of the young King, and when this offer was rejected, he instead openly schemed to displace his brother. He also went to great lengths to ingratiate himself with the King, making him gifts of money and speaking disrespectfully of the Protector, whose overbearing and autocratic manner was beginning to annoy the young Edward VI.

Freely discussing his plans with anyone who he felt might assist him, he sounded out the other Councillors with imprudent openness, questioning their loyalty to Edward Seymour. Even before Catherine died, Thomas had bribed Sir William Sharington, the Vice-Treasurer of the Mint in Bristol, to coin money that could be misappropriated to fund his plans to overthrow his brother. It was said he had a map of England that indicated which areas he could rely on for support in the event of an uprising (and the money embezzled from the Mint could be put to use bribing anyone who wavered in their support). Thomas and Sharington managed to embezzle £4,000 from the Mint before the plot was uncovered. Sharington later informed the authorities that Thomas had said, 'If we had £10,000 in ready money, that were well.'[23]

Thomas's plans were wide and varied, however, and Lady Jane Grey, Elizabeth and her half-sister, Mary, also entered the frame at one point or another. On Catherine's death, Jane had returned to her parents, but Thomas persuaded them to return her to his guardianship by promising to arrange her marriage to Edward VI. In reality this was unlikely, as a possible union between Edward and Mary, Queen of Scots had already been mooted, something that would never come to pass due to the deteriorating relations between England and Scotland.

Thomas had also renewed his attentions towards Elizabeth after Catherine's death. Not content with seeking to rule through

55

Edward VI, he was looking to the future. Lady Mary, the next in line to the throne, suffered from poor health and was a committed Catholic in a now Protestant country. If Edward VI should die young or without heirs, there was a good chance that Mary would be removed from the succession or die before she could produce an heir, and Elizabeth would inherit the crown. Why should Thomas restrict himself to the power behind the throne when he might have the throne itself?

However, Thomas's desire to be Elizabeth's suitor raised suspicions about his political intentions. In November 1547, riding in the procession to Parliament, Thomas found himself next to the Lord Privy Seal, Sir John Russell, who warned him that he should take care: 'My Lord Admiral, there are certain rumours bruited of you which I am very sorry to hear … if you go about any such thing [seek to marry princesses Elizabeth or Mary], ye seek the measure to undo yourself and all those that shall come to you.'[24]

Thomas denied that there was any such plot and angrily demanded to know the identity of his accuser. Russell managed to calm him down, but several days later Thomas sought him out as they rode from Edward Seymour's house to Westminster and asked him again who his accuser was.[25] Russell refused to say. Thomas stated that he was not planning anything untoward, but commented that it was better that the princesses chose to marry someone 'within the realm than in any foreign place', further adding 'And why might not I, or another, made by the King their father, marry one of them?'[26]

Russell replied that this was unthinkable. For one thing, it would arouse suspicions that Thomas might be plotting to gain power, and also there was the matter of a dowry. When Thomas said he would expect £3,000 a year, Russell disabused him. The princesses' dowries were to be 'ten thousand pounds in money, plate and goods, and no land.'[27] Thomas insisted there must be an additional £3,000 a year, and Russell firmly replied there would be no such thing as it would be 'clean against the King's will.'[28] This conversation did not discourage Thomas, however. He began to woo Elizabeth in earnest and solicited the Privy Council for permission to marry her.

Kat Ashley proved a valuable ally in Thomas's courtship. She frequently spoke to Elizabeth on the subject of their marriage, which she seemed to believe would eventually be approved by the Council. Her husband, Sir John Ashley, Elizabeth's senior gentleman attendant, was less certain. He warned his wife to be careful, 'to take heed, for he did fear that the Lady Elizabeth did bear some affection to my Lord Admiral. She seemed to be well pleased therewith, and sometime she would blush when he were spoken of.'[29] Sir John could see the danger of Elizabeth allowing herself to become embroiled in the plots of Thomas Seymour, even if Kat, his romantic wife, could not.

Thomas, recalling what Russell had told him about Elizabeth's dowry, spoke to her Cofferer, Thomas Parry, to offer several suggestions. As part of Henry VIII's will, each of his daughters had been awarded lands worth £3,000. The law moved slowly in confirming the ladies' inheritance and Thomas wanted to know how much the lands were worth and where they lay. If the titles had not yet been finalized, he suggested that Elizabeth should ask to exchange them for better, richer lands in the West Country and Wales, closer to his own properties, in order to form a future power base.

In order to speed this plan along, Thomas made another suggestion to Parry. Elizabeth wanted to go to London to see Edward VI, but her town house, Durham House, had been appropriated by the Crown to act as a Mint. Thomas suggested that Elizabeth should apply to Edward Seymour for another house, befriending Anne, Edward's wife, who might lend her support to the request. Once friends, Elizabeth could ask Anne to use her influence with her husband to exchange her lands for more desirable ones.

When Parry next met with Elizabeth, he asked if she would like to marry Thomas. She replied rather cryptically, 'I will do as God shall put into my mind.'[30] She pressed Parry as to why he was quizzing her on the matter, and he told her about Thomas's suggestion regarding Anne Seymour. Elizabeth was extremely angry and told Parry to inform Thomas that this was a plan that she would not countenance. She also told him to tell Kat Ashley everything immediately 'for I shall know nothing but she shall know of it. In faith, I cannot be quiet until ye have told her of it.'[31]

While Parry may have been prepared to discuss such potentially treasonable matters in secret, Elizabeth was not. She could not be seen to be part of any plot against the King, the Crown or the Council.

Kat was in London at the time, where she had been summoned by Anne Seymour. Anne had heard rumours that Elizabeth had been permitted to go out unchaperoned at night in a barge on the Thames with Thomas. Anne informed Kat that if 'she was not worthy to have the governance of the King's daughter … another should have her place'.[32] Kat did not seem unduly worried, however; the complaints against her were petty, and Elizabeth would never allow her beloved Governess to be taken from her.

Of more concern was information Kat had obtained from Lady Tyrwhitt and Mary Hill, the wife of Sir John Cheke, Edward VI's tutor and friend. Rumours were circulating that Thomas had simply kept on the female servants of Catherine Parr's household in anticipation of them serving Elizabeth when she became his wife. The fact that the matter was being discussed so openly at Court must have sobered Kat. When she returned to Elizabeth she told the young girl that there should be no more talk of her marrying Thomas 'till the King's Majesty [Edward VI] came to his own rule.' The King's Protector and the Privy Council would never consider allowing her marriage to Thomas or anyone else.[33]

Later, when questioned during the enquiry into Thomas Seymour's treasonable activities, Sir Thomas Parry recalled a conversation he had had with Kat Ashley in January 1549. Parry believed that some affection existed between Elizabeth and Thomas. Kat had agreed with him, adding, 'I would wish her his wife of all men living.' Parry countered this by saying that he had heard Thomas 'was not only a very covetous man and an oppressor, but also an evil, jealous man; and how cruelly, how dishonourably and how jealously he had used the Queen [Catherine Parr].'[34]

Kat rose to Thomas's defence, insisting, 'I know him better than ye do, or those that so report of him.' Thomas loved Elizabeth, she said, too well and had done so for a long time. She told Parry about Catherine Parr's jealousy when she had found Thomas and Elizabeth in an embrace, which had led her to send Elizabeth away. Parry, sensing a scandal, pressed her, 'Why, hath there been such familiarity indeed between them?' Realizing she had said too much (she 'seemed to repent that she had gone so far'), Kat swore Parry to secrecy and begged him several times never to repeat what she had said, 'for her Grace should be dishonoured for ever and likewise she undone.'[35]

By now, Thomas Seymour's various schemes had been reported to the Privy Council, and the Bristol Mint had been investigated. Sir William Sharington, arrested for embezzling, had informed against Thomas. But it was Thomas himself who made matters worse and, in a sense, brought about his own downfall. On the evening of 16 January, Thomas broke into Hampton Court Palace and tried to seize the King from his bed as he slept. He and a small gang used stolen keys to get as far as the antechamber, and when one of Edward's dogs began to bark, Thomas shot it. The King's guards rushed in and escorted Thomas out as he pled, 'I wished to know whether his Majesty was safely guarded.'[36]

On the following day, an order was issued for Thomas's arrest. He was dining with the Earl of Dorset when troops came to take him to the Tower of London. Within two days, William Paulet, Lord St John, Sir Anthony Denny and Sir Robert Tyrwhitt had arrived at Hatfield to interview Elizabeth and those in her service: they were suspected of being involved in Thomas's schemes – particularly his plot to marry Elizabeth.

Kat Ashley and Thomas Parry were arrested and taken to London. Sir Robert Tyrwhitt remained at Hatfield to take a statement from Elizabeth, a task he found increasingly onerous. At first Elizabeth 'was marvellous abashed and did weep very tenderly a long time' when she heard that Parry and Kat Ashley had been arrested. Elizabeth acknowledged she had written to Thomas Seymour regarding the help he was to give her in getting Durham Place back. She also recalled that Kat had written to him to warn him against visiting 'for fear of suspicion', and that she had been angry with her Governess for being so presumptious.[37]

By 22 January, Tyrwhitt was fighting his frustration as he tried to get Elizabeth to utter an admission of guilt or prior knowledge of the plot.

> I did require her to consider her honour and the peril that
> might ensue, for she was but a subject … I further declared
> what a woman Mistress Ashley was … saying that if she
> would open all things herself, all the evil and shame should
> be ascribed to them and her youth considered both with the
> King's Majesty, your Grace and the whole Council. But in

no way she will not confess any practice by Mistress Ashley or the Cofferer concerning my Lord Admiral; and yet I do see it in her face that she is guilty, and do perceive as yet she will abide more storms ere she accuse Mistress Ashley.[38]

The next day Tyrwhitt tried a kinder approach, 'All I have gotten yet is by gentle persuasion, whereby I do begin to grow with her in credit.' Elizabeth confirmed that Thomas had offered to lend her his house in London and reported Parry's account of their conversation. Tyrwhitt was pleased, even though there was nothing new in her account. He reported, 'this is a good beginning, I trust more will follow … I do assure your Grace, she hath a very good wit, and nothing is gotten of her but by great policy.'

For a week Tyrwhitt tried to extract a confession, to no avail. On 28 January he wrote, 'I do verily believe that there hath been some secret promise between my Lady, Mistress Ashley and the Cofferer, never to confess till death; and if it be so, it will never be gotten of her, but either by the King's Majesty, or else by your Grace.'[39]

On receiving Tyrwhitt's report, the Protector wrote to Elizabeth himself 'as an earnest friend', and she replied on 28 January, effectively laying out what she had already told Tyrwhitt about her relationship with Thomas. She also made reference to the rumours regarding a possible child borne of her relationship with him:

… Master Tyrwhit and others have told me that there goeth rumours abroad which be greatly both against my honour and honesty, which, above all other things, I esteem, which be these, that I am in the Tower, and with child by my lord admiral [Thomas Seymour]. My lord, these are shameful slanders, for the which, besides the great desire I have to see

the king's majesty, I shall most heartily desire your lordship
that I may come to the court after your first determination
that I may shew myself there as I am.[40]

The Protector wrote back to her to say that if Elizabeth could
identify anyone who uttered such slanders against her, the Council
would have them punished. Elizabeth was unwilling to accuse
specific people in case it made her look vindictive. She came up
with a better plan, asking the Council to stop the gossip instead:

> ... if it might seem good to your lordship, and the rest of the
> council, to send forth a proclamation into the countries that
> they refrain their tongues, declaring how the tales be but
> lies, it should make both the people think that you and the
> council have great regard that no such rumours should be
> spread of any of the King's majesty's sisters (as I am, though
> unworthy) and also that I should think myself to receive
> such friendship at your hands as you have promised me,
> although your lordship shewed me great already. [41]

By early February, both Parry and Kat Ashley had made full and
detailed statements to the Council. On 5 February, Tyrwhitt
showed copies of their confessions to Elizabeth, hoping that their
written disclosures might cause her to break down. Tyrwhitt was
pleased to see that 'she was much abashed and half breathless and
perused all their names particularly.'

Tyrwhitt allowed Elizabeth one night to think matters over, but
when they next met Elizabeth was once more in command of
herself. What had been reported was not treasonable, after all, and
there was no evidence that Elizabeth was involved in a marriage
plot. The exasperated Tyrwhitt wrote, 'They all sing the same song

and so I think they would not do, unless they had set the note before.'[42]

After the investigations both Kat and Parry remained in prison. The Council decided that Kat had been lax in her care of Elizabeth and that she should be replaced as Governess by Lady Tyrwhitt, who had served Catherine Parr and was a puritanical Protestant. When she was told, Elizabeth replied, 'Mrs Ashley was her mistress and she had not so demeaned herself that the Council should now need to put any more mistresses unto her.' Rather lacking in tact, Lady Tyrwhitt replied, 'seeing she did allow Mrs Ashley to be her mistress, she need not be ashamed to have any honest woman to be in that place.' The teenage Elizabeth wept and then sulked. Tyrwhitt reported her despair at losing Kat and her hope that she might recover Kat as her mistress one day: 'The love she beareth her is to be wondered at.'[43]

Tyrwhitt noted that she was also protective of Thomas Seymour: 'She beginneth now a little to droop by reason she heareth that my Lord Admiral's house be dispersed. And my wife telleth me now that she cannot bear to hear him discommended but she is ready to make answer therein; and so she hath not been accustomed to do, unless Mistress Ashley were touched, whereunto she was very ready to make answer vehemently.'[44] Elizabeth was loyal to those she counted as friends. She wanted Kat Ashley back, a woman who had been like a mother to her in many ways, and she would not hear anything against Thomas, who may have been the first man she loved.

Others were not so loyal, and so Thomas's fortunes were doomed from the moment of his arrest. While Elizabeth and servants such as John Harington might stand firm, others did not – the nobles with whom he had discussed his plans came forward, his servants spoke out against him, and even the King reported

63

conversations with Thomas that indicated some treasonable intent. The Council charged him with treason, producing 39 articles of treasonable activities, including that he 'had attempted and gone about to marry the King's Majesty's sister, the Lady Elizabeth, second inheritor in remainder to the Crown.'[45]

Thomas demanded an open trial to face his accusers. The Council, headed by Thomas's brother, Edward Seymour, asked the King for an Act of Attainder to bypass the need for a trial, which was granted. Thomas finally spoke out: he had meant no harm to the King or the Protector, and had long given up his pursuit to share power. To prevent Edward Seymour showing leniency to his brother, the other Council members went to the King on 10 March to ask for the authorization to act without him. This, too, was granted.

On 20 March, Thomas Seymour was beheaded on Tower Hill. Even on the scaffold, Thomas refused to make the usual confession, leading Bishop Latimer to say of him, 'Whether he be saved or no, I leave it to God, but surely he was a wicked man, and the realm is well rid of him.'[46]

3

The First Child?

℘

Elizabeth's reaction to Thomas Seymour's execution remains a matter of conjecture. Whether or not she had been privy to, or part of, a secret marriage plot with Thomas, this was without a doubt her first intimate relationship with a man and as such would influence the way she thought of men in her future dealings with them, both before and after she became Queen. Fraught, as they were, with political intrigue and emotional turbulence, her experiences with Seymour, even without the added complications of a possible secret pregnancy and child, were not likely to change the difficult and unhealthy vision of marriage that Elizabeth had formed, while still a child, as she observed firsthand the tragic outcomes of her father's relationships with his wives.

If, as rumours at the time suggest, Elizabeth did have an illegitimate child with Thomas Seymour, it was most likely to have been conceived in 1548, when she was living in Catherine Parr's household. There is no doubt that Elizabeth felt a fascination for Thomas, who was an extremely attractive and virile man, moreover one extremely popular with women. Whether his subsequent behaviour in visiting her bedroom while she was in bed and his other advances were solicited or not, it appears that Elizabeth did feel some form of passion for him. A more principled man would have made sure that if a young girl, particularly his wife's ward, developed a crush on him nothing came of it, but Thomas seemed singularly lacking in principles; in any case, he was pursuing an agenda of his own.

Common sense and a well-developed sense of self-preservation should have told Thomas that the King's sister should be off-limits. Thomas, however, was arrogant to the point of being self-destructive. His impulsive personality and imperious manner meant that he simply went ahead with his desires: if he had wanted Elizabeth and she had seemed willing, he would have justified his actions by arguing that when his plans matured, he would be a major power in the country and no one would be able to punish either of them for any untoward behaviour.

In order to find out the truth and extent of Thomas and Elizabeth's relationship, we need to explore what was said during the discussion that took place between Elizabeth and Catherine in May or June 1548, just before Elizabeth was sent away from Chelsea. None of Catherine's letters to Elizabeth survive, but the first letter from Elizabeth to her stepmother after their parting shows no sign that they parted bitterly. If anything, Elizabeth seems to be thanking Catherine for being kind and supportive. This supports the contention that Elizabeth was sent away not as a result of Catherine's own jealousy, but to save her. But, if that is the case, what was Catherine trying to protect Elizabeth from? The loss of her reputation? Thomas? Or was she protecting a young girl in possession of an explosive secret – should it become common knowledge?

Is it possible that when they spoke, Elizabeth broke down and told Catherine that she might be pregnant? That would explain Catherine's desire to get Elizabeth away from the house – and from Thomas Seymour – as soon as possible to the Dennys, a safe place. It could also explain Catherine's promise to let Elizabeth know 'of all evils' people might speak of her – that is, to warn her if any hint of the pregnancy ever surfaced. It could also demonstrate a closing of ranks by Catherine and Elizabeth to protect Thomas despite his selfish, philandering behaviour.

The timeframe also works: Catherine and Thomas had married in April or May 1547 and, as Catherine gave birth in August 1548, she probably fell pregnant in December. Thomas appears to have begun his pursuit of Elizabeth as early as the summer of 1547, but it would most likely have been after his wife knew that she was pregnant, in February or March 1548, that he began a physical relationship with Elizabeth.

If Elizabeth had fallen pregnant soon after that, by May or June when she left Catherine's household, she may have been about three months along, a time when a pregnancy would have begun to show. She may have had no choice but to tell Catherine of her situation, but very few people other than her stepmother needed to be involved in keeping the secret. She would, of course, have needed the help of Blanche Parry and Kat Ashley (the latter was so loyal she would later continue to protect Elizabeth while interned in the Tower of London). Finally, Lord and Lady Denny, who were the sister and brother-in-law of Kat Ashley, gave her sanctuary and also closed ranks around the teenage princess, allowing her to take to her bed over the next six months.

In September, when Catherine died and Elizabeth was said to be suffering bouts of ill health, she could have been seven or eight months pregnant. No one but her closest servants would ever have seen her unclothed. Even a doctor would have been forbidden to look at a naked female patient. The 'illnesses' would explain any sickness or prolonged bed rest; any apparent 'swelling' of her abdomen could be explained away as resulting from a kidney complaint.

This timing would put the birth of the child in October or November 1548. If this was the case, it would tie in with Elizabeth's letter to the Protector in January 1549, when she wrote concerning rumours '... that I am ... with child by my Lord Admiral. My lord, these are shameful slanders, for the which

67

besides the great desire I have to see the King's Majesty, I shall most heartily desire your lordship that I may come to Court after your first determination, that I may show myself there as I am.'¹

In January Elizabeth would have been able to face her interrogators in person; she could come to Court and show that she was not pregnant; she may even have permitted a discreet examination of her person, because by that time she was not pregnant any more.

⤜

Even at this young age, Elizabeth had political enemies who would have been happy to see her removed from the succession, disgraced or dead. To the latter group belonged the Catholics who feared that the Protestant Edward VI might decide to pass over the Catholic Princess Mary or Mary, Queen of Scots and leave the throne to Elizabeth. Another faction supported an alternative Protestant heir, particularly Frances Grey, Duchess of Suffolk, and her eldest daughter, Lady Jane Grey.

Elizabeth's supporters, on the other hand, came from a wide spectrum of Court and country. Many Protestants preferred Elizabeth over her Catholic half-sister Mary as Edward VI's successor, should he die without an heir. There were even some who saw her as a possible focal point for an as yet unplanned rebellion. Elizabeth's mother's paternal family, the Boleyns, and her extended maternal family, the Howards, also saw her as their chance to recapture their old greatness if she came to the throne. But at the heart of things, it was Elizabeth's personal servants and their families who were personally devoted to her and who helped her most at Cheshunt. There, Elizabeth would have been surrounded by well-wishers who could cover up her pregnancy and help her place the child in a suitable home, once it was born.

If it was true that Thomas had made her pregnant, at some point in October or November 1548, Elizabeth gave birth to a child. Directly afterwards, Elizabeth left Cheshunt and moved to Hatfield. This arguably might have served to draw all eyes away from the Dennys and their task of placing the baby somewhere safe, but there were rumours, both at the time and later on regarding this. There was the story of a London midwife, taken one night to the Great House in the village of Hamstead Marshall in Berkshire, where she was called upon to assist a fair young lady give birth. As soon as the child was born, it was reportedly murdered by a ferocious gentleman who attended the lady. The horrified midwife was generously rewarded and returned home, only to die several days later after being poisoned.[2] That the 'fair young lady' might have been Elizabeth seems to be supported by the fact that the Great House at Hamstead Marshall belonged to Sir Thomas Parry. However, the house only passed to Parry in 1559, long after these events were said to have taken place. Furthermore, rumours like this were not uncommon.

This story might not be as wild as it seems, though. *The Life of Jane Dormer, Duchess of Feria*, a biography of one of Mary I's ladies-in-waiting who married the Spanish Duke de Feria, was written during Elizabeth's lifetime. It includes the passage:

In King Edward's time what passed between the Lord Admiral, Sir Thomas Seymour and her Doctor, Latimer preached in a sermon, and was a chief cause the parliament condemned the Admiral. There was a bruit of a child born and miserably destroyed, but could not be discovered whose it was; only the report of the mid-wife, who was brought from her house blindfold thither, and so returned, saw nothing in the house while she was there, but candle light;

only, she said, it was the child of a very fair young lady. There was muttering of the Admiral and this lady, who was then between fifteen and sixteen years of age. If it were so, it was the judgment of God upon the Admiral; and upon her, to make her ever after incapable of children ... The reason why I write this is to answer the voice of my countrymen in so strangely exalting the lady Elizabeth, and so basely depressing Queen Mary.[3]

Dating from the early 1600s, the account is close to contemporary with Elizabeth's life, but it should be noted that Jane Dormer was one of Mary I's closest friends and a fanatical Catholic who disliked Elizabeth enormously while the references to Elizabeth may have been meant to discredit her. They probably also act as a gauge of public rumours at the time.

Another possibility is that Elizabeth did fall pregnant, but she never carried the child to term, either miscarrying while she was at Cheshunt, or aborting it and this might explain why there is no positive trace of her child. In any event, by January 1549 Elizabeth could demonstrate that she was not pregnant.

Those researchers who believe that Elizabeth did give birth to a healthy child have endeavoured to identify it over the years. Historian Paul Streitz suggests that the infant boy was given to John de Vere, 16th Earl of Oxford, and his wife, Margery Golding (who later became a maid of honour to Elizabeth I), and was brought up as Edward de Vere, 17th Earl of Oxford.

The young de Vere did seem to have a 'guardian angel' – or an influential parent. When John de Vere died in 1562, Edward became a ward of Court and was placed in the household of

William Cecil, Elizabeth I's Secretary of State and one of the most influential men in England. De Vere later attended Queen's College, Cambridge, and was awarded a Master of Arts degree from both Cambridge and Oxford. He continued his education at the Inns of Court, where, in July 1567, he killed a cook named Thomas Bricknell while fencing. The jury was told the far-fetched story that an intoxicated Bricknell had thrown himself onto de Vere's blade,. The resulting verdict was suicide and by this decision, Bricknell's pregnant widow and child were stripped of his possessions by the state.

In 1571, the 21-year-old de Vere married Cecil's favourite daughter, 15-year-old Anne. The couple had a son and four daughters, but de Vere accused her of adultery (at one time he refused to acknowledge one of his daughters) and abandoned her several times. He had innumerable affairs with women and men, and in 1581 he had an illegitimate son (Sir Edward Vere) by Anne Vavasour. After spending some years travelling abroad, he became a Catholic for a short time before confessing all to Elizabeth I, giving up the Catholic Church and betraying his Catholic friends as traitors.

By the 1590s de Vere had lost most of his wealth, but he managed to retrieve his position by marrying the wealthy heiress Elizabeth Trentham, who would give him his heir, Henry de Vere, in 1592. De Vere died at King's Place, Hackney, on 24 June 1604. During his last years he received no financial assistance from Elizabeth I and was rejected as a Knight of the Garter. He is most probably best remembered as one of the great Elizabethan courtier poets – and, some claim, as the author of the works attributed to Shakespeare.

One problem with this theory is that the accepted date of birth for Edward de Vere is 12 April 1550, at Castle Hedingham, Essex

71

(home of the Earls of Oxford). The timeline for Elizabeth's affair with Thomas Seymour suggests that makes it impossible for de Vere to be Elizabeth's child. Elizabeth was sent away from Chelsea in May or June 1548; Thomas was arrested on 17 January 1549 and executed in March. Early January is therefore the last time they could have had sexual relations, meaning that the very latest birth date of their child would have to be October 1549, a good six months before de Vere was born.

Furthermore, evidence suggests that if Thomas and Elizabeth did have a sexual relationship, it occurred before Elizabeth left Catherine Parr's household in mid-1548, putting the birth no later than early January 1549 (before her interrogation and subsequent house arrest began). Although it might be possible to disguise the date of a baby's birth by a few months, it would be impossible to persuade anyone that a child of a year or more might be newborn.

If we assume that Elizabeth gave birth late in 1549, and that the baby survived, I believe there are other candidates who better fit the bill.

The Bisham Babies

On his *Royal Berkshire History* website David Nash Ford records, 'The parish church at Bisham [near Marlow], claims among its many huge monuments a "small sculptured memorial" to Queen Elizabeth's two sons, which sadly I have been unable to locate.'[4] Bisham Church is famous for its magnificent monuments to the Hoby family, who lived in nearby Bisham Abbey, a monastic building that fell into private hands with the Dissolution of the Monasteries under Henry VIII.

Sir Thomas Hoby was a noted diplomat, ambassador and leading light in the Protestant Reformation, as well as a personal friend to many of the leading reformers of the time. His wife,

Elizabeth, was one of the four daughters of Sir Anthony Cooke, a prominent Councillor to Edward VI (the other daughters married Sir William Cecil, Sir Nicholas Bacon and Sir Henry Kiligrew).

During the reign of Mary I, Hoby remained on good terms with Elizabeth. She stayed at Bisham Abbey sometime between 1555 and 1558, under a loose form of house arrest ordered by Mary I, and years later, when Elizabeth herself was Queen, she is reported to have said to Hoby, 'If I had a prisoner whom I wanted to be most carefully watched, I should entrust him to your charge.' Then she added, perhaps with a smile, 'If I had a prisoner I wished to be most tenderly treated, I should entrust him to your care.'[5] It is known that Elizabeth I visited and stayed at Bisham Abbey several times; her cousin, Margaret, daughter of Henry Carey, 1st Baron Hunsdon, married Thomas and Elizabeth Hoby's son, Sir Edward.

Close as Elizabeth may have been to the Hobys, in 1549, the house belonged to someone who loved her better and in whom she could trust even more. Henry VIII had given Bisham Abbey to Anne of Cleves as part of her divorce settlement. It was not until 1552 that Anne gave the house to Thomas Hoby as part of an exchange of lands. Anne of Cleves would have been the perfect person to take care of Elizabeth's child; she was a dear and trustworthy friend and was widely known to take in orphans, a fact that could easily explain a new baby appearing in her care.

It would have been easy for the Dennys, abetted by the Ashleys, to arrange for the child to travel the 50 miles from Cheshunt to Bisham. From Bisham, it was only about 30 miles to Anne of Cleves' principal home at Richmond Palace where her orphans' school was based. The baby could easily have been transported to Richmond, again confusing its place of origin.

Sadly, as so frequently happened in those times, the child did not survive his infancy. According to the legend, he was interred in

Bisham Church, where Anne would have arranged for the burials of any of her household servants or the orphans she cared for that died while living at Bisham. This child, however, young as it was, was given a monument, which suggested to the local people that there was something special about him. Rumour had it that he was the child of someone important.

If the burial took place early in 1550, rumours of Elizabeth having given birth the previous year would tie in with the Bisham baby. But the legend refers to two baby boys buried at Bisham. Could it be that the baby was buried with another genuine orphan who died at the same time? Were two different children buried here at different times? Or did Elizabeth perhaps give birth to twins?

74 **Hester Harington**

Bisham offered the necessary safety for placing a royal bastard: reliable foster parents and a secret location, but it is not the only possibility. There were other people who could be trusted to care for a royal infant, who lived far enough away from Court to protect the child from exposure – moreover, among them, someone who resembled Henry VIII as much as Elizabeth did, should a likeness ever be commented on.

In 1534, while Anne Boleyn held him at arms' length, Henry VIII had an affair with a lady named Joanna Dingley. In 1535, she gave birth to the King's daughter, Etheldreda, who was fostered out to the household of his tailor, John Malte. In 1548, after Henry's death, the well-dowered Etheldreda was married to John Harington, once a servant to the King, and now an attendant to Thomas Seymour. When Thomas was arrested in January of 1549, Harington was also taken into custody and imprisoned in the Tower for his links to Thomas; he spent the next year there and was released in early 1550. His release may have been triggered, in part, by his wife having need of him at home, near Bath.

Etheldreda would have been about 14 at the time and married for about a year. With her husband in prison and in some peril as a close associate of Thomas Seymour, who had been executed in March 1549, perhaps a bargain was struck. Etheldreda would take in an anonymous child and pretend it was hers if the Parrs, Ashleys, Dennys and all their influential connections would ensure that her husband was saved from a death sentence and released. What is known is that John Harington and Etheldreda Malte, in their seven years of marriage (Etheldreda died in 1555), only had one child, a daughter, Hester. The birthdate of the child was never recorded.

John Harington was completely loyal to Thomas Seymour: even after the latter's execution, he could be trusted absolutely to protect his master's illegitimate child. He was also loyal to Elizabeth. In 1554, he would be imprisoned in the Tower a second time, purportedly for delivering a letter to Elizabeth, who was suspected of plotting against Mary I.

Etheldreda, herself the illegitimate child of Henry VIII, was trusted by her royal siblings. Furthermore, if anyone noticed any resemblance between the little Hester and the Tudors, it could have been easily explained by Etheldreda's paternity – she was in fact the half-sister of Elizabeth. Etheldreda and John Harington would have made ideal guardians for the infant: financially well off, living a long way from Court, discreet and unflinchingly loyal.

After Etheldreda's death, John Harington married Isabella Markham. They would go on to have one daughter and three sons (one of whom, John Harington, would become Elizabeth's godson; he is discussed in more detail in Chapter 12). In 1568, it is known that Hester was still alive as her name was joined with her father's on a property deed. There is no further record of her, but in May 1569, John bought a wardship for the 20-year-old William Brouncker of Erlestoke in Wiltshire, most likely with the aim of acquiring the right to arrange William's marriage. One might imagine that he had Hester in mind as William's future wife, but as William's burial monument records his wives as Catherine Moore and Martha Mildmay, it could be deduced that Hester Harington, possible illegitimate daughter of Elizabeth and Thomas Seymour, died late in 1569, aged 20, unmarried.

Hugh Bethell

An essential aspect of successfully concealing the birth of a contentious illegitimate child is to make sure it is brought up as far away from the parents as possible. Ideally there should never be an occasion when the parents and child meet. The Bisham baby (or babies) was hidden among humble orphans and Hester Harington was brought up in the Somerset countryside. A third candidate also fulfils this requirement – Hugh Bethell (or Ap Ithil in the original Welsh spelling).

Hugh's father, Thomas, lived in Maunsel in Herefordshire. He married Elizabeth Rogers, who had five sons, John, Nicholas, Hugh, Roger and Andrew. Hugh's birthdate is unknown and he is quite a remarkable member of an otherwise ordinary family. What makes him stand out is that he was one of the principal beneficiaries in Blanche Parry's will. Hugh trained as a lawyer and a surveyor, and Blanche used her influence to get him his first job in 1572 as Particular Surveyor in East Riding in Yorkshire. In 1576, he was Surveyor for repairs to the castle at Kingston-upon-Hull. Under Elizabeth I, Hugh was granted the Yorkshire manor of Ellerton, while Blanche left him the Yorkshire manor of Rise and lands at Wheldrake in her will.

The question remains why would Blanche Parry have made Hugh Bethell a beneficiary? Extensive research carried out by historian Ruth Richardson has failed to find any solid link between the Parrys and the Bethells that might suggest that Hugh was a relative.[6] In her will, Blanche calls this man 40 years her junior her 'friend', one in whom she took quite an interest.

From at least 1566, Hugh Bethell was a friend of Blanche's favourite nephew, John Vaughan. John's prominent position in Herefordshire and the influence of his aunt may be indicated by his marriage to Anne, daughter and heiress of Sir Christopher Pickering and the widow of Francis Weston (one of Anne Boleyn's supposed lovers, executed in 1536) and Sir Henry Knyvett.

Despite their closeness, John and Hugh are unlikely to have been the same age, as John died in 1577 and Hugh in 1611, which would make them a generation apart. Perhaps Blanche Parry's favourite nephew, already established as a political force in his own right, took the young Hugh, a contemporary of his own son, under his wing for other reasons, as a favour to someone his mother loved?

So, if not a relative, why would Blanche and John be so kind to Hugh? If Elizabeth had a child in late 1548, she knew she could rely on Blanche Parry to help her conceal it and make sure it was well cared for and brought up in a useful profession. Blanche might have selected a family with two sons, known to her from her home county of Herefordshire (Bacton, the home of Blanche's family, and Maunsel, the home of the Bethells, are within 15 miles of each other), presenting them with a third. When two more boys followed, the third son would be even less noticeable. But this boy was different in some way; he would be befriended by Blanche's nephew, John, and patronized by Blanche herself. When Blanche was given lands by Elizabeth I, at least one in Yorkshire was managed by Hugh. If he was Elizabeth's son, he could be set up on sufficient lands for him to live well, far away from London and the Court, without needing to involve the Queen, and Blanche could keep Elizabeth informed about how the young man was doing.

77

In any event, Hugh Bethell married twice, first of all to Joan Stephens of Devonshire, and then in around 1580 to Anne, daughter of Sir William Mallory of Studley, Yorkshire. His only surviving child was his daughter, Grissel, who married Sir John Wray. Hugh died in 1611, which, if he was born in 1548, would have made him 63, and he was succeeded in his lands and titles by the son of his elder brother, Nicholas. When this family line died out, the Bethell lands passed to the descendants of the fourth brother, Roger. There are Bethells at Rise in Yorkshire to this day, but they cannot claim descent from the Tudors. The descendants of Grissel Wray, however, are still going strong – and some people claim that a direct descendant of Sir Hugh Bethell is Camilla Shand, HRH The Duchess of Cornwall, wife of Charles HRH The Prince of Wales.[7]

4

The Discreet Princess
1549–58

༄

Elizabeth began to campaign to reinstate her reputation after Thomas Seymour's execution and her own exoneration from any involvement in his treasonous activities. If she had had a child with Seymour, with it now out of the way, either dead or, more likely, placed in safe hands, Elizabeth began to rebuild her old life, starting with the return of her old governess Kat Ashley. On 7 March 1549, Elizabeth wrote to the King's Protector, Edward Seymour, listing the reasons why Kat should return to her:

First, because that she hath been with me a long time, and many years, and hath taken great labour and pain in bringing me up in learning and honesty; and, therefore, I ought of very duty to speak for her ... The second is, because I think whatsoever she hath done in my Lord Admiral's matter, as concerning the marrying of me, she did it because knowing him to be one of the Council, she thought he would not go about any such thing without he had the Council's consent thereunto ... The third cause is, because that it shall, and doth make men think, that I am not clear of the deed myself; but that it is pardoned to me because of my youth, because she that I loved so well is in such a place.[1]

Elizabeth's well-reasoned pleas succeeded, and by autumn Kat was back in her service, as was Sir Thomas Parry, although Tyrwhitt was quick to note that, apart from being an indiscreet gossip, Parry was a hopeless bookkeeper and had got Elizabeth's finances into a mess 'so indiscreetly made that it doth well appear he had little understanding to execute his office.'[2] Soon one of Tyrwhitt's clerks took over the bookkeeping and Parry became Elizabeth's secretary instead.

During this period, more references appear relating to Elizabeth's poor health, mostly relating to her trouble with migraines and eye problems. She mentions in letters that she is unable to write more often because of the pain in her 'evil head' and complains of 'a disease of the head and eyes'.

In spite of these ailments, Elizabeth kept up with her studies, working diligently with her tutor, Roger Ascham. In 1548, he had written to a friend that he was unable to leave Hatfield 'because she [Elizabeth] never lets me go anywhere.'[3] Nonetheless, he had only praise for his pupil. He wrote to John Aylmer, 'I teach her words, and she me things. I teach her tongues to speak, and her modest and maidenly looks teach me works to do. For I think she is the best disposed of any in all Europe.' In January 1550, however, he was removed from his post, as he put it, 'overcome by court violence and wrongs', having got on the wrong side of Thomas Parry, who did not like him.[4]

In April 1550, Ascham wrote a tender and laudatory letter about his erstwhile pupil to Johann Sturm at the University of Strasbourg:

> She [Elizabeth] has just passed her sixteenth birthday and shows such dignity and gentleness as are wonderful at her age and in her rank. Her study of true religion and learning is most energetic. Her mind has no womanly weakness, her

perseverance is equal to that of a man, and her memory long keeps what it quickly picks up. She talks French and Italian as well as English; she has often talked to me readily and well in Latin, and moderately so in Greek. When she writes Greek and Latin, nothing is more beautiful than her handwriting. She is as much delighted with music as she is skilful in the art. In adornment she is elegant rather than showy, and by her contempt of gold and head-dresses, she reminds one of Hippolyte rather than of Phaedra ... She likes a style that grows out of the subject; chaste because it is suitable, and beautiful because it is clear ... I am not inventing anything, my dear Sturm, it is all true.[5]

Ascham remained on good terms with Elizabeth, so much so that on her later accession to the throne she appointed him her Greek Secretary, and when he died in 1568, she is reputed to have said of him, 'I would rather have cast ten thousand pounds in the sea than parted from my Ascham.'[6]

Ascham's letter mentions a valuable part of Elizabeth's plan to rehabilitate her reputation after an anxious period as the subject of political and sexual gossip scandals. She now declined to wear elaborate, fashionable clothes, preferring her gowns to be plain and elegant. She also refused to wear ostentatious jewellery or have her hair curled and puffed in the day's fashion.

Others also remarked on her plain dress and simple style. In 1551, Mary of Guise, Regent of Scotland, visited the English Court on her way from France to Scotland. At the time, French fashion was all the rage, but Elizabeth 'kept her old maiden shamefastness.'[7] Dr John Aylmer, tutor to Lady Jane Grey and later Bishop of London, wrote in his book *A Harbour for Faithful Subjects*:

The King left her [Elizabeth] rich cloths and jewels; and I know it to be true, that in seven years after her father's death, she never in all that time looked upon that rich attire and precious jewels but once, and that against her will. And that there never came gold or stone upon her head, till her sister forced her to lay off her former sombreness, and bear her company in her glittering gayness. And then she wore it, as every man might see that her body carried that which her heart misliked. I am sure that her maidenly apparel which she used in King Edward's time, made the noblemen's daughters and wives to be ashamed to be dressed and painted like peacocks; being more moved with her most virtuous example than with all that ever Peter or Paul wrote touching the matter.[8]

Elizabeth lived quietly, moving from house to house, with a particular preference for Hatfield and Ashridge. Now that she had been vindicated of any part in Thomas Seymour's plans, she was able to resume her visits to Court to see her brother. Elizabeth and Edward had remained close, frequently writing to each other when they were apart. When Edward asked for a portrait of her, Elizabeth sent one with this accompanying letter:

For the face, I grant, I might well blush to offer; but the mind I shall never be ashamed to present. For though from the grace of the picture the colours may fade by time ... yet the other nor time with her swift wings shall overtake, nor the misty clouds with their lowerings may darken ... And further I shall most humbly beseech your Majesty that when you shall look on my picture you will witsafe to think, that as you have but the outward show of the body afore you, so my inward mind wisheth, that the body itself were oftener in your presence.[9]

Keeping abreast of Court activity, in early 1550 Elizabeth became friendly with the new leader of the Council, John Dudley, now 2nd Earl of Warwick. He was given Hatfield, her favourite house, and when she wrote to the Council in June offering to exchange a manor in Lincolnshire for Hatfield, Dudley was pleased to agree. Elizabeth and the King's Protector, Edward Seymour, had not always been on the best terms, and she found Dudley much easier to deal with. Their good relations were well known, so much so that Jehan Scheyfve, the Imperial Ambassador, wrote in his dispatches, 'I have heard from a safe source that my Lord Warwick is about to cast off his wife and marry my lady Elizabeth, daughter of the late King, with whom he is said to have had several secret and intimate personal communications; and by these means he will aspire to the Crown.'[10]

While it was a fascinating piece of gossip, there were other plans afoot for the 17-year-old Elizabeth to marry – and not to an English nobleman. Preliminary negotiations were taking place for her to marry into a powerful European family: either a French Duke or Frederick, Crown Prince of Denmark.[11] Neither plan would progress very far, but political observers would have been aware that, as a Protestant, Elizabeth's position in the royal line was strong.

When Elizabeth visited London in January 1551, Ambassador Scheyfve wrote that she 'was most honourably received by the Council who acted thus in order to show the people how much glory belongs to her who has embraced the new religion and is become a very great lady.'[12] There is no doubt that the 13-year-old Edward loved his sister Mary, but the question of her unyielding Catholicism was souring relations between them. Elizabeth worshipped according to the King's royal decree, made no great public shows of her faith and stayed discreet. Edward was said to have called her 'his sweet sister Temperance'.

During this period of her quiet life in the country, Elizabeth was to develop what would become one of the key relationships of her reign. In 1550, Elizabeth hired William Cecil as Surveyor for her lands and properties at a salary of £20 a year, a post that was quite a valuable sinecure at the time. A letter dating from 1548 suggests that Elizabeth and Cecil were already known to each other, probably through his post as Secretary to the Protector. He was a skilled administrator and was eventually appointed as one of the principal secretaries to the Council and its leader, John Dudley. His position allowed Cecil privileged access to the Council members, making him a valuable ally to anyone who wished to keep abreast of the political mood of the Court. As his power grew, he would become a powerful connection for Elizabeth.

At this time, the kingdom was in difficulty. Royal finances had been depleted by war with Scotland and France, and in 1549, social unrest at home culminated in several armed revolts spurred by religious and agrarian issues. The blame was placed on the government of the Protector, Edward Seymour. On 22 January 1552, he was executed, and the leader of the Council, John Dudley, became the major force in the English Court. Before long, he was granted the title of 1st Duke of Northumberland and, although he never took up the title, he became Protector in all but name.

Dudley gave Edward VI more apparent freedom than his predecessor had, letting him take part in 'manly' pursuits such as hunting and jousting, and was better liked by the King. But Edward's new liberty would be brief. In April 1552, he fell ill with measles, and then recovered. He spent a strenuous summer, and by late autumn was ill again. By January 1553, he was bedridden with a terminal illness, probably tuberculosis.

Now Dudley was faced with a dilemma. If Henry VIII's will was followed to the letter, the heiress to the throne was to be Princess Mary, a formidable Catholic who would doubtless put an end to the Protestant Reformation in England. He considered the option of Elizabeth as a viable alternative to the next queen, perhaps even with himself as the power behind the throne. Sources indicate that Dudley was considering marrying Elizabeth to his eldest son or even 'that he might find it expedient to get rid of his own wife and marry Elizabeth himself.'[13]

However, Dudley may have suspected that if Elizabeth was monarch, she would be unlikely to play the puppet; she would choose her own ministers and marry whom she wanted, with the result that he would cease to wield any real power. An even more bizarre plan by Dudley was alleged in a book published around 1584. A passage suggests that Dudley intended to wed Mary to retain power: ' the Duke of Northumberland had strange devices in his head ... for bringing the crown to his own family. And among other devices it is thought that he had most certain intention to marry the Lady Mary himself ...' As to the fact that John Dudley was married at the time: 'These great personages, in matters of such weight as is a kingdom, have privileges to dispose of women's bodies, marriages, lives and deaths, as shall be thought for the time most convenient.'[14]

Another alternative was to find Elizabeth a husband outside of England, getting rid of her so that she and Mary could be removed from the succession more easily. Dudley considered the possibility of Elizabeth marrying Francesco d'Este, Prince of Massa Lombarda and son of Alfonso d'Este, Duke of Ferrara and Lucrecia Borgia. There was, however, little support for the marriage.

Early in 1553, Dudley opted for a different approach and began working to persuade the King to change the succession. Edward VI was reminded that Mary and Elizabeth were both illegitimate, and more importantly, that Mary would bring Catholicism back to England. Dudley reasoned that if Mary were to be struck out of the succession, how could Elizabeth, her equal, be left in? Futhermore, he argued that both the princesses would seek foreign husbands, jeopardizing English sovereignty.[15]

As part of his plan, Dudley determined to keep the dying Edward away from Elizabeth, in case he decided to exclude Mary but insist on making Elizabeth his heir out of love and respect. Dudley made sure Elizabeth's and Edward's letters to each other were never delivered. A letter survives from Elizabeth to Edward, showing that she was on her way to visit him when she heard he was seriously unwell, but was turned back by a messenger who said he had been sent by the King:

> Two chief occasions moved me much and grieved me greatly – the one, for that I doubted your Majesty's health – the other, because for all my long tarrying I went without that I came for. Of the first, I am relieved in a part, both that I understood of your health … Of my other grief I am not eased … For if your Grace's advice that I should return (whose will is a commandment) had not been, I would not have made the half of my way the end of my journey …[16]

By April, Edward was vomiting phlegm, black bile and blood, and Dudley's desperate search for a Queen he could control and manipulate intensified. He persuaded the dying Edward to name his cousin Lady Jane Grey (Henry VIII's great-niece, who also happened to be married to Dudley's youngest son, Guildford

Dudley) as his successor, thereby excluding his two half-sisters, Mary and Elizabeth. Finally, after months of agony, the 15-year-old Edward VI died on 6 July 1553, leaving the throne to the Protestant Lady Jane and her sons.

Dudley immediately put his plans into action, withholding the official notification of the death of the King and sending messages to Mary and Elizabeth to summon them to London, presumably to take the two princesses into custody. But the luckless Lady Jane, proclaimed Queen on 10 July, would rule for only nine days.

As Elizabeth avoided trouble by taking to her bed at Hatfield and claiming to be too ill to travel, Mary set off for London, but was warned of the plot at Hoddesdon and fled to Kenninghall to plan her strategy. So loyal were the people of England to Henry VIII's daughter, she was able to raise an army from her base at Framlingham and march on London. With her base growing, Parliament proclaimed Mary as Queen, and Lady Jane was placed under arrest.

87

✒

The Catholic Mary I (Queen of England and Ireland 1553–58) acceded to the throne on a wave of popular support. Catholics, who had suffered under the rule of Edward VI's ministers, welcomed her with open arms. They expected that she would re-establish the Catholic Church, give back the monastic lands and effectively turn the clock back 20 years. Many Protestants also supported her right to rule, but hoped the Council would keep her from bringing back the Catholic religion and from punishing the growing numbers of Protestants. As the daughter of Henry VIII, everyone was prepared to support Mary.

By 24 July 1553, Dudley's powerbase had crumbled and he was arrested. Mary I was able to disband most of her army, safe in the knowledge that she had the support of the vast majority of the nobles. She moved slowly, arriving in London on 3 August. Elizabeth, once she had received confirmation of Mary's success, left Hatfield on 30 July for London, staying at Somerset House. She rode out to meet Mary with an entourage of 1,000 horsemen, knights and ladies. The sisters met at Aldgate, embraced, kissed, and rode into London together. Mary I, dressed in purple and gold and laden with jewels, was 37 years old; Elizabeth was 20. The cortege proceeded to the Tower, where prisoners including John Dudley and Jane Grey were held. Dudley would be beheaded on 22 August, charged with high treason.

At first Mary and Elizabeth's interactions were friendly. Mary, who at the age of 20 had been responsible for the household of the 3-year-old Elizabeth when Anne Boleyn was executed, seems to have had great affection for her younger half-sister, whom she possibly at one stage may have viewed as a surrogate child. The relationship, however, was never straightforward. In spite of her reconciliation with Henry VIII after Anne Boleyn's death, Mary always blamed Elizabeth's mother for the breakdown of her parents' marriage and Catherine of Aragon's subsequent miserable death in poverty and loneliness.

At times, Mary could put this aside and enjoy the company of her younger sister, sending her small gifts, giving her pocket money and exchanging letters. The feeling seems to have been mutual, with Elizabeth writing to Mary in 1552 to commiserate with her for another bout of a longstanding illness. This may refer to Mary's migraine headaches, or to the monthly period pains that she had suffered from the time she was about 16 years old:

> Good sister, As to hear of your sickness is unpleasant to me,
> so is it nothing fearful, for that I understand it is your old

guest that is wont oft to visit you, whose coming, though it be oft, yet is it never welcome ... Good sister, though I have good cause to thank you for your oft sending to me, yet I have more occasion to render you my hearty thanks for your gentle writing, which how painful it is to you, I may well guess by myself. And you may well see by my writing so oft, how pleasant it is to me. And thus I end to trouble you, desiring God to send you as well to do as you can think and wish or I desire or pray ... Your loving sister, Elizabeth.[17]

The letter is light, cheerful and lacks the heavy formality of Elizabeth's letters to her father, stepmother and brother – and her later letters to Mary as Queen. At the time of Mary's accession, Elizabeth counted her sister a friend.

At Mary I's coronation, Elizabeth enjoyed a prominent role, riding in the procession in a carriage draped with silver cloth together with Anne of Cleves (as part of her divorce settlement, Anne of Cleves, the King's 'sister', was acknowledged to rank only below Mary and Elizabeth, the King's daughters), and sitting at the Queen's table during the banquet in Westminster Hall.

However, when Mary's rule began in earnest, her relationship with Elizabeth changed. She became obsessed with restoring Catholicism to England and soon fell under the influence of her cousin, the Holy Roman Emperor Charles V, King of Spain, and his Imperial Ambassador Simon Renard, who had replaced Eustache Chapuys at the English Court. From the outset, Renard advised Mary that Elizabeth was not to be trusted, that she had 'a spirit full of enchantment ... clever and sly', and that she should be watched as she would prove disloyal.[18]

Mary's Council, which comprised both previously serving and new members, found itself sidelined in favour of Spanish advisers.

89

Mary sought to restore Catholicism immediately, even wanting to bury the Protestant Edward VI with Catholic rites. Renard persuaded her against this, and so the King had a Protestant funeral 'with scant ceremony' after remaining unburied for more than a month.[19] Within weeks of her accession, the significant changes that Mary instigated, such as the reintroduction of Catholic priests and ceremonies, resulted in violent protests on the streets of London.

Amongst this religious upheaval, Elizabeth found herself in an extremely delicate position. She did not wish to throw herself wholeheartedly into Catholic worship, partly because she had been brought up as a Protestant, but also because she knew that by allying herself too closely with the Catholic faction she would destroy the support she had from the kingdom's large number of Protestants. She endeavoured to walk a fine line, just Catholic enough to please Mary, but not so much as to alienate the Protestant faction. She explained to Mary that it would take time for her to assimilate and accept the different faith, and asked for books and instruction.

On 8 September 1553, Elizabeth attended her first Mass, although on the day she was suffering from a severe stomach upset that meant she was unable to enjoy the service, as Renard noted.[20]

The angry French Ambassador, who found himself marginalized by the Spaniards, wrote to Henri II (King of France 1547–59), 'everyone believes that she is acting from fear of danger and peril from those around her than from real devotion.'[21] However, it should be kept in mind that the French had ulterior motives in portraying Elizabeth in a bad light and in encouraging plots that might implicate her: if Elizabeth was removed from the succession, the next lawful heir was another Catholic Mary (Mary, Queen of Scots), who just happened to be married to the French Dauphin, François.

Apart from the religious turmoil, one of the first priorities of the English Council was the marriage of the new Queen, who was 37 years of age. The most obvious English candidate was Edward Courtenay, Mary's second cousin, who had recently been released from the Tower after a 15-year imprisonment following his family's implication in a Catholic uprising in 1538. Courtenay was the last of the legitimate York bloodline, and their union would reunite the Royal Houses, as the marriage of Henry Tudor and Elizabeth of York had done previously, in 1486. There was some support for this among the English nobles, and particularly among Mary's ladies-in-waiting, who included Courtenay's mother, the Dowager Marchioness of Exeter.

The problem with this plan, however, was twofold. Firstly, on his release from the Tower, Courtenay set about making up for all the years he had spent in prison. He began drinking, wenching, and generally behaving so badly in public that it became an open scandal. Secondly, Mary did not find him attractive, despite his fair good looks and his Catholicism.

Another potential English candidate was Reginald Pole, the son of Mary's Governess, Margaret Pole, 8th Countess of Salisbury. Unfortunately, he was living in Rome, had taken holy orders and had been elected a Papal Cardinal.

At this timely juncture, Renard showed Mary a portrait of Philip, the son of Charles V, and suggested that this handsome young prince might make a good husband. Charles V also dissuaded potential suitors from making Mary marriage offers, using his immense influence to win the throne of England for his own son. On 10 October 1553, a formal proposal of marriage was submitted to Mary, and on 28 October she accepted. Although some Councillors tried to discourage her, and the House of Commons formally requested that Mary take an English husband, it was to no avail. On 16 November, Mary publicly announced that she would take Philip as her husband.

Now that the question of marriage was settled, Renard could concentrate on alienating Mary from her sister. The Queen's Spanish advisers fuelled her suspicions of Elizabeth's dishonest intentions, asserted that she should be removed from the succession and even suggested that Elizbabeth be executed. Allowing her hatred of Anne Boleyn to surface and encouraged by Elizabeth's detractors, Mary said to Renard 'that it would be a scandal and a disgrace to the kingdom to allow Elizabeth to succeed, for she was a heretic, a hypocrite and a bastard.'[22]

In one of her more paranoid ramblings about her sister, Mary claimed that Elizabeth was not Henry VIII's child and that she looked exactly like Mark Smeaton, the lowliest of Anne Boleyn's alleged lovers. Elizabeth, however, was said to resemble Henry VIII greatly – more so, it was sometimes said, than Mary I.

Elizabeth quickly became aware of Mary's mounting hostility, and after the coronation she requested permission to retire from Court. Mary responded by reducing her status (as had been done to Mary when Elizabeth was born), openly indicating that she considered Elizabeth, her legal heir, to be of no importance. In official state processions, Elizabeth would no longer walk directly behind the Queen, but instead behind Margaret Douglas, Countess of Lennox (the daughter of Margaret Tudor, Henry VIII's elder sister) and Frances Grey, Duchess of Suffolk (the mother of Lady Jane Grey, who had been convicted for high treason and was imprisoned in the Tower).

This was a terrible slight. Elizabeth did the only thing she could to retain her dignity and stayed in her rooms as much as possible. With this stalemate in place, in December, Mary allowed Elizabeth to leave Court for Ashridge in Hertfordshire. This was not only to remove her from Court, but also to allow Elizabeth the illusion of freedom and become embroiled in the plots that the Spanish advisers so wanted her to become involved in and they hoped that would lead to her eventual downfall.

One such plot was already forming. The French Ambassador de Noailles, who had his ear to the ground and had noted the English people's horrified reaction to the Queen's plans for a Spanish marriage, wrote, 'From what I hear, it only requires that my Lord Courtenay should marry her [Elizabeth], and that they should go together to the counties of Devonshire and Cornwall. Here it can easily be believed that they would find many adherents, and they could then make a strong claim to the crown, and the Emperor and Prince of Spain would find it difficult to suppress the rising.'[23]

Indeed, Courtenay, who thought Mary would wed him, had been furious when she had chosen Philip, and rumours suggested that he was already preparing a revolt against the new monarch. However, as a conspirator he was a disaster. Even de Noailles, who would have loved such a plot to come to fruition, said of him, 'Courtenay is of such a fearful and timid disposition that he dare not make the venture … There are many, of whom I know, who would be ready to give him encouragement and all help in carrying out some plan to his advantage, and I do not see what should hinder him, except his weakness, faint-heartedness and timidity.'[24]

As for Elizabeth, she had survived the Seymour enquiry and she would never allow herself to be linked to so feeble a co-conspirator when she had so much to lose. She was also wise enough to realize that any plots against Mary's reign had little hope of success, and if it could be proved that Elizabeth had supported any of them, she would most likely lose her life.

93

On 2 January 1554, Charles V sent his envoys to London to undertake negotiations, and on 12 January a treaty of marriage was signed. Protestants fearing Catholic repression planned a rebellion, with simultaneous risings in Devonshire, led by Sir Peter Carew; in Kent, by Sir Thomas Wyatt; and in Wales, by Sir James Crofts. However, Courtenay, displaying his usual vacillation, went to his mentor Bishop Gardiner and told him everything. With Courtenay out of the equation, the rising in Devonshire was doomed to failure. Sir Peter Carew backed out and fled to France, followed by Sir William Pickering, another conspirator and a friend of Elizabeth's. Sir Thomas Wyatt, believing that the revolt would unleash a popular uprising in opposition to the Spanish marriage, went ahead. His rebellion was crushed and he surrendered.

At Ashridge, Elizabeth had her usual reaction in time of crisis: she took to her bed with a serious illness. False rumours flew to London – that Elizabeth had fortified Ashridge to withstand a siege, or that she was on her way to the more easily defended Donnington Castle. In fact, she stayed put, suffering from blinding headaches and swelling in her face, arms and legs, which might have been nephritis or, perhaps, inflammation of the kidneys.

Mary sent a message saying that she should come to London for her own safety, although probably with the intention of arresting her for treason. The message came back that Elizabeth was far too ill to move. She requested the Court's doctors to attend her, but the Council refused. When it was suggested she see local doctors, she replied, 'I am not minded to make any stranger privy to the state of my body.'[25]

Mary arranged for Dr George Owen and Dr Thomas Wendy to come and examine Elizabeth and oversee her travel, accompanied by Lord William Howard (Elizabeth's great-uncle), Sir Edward Hastings and Sir Thomas Cornwallis. Lord William wrote to the Queen that he found Elizabeth very willing, but that she had feared that she was so weak as to be unable to travel without fear for her life. She 'therefore desired some longer respite until she had better recovered her strength; but in conclusion, upon the persuasion ... she is resolved to remove hence tomorrow towards your Highness ...'[26]

It was agreed that Elizabeth could move, but only very slowly and carefully. On 12 February, they set out, although when Elizabeth was brought to the litter 'she was very faint and feeble and in such case that she was ready to swound three or four times.' They had 30 miles to travel, which Lord William estimated would take 5 days: in fact, it took 10.[27]

At the outskirts of London, Elizabeth had the curtains of the litter drawn back so that she could be seen lying there, thin and pale. She was dressed in white, the colour of innocence and purity. This gesture was, in part, in response to new rumours that she was pregnant, this time by Courtenay. Renard had reported as much to Charles V: 'Wyatt [who had been arrested] cannot be executed until he has been confronted with the Lady Elizabeth, who is so unwell that she only travels two or three leagues a day, and has such a stricken conscience that she refuses meat or drink. It is taken for certain that she is with child.' A week later Renard reported that a French plot had been uncovered regarding Courtenay and Elizabeth, 'who, they say, has lived loosely like her mother, and is now with child.'[28]

For a princess suspected of treason, with powerful enemies, London was horrific. There were gallows on the streets with the hanged bodies of traitors. Courtenay had been arrested and was incarcerated in the Tower, as was Henry Grey, 1st Duke of Suffolk, who had tried to raise a rebellion in the Midlands with the aim of restoring his daughter, Lady Jane Grey, to the throne. His lunatic

95

scheme led to both of their deaths on the block. On 12 February 1554, Lady Jane Grey and her husband, Guildford Dudley, were executed in the Tower. On 21 February, two days before Elizabeth arrived in London, the French Ambassador de Noailles described the gibbeted bodies and severed heads on display, adding '... the Princess Elizabeth, for whom no better fate is foreseen, is lying ill, about seven or eight miles from hence, so swollen and disfigured that her death is expected ...'[29]

Elizabeth was taken to Whitehall Palace, where she was confined to her rooms, and her servants were sent away and replaced with supporters of the Queen. The evidence against her in plotting to overthrow Mary was circumstantial; a letter from her to Mary had been found in the possession of the French Ambassador's messenger, suggesting she had been in written contact with him. The rebel Wyatt had also sent letters to her at Ashridge, and another rebellion leader, Sir James Crofts, had actually visited the house.

On 15 March, Bishop Gardiner came to Whitehall with about 20 of the Councillors and confronted Elizabeth, accusing her of being party to the uprisings of Sir Peter Carew and Sir Thomas Wyatt. Elizabeth was due to be sent to the Tower the following day, but managed to delay matters by writing a letter to the Queen. Her guardians, William Paulet, 1st Marquess of Winchester, and Thomas Radclyffe, 3rd Earl of Sussex, were divided over whether the letter should be sent, with the latter winning out. Elizabeth pleaded for her sister to hear her out:

If any ever did try this old saying, 'that a King's word was more than another man's oath', I most humbly beseech your majesty to verify it to me, and to remember your last promise and my last demand, that I be not condemned without answer and due proof, which it seems that I now am; for without cause proved, I am by your Council from you commanded to go to the Tower, a place more wanted for a false traitor than a true subject, which though I know I desire it not, yet in the face of all this realm it appear proved I pray to God I may die the shamefullest death that any ever died, if I may mean any such thing; and to this present hour I protest before God (who shall judge my truth, whatsoever malice may devise), that I never practiced, counselled, not consented to anything that might be prejudicial to your person any way, or dangerous to the state by any means ... I pray God the like evil persuasions persuade not one sister against the other, and all for that they have heard false reports, and the truth not known. Therefore, once again, kneeling with humbleness of heart, because I am not suffered to bow the knees of my body, I humbly crave to speak with your Highness, which I would not be so bold as to desire if I knew not myself most clear, as I know myself most true ...

Your Highness's most faithful subject, that hath been from the beginning, and will be to my end, Elizabeth. I humbly crave but only one word of answer from yourself.[30]

This desperate attempt to prick the Queen's conscience gained Elizabeth 24 hours, but infuriated Mary, who lashed out at the nobles who delivered the letter, saying they would never have dared thwart her father in such a manner.

Thus, on 17 March, Elizabeth, accompanied by her guardians, went by river to be imprisoned in the Tower. She was attended by three of her ladies-in-waiting, three of the Queen's, a gentleman usher and two grooms. Sir John Gage, the Lord Chamberlain and acting Constable of the Tower, was with them. Radclyffe, mindful that Elizabeth might survive and become heir to the throne, reminded them that they should remember who they were dealing with. If Elizabeth was found guilty of treason, it would be the perfect opportunity to rid themselves of her permanently. Renard and the Spanish delegation put pressure on Mary, warning that Philip would be unwilling to come to England as her husband as long as traitors like Elizabeth posed a threat, and that even if Elizabeth's part in Wyatt's rebellion could not be proved, she was still a possible focus for future uprisings. Renard wrote in his dispatches '... that it was of the utmost importance that the trials and executions of the criminals, especially those of Courtenay and Elizabeth, should be concluded before the arrival of the prince ... as long as Elizabeth was alive, there was no hope that the kingdom could be tranquil.'[31]

Bishop Gardiner, desperate to protect a precariously Catholic England, was convinced of Elizabeth's guilt and sought to find solid proof against her, beyond the circumstantial evidence that he had. The incriminating letter held by the French Ambassador was a copy, so it might not have come from Elizabeth since it could have been copied by anyone, including any number of spies at Court hired by the French. Equally, although Wyatt had sent letters to Ashridge, there was no evidence that they had ever reached Elizabeth or that she had responded to them. Crofts might have visited Ashridge, but even he admitted that he had spoken only to one of Elizabeth's servants and had no idea if she had ever got his message or if she supported him. As for the alleged link between Elizabeth and Courtenay, Lord William Paget had to admit that he had once, on instructions from the Council, asked Courtenay if he might consider marrying Elizabeth, and Courtenay had very firmly refused.

Even the accusation that Elizabeth wanted to flee to the well-fortified Donnington Castle proved to be suspect; whatever the rebellion leaders might have wanted, Elizabeth had not gone anywhere. The interrogations carried on, but there was no additional evidence, and what little there was became more shaky by the day. When the rebellion leader Sir James Crofts was brought to the Tower to confront Elizabeth with his evidence, he knelt to her, and according to the report confessed that: 'He was heartily sorry to be brought in that day to be a witness against her Grace, but he took God to record that he never knew anything of her, worthy the least suspicion.'[32] On 11 April 1554, Wyatt was executed; eyewitnesses reported that on the scaffold he exonerated Elizabeth from any part in the plots.

While her enemies lobbied for her execution, Elizabeth's life in the Tower improved slightly. She was permitted to walk through the adjacent rooms, and eventually she was allowed to go out into a small, walled garden. The five-year-old son of the Keeper of the Wardrobe and two little girls visited her until they were forbidden to do so: it was thought they might be passing her messages from Courtenay, who was also in the Tower at the time.

Outside, there was chaos among the Councillors. Renard wrote to Charles V that '… quarrels, jealousy and ill-will have increased among the Councillors, becoming so public that several of them, out of spite, no longer attend the meetings. What one does, another undoes; what one advises, another opposes; one strives to save Courtenay, another Elizabeth; and such is the confusion that one can only expect the upshot to be arms and tumult.'[33] The political vacillation was due to the fact that everyone recognized that Elizabeth was still heir to the throne until Mary married and produced a child.

Despite Mary's reverence for Charles V, her burgeoning love for Philip and her respect for Renard, she would not agree to

99

Elizabeth being tried for treason when there was so little evidence against her. While Mary would have preferred to find Elizabeth guilty, she could only do so, in all conscience, in the face of serious and convincing proof. Without this, Mary stood firm.

Realizing that Elizabeth might escape execution, Renard devised a back-up plan and proposed that she should be married, preferably to a Spanish dependent, and should live abroad. The primary candidate was Emmanuel Philibert, Duke of Savoy and Prince of Piedmont, which were grand-sounding titles for a ruler without a kingdom. He was, however, Philip's cousin. His mother, Beatriz, was the sister of Philip's mother, Isabel, both daughters of Manuel I (King of Portugal 1495–1521) and Maria of Aragon, Catherine of Aragon's sister. Elizabeth, however, refused to entertain the marriage, knowing that she would have the support of the Council, who would oppose any attempt to have her married abroad to an insignificant Spanish nobleman.

After two months of uncertainty and fear in the Tower, Elizabeth was appointed a new jailer, Sir Henry Bedingfield. On 19 May 1554, they left the Tower for the palace of Woodstock, where Elizabeth was to be held under house arrest. Bedingfield had hoped for a quiet, anonymous journey, but he was rudely disabused of this almost immediately. Passing through Windsor, the boys of Eton College turned out in force to cheer the princess, while local women made cakes and 'wafers' (biscuits) for her and tossed them into her litter. At Aston, they rang the church bells, and a frustrated and angry Bedingfield ordered that the bell-ringers be arrested. At Ricote 'Her Grace was marvellously entertained' at the house of Sir John Williams, Baron Williams of Thame, who had accompanied Bedingfield from the Tower. Somewhat annoyed at the turn of events, Bedingfield told Williams that Mary I might not care for his actions. Williams replied that 'he was well advised of his doing and that her grace [Elizabeth] might and should in his house be merry.'[34]

All along the route to Woodstock, people came to cheer Elizabeth. Mary I had become increasingly unpopular with the people because of her violent repression of non-Catholics. During her rule, hundreds of Protestants were burned at the stake, earning her the name 'Bloody Mary'. For Elizabeth, the obvious and public signs of the people's affection were a clear indication of her popularity over Mary and would surely help her endure the months to come.

Arriving at their destination, they found the palace had virtually fallen into ruin; Elizabeth and her servants were obliged to make their home in four rooms in the gatehouse. While Bedingfield proved an exasperating, pedantic guardian, checking even the smallest request with the Council before granting or refusing it, he meant her no harm and was not cruel to her. She might not be allowed to send or receive letters without permission, but she was able to read any book she could get her hands on and to take walks in the gardens and orchard when the weather permitted.

Elizabeth was always aware of spies around her, reporting every word and deed to the Council and to the Imperial Ambassador. As if to reinforce her claim of innocence, she is reported to have written a short verse in charcoal on the wall of one of her chambers (others say on a window shutter). Although it faded with time, copies were made in the 1590s and early 1600s. The verse starts by blaming Fortune for causing the writer to be at Woodstock, a helpless prisoner:

> ... *Thou causedst the guilty to be loosed*
> *From lands where innocents were enclosed,*
> *And caused the guiltless to be reserved,*
> *And freed those that death had well deserved.*

101

> *But all herein can be naught wrought,*
> *So God grant to my foes as they have thought.*
> FINIS ELISABETHA A PRISONER 1555[35]

The verse ends with a version of the saying that God will send 'evil to he who evil thinks'. The message is clear – although surrounded by evildoers, the innocent will have the final vengeance.

By the end of June, Elizabeth was ill again, 'daily vexed with swelling in the face and other parts of her body.'[36] Her favourite doctors could not attend to her, but they recommended two others from Oxford who were never summoned. Elizabeth disliked strangers and would, she said, rather leave the outcome of her illness to God.[37]

102

Exacerbating her dire situation was that money from London was slow in coming. Wages for servants and guards did not arrive and Bedingfield had to pay for supplies out of his own pocket. This neglect by the Council may have been due in part to the fact that on 25 July 1554, Philip and Mary were married in a grand ceremony at Winchester Cathedral, with all the great nobles of Europe present. Elizabeth was not invited, of course. The couple travelled slowly back to the capital, arriving in London on 18 August. By November, Mary reported that she was pregnant. The Court did not have much time to consider Elizabeth's well being, out of sight and mind, as she was, at dreary Woodstock.

In the months to follow, Bedingfield and Elizabeth continued to live in a state of heightened irritation with each other. She made numerous requests, many of which he believed were frivolous and meant to annoy. He refused to allow her to do even simple things without seeking permission from the Council, a process that usually took weeks. As time passed, Elizabeth's friends and servants, particularly Sir Thomas Parry, began to appear in

Woodstock village, staying at the local inn, The Bull. Bedingfield could not prevent them from coming, so had the added worry that they might try to communicate with the princess.

In a ruined palace, short of money, constantly rubbing each other up the wrong way, Elizabeth and her governor each existed in a state little short of martyrdom. When she became Queen, Elizabeth is reported to have said to him, 'If we have any prisoner whom we would have sharply and straitly kept, we will send for you.'[38] However, as she never punished him, perhaps she recognized that his lack of malice outweighed his infuriating insistence on following rules.

Finally, in April 1555, Elizabeth was allowed to leave Woodstock to come back to Hampton Court and attend the Queen in her late pregnancy. Mary had little choice but to attempt to mend fences with her sister. Childbirth was dangerous at the time, and a new mother, bearing her first child at about the age of 40, was in particular danger. The Queen and Philip had to consider the implications of mother and child dying, since the Council and Parliament had rigorously refused to make Philip King Regnant, which would have allowed him to rule England if Mary and their child died. Mary's successor, despite all her attempts to change the fact, was Elizabeth. Philip may also have softened Mary's attitude towards her sister for political motives – Spain was wary of France at the time, and as the other heiress to the English throne was the French ally Mary, Queen of Scots, he may have felt that Elizabeth was the lesser of two evils.

When she arrived at Hampton Court, Elizabeth was met by Philip. Later she was confronted by Bishop Gardiner and the Council, who requested that she admit her 'offences' and beg the Queen for forgiveness. Elizabeth reminded them that she had not committed any offences and so had nothing to confess; she would

103

prefer to remain a prisoner all her life than admit to something she had never even entertained.

Finally, at 10 p.m., Elizabeth was taken to meet Mary. The Queen accused Elizabeth of conspiring against her; Elizabeth wept and swore her loyalty. The meeting ended with the Queen saying 'God knows' in Spanish, leading to the legend that Philip was hidden somewhere in or near the room, eavesdropping on their conversation to try to get a better understanding of his sister-in-law. [39]

The whole Court awaited the imminent birth of an heir. Elizabeth had very few visitors, although she was allowed to receive who she liked. She stayed in her rooms and waited with the rest. Mary, ecstatic in her pregnancy and believing the birth of a son to be only a few weeks away, felt secure enough to release Courtenay and exile him; he died in Padua in September 1556. She also released the Dudley brothers from the Tower, where they had been imprisoned with their father when he had tried to put Lady Jane Grey on the throne; Guildford had already been executed, John died shortly after his release, but Ambrose, Robert and Henry joined the English army in France.

As April progressed, there were no signs of labour, but it was not easy to calculate when the full-term of a pregnancy was due, so May came and went before it became clear that all was not well. Throughout June, Mary desperately clung to her fading hope, but by July it became obvious that, whatever this was, it was not a pregnancy. Mary was devastated.

While Mary kept to her rooms, praying for a child, her husband Philip began to get to know his sister-in-law. He and Elizabeth spent a lot of time together, not without comment. In 1557, Giovanni Michiel, the Venetian Ambassador, would write to the Doge, 'at the time of the Queen's pregnancy, Lady Elizabeth … contrived so to ingratiate herself with all the Spaniards, and especially with the King, that ever since no one has favoured her more than he does.' He also thought that Philip did 'not only ... not permit, but opposed, and prevented the Queen's [Mary's] wish to have her [Elizabeth] ... declared a bastard by Act of Parliament ... and consequently ineligible to the throne, which, besides affection, argued some particular design on the part of the King with regard to her.'[40]

Philip himself later acknowledged that while his wife waited to give birth, he flirted with her younger, more attractive sister, and that Elizabeth did nothing to stop him. Thomas Cecil, William Cecil's eldest son, reported that he heard Philip say 'whatever he suffered from Queen Elizabeth was the just judgement of God, because, being married to Queen Mary, whom he thought a most virtuous and good lady, yet in the fancy of love he could not affect her; but as for the Lady Elizabeth, he was enamoured of her, being a fair and beautiful woman.'[41]

Mary's anguish and the desperate need of her Catholic supporters for her to have a son led to a strange rumour surfacing. It is recorded in Foxe's *Book of Martyrs* in the section 'Concerning the Child-bed of Queen Mary':

> There came to me whom I did both hear and see, one Isabel Malt, a woman dwelling in Aldersgate street in Horn Alley ... who before witness made this declaration unto us, that she being delivered of a man-child upon Whitsunday in the morning, which was the 11th day of June 1555, there came to her the Lord North [Edward North, Baron North of Kirtling, a member of Mary's Council], and another lord of her unknown, dwelling then about Old fifthstreet, demanding of her if she would part with her child, and would swear that she ne'er knew nor had any such child.

Which, if she would, her son (they said) would be well provided for, she should take no care for it, with many fair offers if she would part with the child. After that came other women also … but she in no wise would let go her son, who at the writing hereof being alive and called Timothy Malt, was of the age of thirteen years and upward. Thus much I say, I heard from the woman herself.[42]

On 3 August, after the fiasco of the false pregnancy had died down, Mary, Philip and the Court moved to Oatlands in Surrey. Elizabeth was not with them. Despite Mary's pleas, on 29 August, Philip left her and returned to Spain. The despairing Queen went to Greenwich where she stayed with Cardinal Reginald Pole, an old friend. Elizabeth joined her and attended Mass at her side. There, she was reunited with an old friend, Ascham, who had also 'embraced' Catholicism and had been allowed to return to Court as the Queen's Latin Secretary. He and Elizabeth took pleasure in reading Greek texts together.

In October, the sisters separated, Mary going to St James and Elizabeth to her beloved Hatfield. Kat Ashley was allowed to return to Elizabeth's service, as was Sir Thomas Parry, while Ascham found time to drop in every now and then. Life resumed a gentler pace, this time with Philip as Elizabeth's friend rather than her enemy. It had become clear that Mary was as unlikely to have a child as she was to enjoy a long life; Philip was covering his bets, making sure he was on good terms with the next Queen of England. Now when Mary railed against Elizabeth, her Spanish advisers tried to calm her down. Renard was replaced as Ambassador, and in November 1555, Bishop Gardiner, Elizabeth's greatest opponent, died.

In March 1556, there was a minor uprising, referred to as Dudley's Rebellion, led by Henry Dudley, a distant relation of John

Dudley. The plotters gave their aim as 'to send the Queen's Highness over to the King [to Spain] and to make the Lady Elizabeth Queen and to marry the Earl of Devonshire to the said Lady.'[43] The rebellion was betrayed early on and came to nothing. Elizabeth was never convincingly implicated.[44]

❧

Plans to marry off Elizabeth and send her out of England were still raised from time to time and after the rebellion in April 1556, the question arose again. In the previous year Mary's husband, Philip, (Philip II, 1556–98) had suggested that 23-year-old Elizabeth marry his 10-year-old son and heir, Prince Carlos (Philip's first wife, before Mary, was Princess Maria of Portugal, who had died giving birth to Carlos). There was an attempt to resurrect this plan. The Venetian Ambassador was less sure, recording that Elizabeth had openly said she did not want to marry.

107

Elizabeth's efforts to stay out of trouble could not always protect her. When a random search was carried out at Somerset House, a quantity of anti-Catholic literature was found. Kat Ashley admitted that it was hers; she spent three months in the Fleet Prison for 'having writings and scandalous books against the [Catholic] religion and against the King and Queen'[45] and on her release she was removed as Elizabeth's Lady Mistress and told to stay away from the princess. She was replaced by 'a widowed gentlewoman', and a new Governor was appointed, Sir Thomas Pope (founder of Trinity College, Oxford, in 1556), 'a rich and grave gentleman of good name both for conduct and religion.' Elizabeth knew and liked Pope, so found her new Governor a pleasure to have in her household. They frequently talked about the new University College he was founding and general issues relating to education.

Pope told Elizabeth when, in July 1556, there was a ridiculous uprising in Suffolk led by a local teacher named Mr Cleobury, who pretended to be Courtenay. His rallying cry was 'the Lady Elizabeth Queen and her beloved bedfellow, Courtenay, King.'[46] This caused Elizabeth to write to Mary on 2 August, not so much pleading her loyalty, but rather wondering how such evil people could exist.[47]

In late November, Elizabeth arrived to stay at Somerset House in London to spend Christmas at Court. Her first meeting with Mary, accompanied by Cardinal Pole, was amicable. The next was less so. On 2 December, Mary summoned her sister to tell her that Emmanuel Philibert, Duke of Savoy, had renewed his offer of marriage and that she and Philip wanted her to accept. Elizabeth broke down in tears, swearing that she had no wish to marry anyone and would be happy to spend her life single.

According to the Venetian Ambassador, Elizabeth told Mary that 'the afflictions suffered by her were such that they had ... ridded her of any wish for a husband.'[48] Mary accused her of treachery and lies, shouting that Elizabeth was just waiting for Mary to die so she could seize the Crown. Mary ordered her to leave the Court. On the following day, Elizabeth returned to Hatfield.

Philip, who was still in Spain, was determined that Elizabeth marry Emmanuel Philibert to get her out of the way. The plan had the additional benefit that if she did inherit the throne, his cousin would rule as her husband and King of England. In March 1557, Philip returned to Mary for four months, primarily to win the support of England in Spain's war with France.

As a secondary concern, he was accompanied by his sister Margaret, Duchess of Parma, and his cousin Louise, Duchess of Lorraine, who were to befriend Elizabeth with the aim of taking her back to Spanish territory to marry Emmanuel Philibert. The

French Ambassador de Noailles warned Elizabeth of a plot to trick her into visiting Flanders where she would be married, sending a message to her via Elizabeth Parr, Marchioness of Northampton. Elizabeth replied to the Ambassador to thank him for the warning and reaffirmed that she would never marry. In this instance her resolve was not tested. Jealous of the attention Phillip paid to the two duchesses, Mary made it clear she did not like them and they never actually got to meet Elizabeth. Philip then tried to order Mary to force Elizabeth into the marriage.

With Spain at war with France and Mary, Queen of Scots, the Dauphine of France and a possible heir to the English throne, it was imperative for Spanish foreign policy that England remain firmly under Spanish influence, but Mary refused. This time Mary again raised her belief that Elizabeth was not the child of Henry VIII. A second husband was offered, Alexander Farnese, son of Ottavio Farnese, Duke of Parma, and Margaret, the illegitimate daughter of Charles V (Philip's half-sister).[49] As with the others, these marriage plans failed to materialize, but Philip did win support for the war with France, and in July, he went back to Spain, never to return.

With Philip gone, Mary dedicated herself to her religion and the possibility of his return. His last visit had not left her pregnant, so even the hope of a child had disappeared. England was now locked into war with France, and in January 1558, Mary received notice that Calais, England's last foothold in France, the relic of what had once been vast English holdings, had been lost. The blow to English pride was severe, and Mary never fully came to terms with it. She is supposed to have said that when she died, they would find the word 'Calais' engraved on her heart, so terrible had been her loss. Certainly the failure of the English troops did serious damage to England's reputation in Europe, and to Mary's own reputation with the English people.

Elizabeth did her best to live quietly, knowing the Queen would do anything she legally could to deny her the throne. In April 1558, with an eye to the future, Gustav I (King of Sweden 1523–60), proposed that Elizabeth should marry his son and heir Prince Eric. However, the King wrote directly to Elizabeth, not to Mary I as he should have. Mary, worried that Philip would not approve and would blame her if the marriage took place, contacted Elizabeth to find out how she felt.

Pope, Elizabeth's Governor, asked her directly, and she reiterated that she had no desire to marry and certainly would not consider the Swedish prince. He asked if she might agree if some suitable match were identified, and Elizabeth replied, 'What I shall do hereafter I know not, but I assure you, upon my truth and fidelity, and as God be merciful unto me, I am not at this time otherwise minded than I have declared unto you. No, though I were offered the greatest prince in all Europe.'[50] Even before becoming Queen, it seems her mind was made up against marrying.

In 1557, we have a rare contemporary description of Elizabeth, written by the Venetian Ambassador Michiel:

> She is at present of the age of twenty-three, and is esteemed to be no less fair in mind than she is in body. Albeit, in face she is pleasing rather than beautiful; but her figure is tall and well proportioned. She has a good complexion, though of a somewhat olive tint, beautiful eyes, and above all a beautiful hand, which she likes to show. She is of admirable talent and intelligence, of which she has given proof by her behaviour in the dangers and suspicions to which she has been exposed. She has great knowledge of languages, especially Italian, and for display talks nothing else with Italians. She is proud and haughty; for in spite of her

mother, she holds herself as high as the Queen and equally legitimate, alleging in her own behalf that her mother would not cohabit with the King save as his wife, and that with the authority of the Church ... so that even if she were deceived having acted in good faith, she contracted a valid marriage and bore her child in lawful wedlock. Even supposing she be a bastard, she bears herself proudly and boastfully through her father, whom she is said to resemble more than does the Queen ... She lives on what her father bequeathed her, and is always in debt; she would be more so but that she keeps down her household not to awaken the Queen's jealousy. For there is no lord, nor knight in the kingdom who would not enter her service, to send there his son or brother; such is the affection and love which is felt towards her. She is always pleading her poverty, in such a dexterous way as to awaken silent compassion and therefore greater affection. For every one thinks it hard that a King's daughter should be so miserably treated. Since Wyatt's rebellion she has never been free; for though she is allowed to live in her house, some twelve miles distant from London, still she has many guards and spies about her, who observe all comers and goers; and she never says or does anything that is not at once reported to the Queen.[51]

Mary was alone in denying that Henry VIII was Elizabeth's father. She would have denied the throne to Elizabeth if she could, but her Council would not allow her to change the succession, and her absent but still adored husband would never accept the alternative represented by Mary, Queen of Scots. Philip put pressure on his wife to name her sister as her successor, which she finally agreed to, just 11 days before her death.

111

In 1558, Mary fell ill. She died just before dawn on 17 November at the age of 42. Her courtiers left in droves to go to Elizabeth at Hatfield. When William Herbert, 1st Earl of Pembroke and Henry Fitzalan, 12th Earl of Arundel, both Catholic ministers in Mary's Council, came to bring Elizabeth the official news of Mary's death at 8 a.m., she praised God for bringing her to such a position.

On the road from London, crowds flocked to her, abandoning the dead Mary I to offer their services to the new Queen. The sight was to make a lasting impression on Elizabeth, one that would affect her policy in naming her own successor for decades to come. At the age of 25, Elizabeth was finally Queen.

Elizabeth

❧

the Queen

5

The New Queen
1558–59

๙๒

When Elizabeth became Queen, she inherited a country with a range of serious internal and external problems. The reigns of Edward VI, followed by Mary I, had both been short, but had been marked by economic difficulties, war, and religious and social unrest. A contemporary memorandum summed up the situation:

> The Queen poor; the realm exhausted; the nobles poor and decayed; good captains and soldiers wanting, the people out of order; justice not executed; the justices unmeet for their offices; all things dear; division among ourselves; war with France and Scotland; the French King bestriding the realm, having one foot in Calais and the other in Scotland; steadfast enmity, but no steadfast friendship abroad.[1]

At her accession, Elizabeth must have recalled the initial joy with which her half-sister's succession had been met, only to end, a scant five years later, in disappointment, disillusion and bitterness. Now it was Elizabeth's turn – and she had no intention of failing.

One strong card that Elizabeth held in her favour was the matter of her parentage. As she was proud to remind everyone, Elizabeth was 'mere English', unlike the half-Spanish Mary I.

The official record of her accession further states that Elizabeth was 'of no mingled blood of Spaniard, or stranger, but born mere English here among us, and therefore most natural unto us.'[2]

Elizabeth's youth, grace and charm, and her undoubted resemblance to Henry VIII, also stood her in good stead with both her subjects and her court. Politician and writer Sir Robert Naunton describes the 25-year-old Queen as 'tall, of hair and complexion fair, and therewithal well favoured, but high nosed; of limb and feature neat, and, which added to the lustre of these external graces, of a stately and majestic comportment, participating more of her father than of her mother.'[3]

Elizabeth was also renowned for her ability to engage with all her subjects, from the highest to the lowest: 'If ever any person had either the gift or the style to win the hearts of the people, it was this Queen ... Some she pitied; some she commended; some she thanked; at others she pleasantly and wittily jested, condemning no person, neglecting no office ...'[4]

Her succession was met favourably and was announced swiftly. Less than half an hour after the official announcement of Mary I's death at 8 a.m. on 17 November 1558, Parliament had confirmed Elizabeth as Mary's successor. On 19 November, heralds proclaimed the Queen at the gates of Hatfield, and it was there that on the following day Elizabeth I held her first Council meeting, one that would prove vital to the successful transfer of power.

It would have been tempting for any new monarch to make a clean sweep of his or her predecessor's Councillors, but even at 25, Elizabeth recognized that their experience, influence and skill were essential to how successful she would be as Queen – in the early days at least. Similarly, as Renard, the Imperial Ambassador, also recognized in his missives home, not all of the Council were hostile to the new Queen.

Displaying the caution that was to mark her reign, Elizabeth strove to achieve a workable compromise. While she removed Councillors who had worked against her during Mary's reign – such as Sir Henry Bedingfield and William Paget (Nicholas Heath, the Catholic Archbishop of York, refused to continue as Lord Chancellor and retired in December 1558), she also retained several. Henry Fitzalan, 12th Earl of Arundel; William Herbert, 1st Earl of Pembroke; William Paulet, 1st Marquis of Winchester; Francis Talbot, 5th Earl of Shrewsbury; Edward Stanley, 3rd Earl of Derby; Sir William Howard, Baron Howard of Effingham; Lord Edward Fiennes Clinton; Sir John Mason; Sir William Petre and Dr Nicholas Wotton (the only remaining churchman) all remained. To those men, she added her own personal supporters: Sir William Cecil as the new Principal Secretary; Sir Thomas Parry; Sir Edward Rogers; Francis Russell, 2nd Earl of Bedford; William Parr, 1st Marquis of Northampton; Sir Richard Sackville; Sir Francis Knollys; Sir Ambrose Cave and Sir Nicholas Bacon

The new Queen's priority was to seek good, experienced counsel and the Council now had 20 members, all of whom, except for Sir Ambrose Cave, had served at least one of the preceding monarchs, either as a Councillor or a household officer (Cave had been Elizabeth's Controller of the Household at Hatfield when she was a princess and was now a country neighbour of the Cecils). William Cecil, 13 years Elizabeth's senior, was the youngest member of the Council. Most were older; some considerably so, such as the 83-year-old William Paulet. Several of the Councillors were also related to Elizabeth through her mother, Anne Boleyn, including William Howard, Henry Fitzalan, Sir Francis Knollys and Sir Richard Sackville.

Elizabeth also rewarded those who had remained faithful to her throughout her early years. Roger Ascham, her old tutor, became her Latin Secretary; Sir Nicholas Throckmorton was made Chief Butler and Chamberlain of the Exchequer; and Lord Cobham, who had been implicated in Wyatt's rebellion and imprisoned in the Tower, became Warden of the Cinque Ports.

Others arrested during Wyatt's rebellion were also rewarded: Sir William St Loe was created Captain of the Guard, and Sir James Crofts became Captain of Berwick. Elizabeth's dear friend William Parr was restored as the Marquis of Northampton. Henry Carey, her cousin, was created Baron Hunsdon and made Captain of the Gentleman Pensioners, the Queen's bodyguard. His sister, Catherine Carey, now married to the new Councillor Sir Francis Knollys, was made a Gentlewoman of the Privy Chamber, with Elizabeth Norwich, wife of Sir Gawen Carew (another of Elizabeth's supporters who was exiled after Wyatt's rebellion). Sir John Ashley, who was related by marriage to Anne Boleyn and who had tried to warn his wife, Kat Ashley, of the perils of permitting Thomas Seymour to grow too familiar with the princess, was rewarded with the posts of Master of the Jewel House, Treasurer of Her Majesty's Jewels and Plate, and Groom of the Chamber.

Kat Ashley, who had endured several periods of imprisonment through her loyalty to Elizabeth, was made Mistress of the Maids of Honour, Chief Gentlewoman of the Privy Chamber and Keeper of the Close Stools. She would remain in Elizabeth's service until her death. The second Gentlewoman and Keeper of Her Majesty's Books was Blanche Parry, who had seen the infant Elizabeth rocked in her cradle. Both of these ladies had considerable sway when it came to influencing the Queen in smaller matters.[5]

The trusted Blanche was devoted to the Queen. Blanche never married and had no title, but over the years she bought land in Herefordshire and Breconshire, where her family came from, and also in Yorkshire, where her beloved nephew John Vaughan lived.

In Blanche's final will, published at her death in 1590, the first item was the bequest of a large diamond to Elizabeth I, a sign of her great devotion to her former charge and Queen.

On attaining the throne, Elizabeth dismissed many of the older staunchly Catholic ladies-in-waiting of the Court of Mary I, and replaced them with friends and family closer to her own age, such as Anne Morgan (wife of Henry Carey, Lord Hunsdon), aged 29; Anne Poyntz (wife of Sir Thomas Heneage), aged about 20; Lettice Knollys (daughter of Catherine Carey and Francis Knollys), aged 19; and the legendary beauty Elizabeth Fitzgerald (third wife of Edward Fiennes Clinton), aged 31.

❧

The greatest of the Queen's Councillors was undoubtedly William Cecil. The Tudor historian William Camden summed Cecil up when he wrote that 'Of all men of genius he was the most a drudge; of all men of business, the most a genius.'[6]

Cecil's grandfather, David, came from the Welsh family of Sitsilt, and had started the family's rise in royal service as one of Henry VIII's sergeant-at-arms in Lincolnshire, Steward to Crown lands and Sheriff of Northampton. Cecil's father, Richard, was a King's Page, Groom of the Wardrobe and Yeoman of the Robes to Henry VIII, Constable of Warwick Castle and Sheriff of Rutland.

In 1535, Richard, wishing to advance his son sent the 15-year-old boy to St John's College, Cambridge. Here he became friendly with such men as John Cheke, Roger Ascham, Matthew Parker (who later became Archbishop of Canterbury under Elizabeth I) and Nicholas Bacon. They became immersed in the Classics and in the Protestant New Religion.

In May 1541, Cecil left Cambridge without taking his final degree and started to study law at the Inns of Court. He had formed a relationship with John Cheke's sister, Mary, whom his family found unacceptable as a wife (her father had been a college beadle and her mother ran a wine shop). In spite of opposition, in August, Cecil married Mary. He was given a post in the Court of Common Pleas. The next year, Mary gave birth to their only child, Thomas, in Cambridge. She died in February 1543.

In 1544, William Cecil's career took an immense leap when his friends John Cheke and Roger Ascham received powerful appointments – Cheke became tutor to Prince Edward, and Ascham tutor to Princess Elizabeth. With influential friends at Court, the 25-year-old Cecil was able to make a significant second marriage in 1545 to 20-year-old Mildred, the eldest daughter of Sir Anthony Cooke, Governor of Prince Edward's household.

On Henry VIII's death in 1547, Cecil became Master of Requests. With his friends and in-laws now in the service of the King, and the King's Protector as his patron, Cecil's future seemed assured. In September 1548, Cecil was appointed Secretary to the Protector, thereby increasing his power and influence. In the following year, when Edward Seymour was ejected from power and replaced by John Dudley, Cecil was arrested, however, and briefly imprisoned. Dudley recognized his value and took Cecil into his own service. But by September 1550, Cecil was Secretary of State.

Roger Ascham, writing to his friend the German scholar, Johann Sturm, in August 1550, offered this description of Cecil:

> ... a young man, indeed, but mature in wisdom, and so deeply skilled, both in letters and affairs, and endued with such moderation in the exercise of public offices, that to him would be awarded ... the fourfold praise: 'To know all that is fitting, to be able to apply what he knows, to be a lover of his country, and superior to money.'[7]

Dudley had also apparently commented that Cecil had shown himself not just a faithful servant, but also a witty councillor 'as was scarce the like within his realm.'[8]

In recognition of their role in the Court administration, in October 1550, both Cecil and Cheke were knighted. Cecil was made Joint-Secretary to the Council with Sir William Petre, who was often ill and unable to attend to his work. Now all the deliberations of the Council passed through Cecil's hands. To be on hand for Council work, he lived in a house in Cannon Row, Westminster, while his wife managed their country house at Wimbledon.

The value of Cecil's work was recognized even by the young Edward VI.[9] When Edward VI died and Dudley was plotting to place his daughter-in-law, Lady Jane Grey, on the throne, Cecil frequently excused himself from the Council, pleading ill health. Along with the other Council officers, he was ultimately forced to sign the document changing the order of succession (cutting out Mary and Elizabeth in favour of Jane), but he was unhappy about it and made sure he had witnesses to his misgivings.

Later, when Mary came to the throne, Cecil was able to demonstrate that he had acted against her only under duress from the bullying Dudley. He had, he said, never actively supported 'Queen' Jane. It appears that Mary believed him – and although Cecil did not retain his post as Secretary of State under her reign, he was not sent to the Tower like Cheke.

During Mary I's rule, Cecil remained discreet, spending much of his time looking after his growing estates. He had no interest in sport, games or such 'pastimes', but he was an avid book collector, and those who knew him well gave him books as gifts, particularly his favourite works on heraldry and genealogy. He also kept up his role as a benefactor to Cambridge University and St John's College. It appears that he was also solicited for his political skills, although

121

he had no official title. An anonymous biographer, possibly one of his servants, reported 'that Mary had a good liking for him as a Councillor, and would have appointed him if he had changed his religion'.[9]

Through these years Cecil kept up his correspondence and friendship with other Protestants who stayed discreetly in England or fled into self-imposed exile. He himself chose not to swim against the tide and took his family and household to services at the newly converted Catholic parish church at Wimbledon.

Cecil's good relations with Elizabeth, which would continue for the rest of his life, began in 1549 when she wrote to him in his role as the Protector's Secretary about matters relating to her brother Edward VI. In 1553, she asked him to look into accusations of extortion and intimidation against one of her stewards, and also appointed him steward of her estates at Collyweston. In the last days of the reign of Mary I, Cecil was a frequent visitor to Hatfield, so much so that when members of the Council arrived to see Elizabeth, they found Cecil already in discussion with her. Therefore, he was a natural choice to become Elizabeth's chief adviser when she became Queen. Not everyone was pleased by this decision. The Spanish Ambassador de Feria complained of Cecil's importance in a 1559 letter to Philip II: 'Cecil is very clever, but a mischievous man, and a heretic, and governs the Queen in spite of the Treasurer [Parry].'[10]

From the outset of Elizabeth's reign, Cecil used his skills to make the transition as easy as possible. He prepared a list of 12 points to help the succession go smoothly, including the contents of the proclamation; which Heads of State should be formally notified; how Mary's funeral should be conducted; who should arrange Elizabeth's coronation and which preacher would be the safest choice to give the sermon at St Paul's Cross.

In her first Council meeting with Cecil acting as her Principal Secretary of State, Elizabeth presented in writing her reasons for choosing him as her closest and most respected servant:

> I give you this charge that you shall be of my Privy Council and content to take pains for me and my realm. This judgement I have of you that you will not be corrupted by any manner of gift and that you will be faithful to the state; and that without respect of my private will, you will give me that counsel which you think best and if you shall know anything necessary to me of secrecy, you shall show it to myself only. And assure yourself I will not fail to keep taciturnity therein and therefore herewith I charge you.[11]

By all accounts, she had chosen well. Throughout his life, Cecil was a respected statesman who gave the Queen sound advice. While he refrained from changing his opinion if it differed from Elizabeth's, Cecil followed her will once she had made a decision.

❧

The first most important issue facing Elizabeth was that of the coronation. The date for the event, so symbolically vital, was placed in the hands of the internationally famous mathematician, astronomer and astrologist Dr John Dee, who had studied at St John's and Trinity Colleges in Cambridge with Cheke.

In 1551, Dee returned to England from Charles V's court, where he had been teaching Ambassador Sir William Pickering mathematics and astronomy. Dee offered two of his books on mathematics to the young Edward VI, who awarded him a pension. The Dee family also gained the favour of John Dudley, although this turned out to be an unfortunate turn of events when

123

Dudley's fall from power also led to Dee's arrest in May 1555 for 'calculating', 'conjuring' and 'witchcraft' in illegally casting horoscopes for Mary I, Philip and the Lady Elizabeth.[12]

With his studies deemed part of the so-called 'Black Arts', he ended up in the custody of the fearsome Bishop Edward 'Bloody' Bonner, Mary's most aggressive inquisitor. But, by November 1555, Dee had embraced Catholicism and was not only one of Bonner's chaplains, but his close friend, a relationship he maintained even after Elizabeth I removed Bonner from office and he was imprisoned in the Marshalsea for debt, where he later died.

Safe in Bonner's esteem in January 1556, Dee wrote a supplication to Mary I asking for the preservation of old writings and monuments, many of which had been destroyed or thrown away during the Reformation and Dissolution of the Monasteries under Henry VIII. He wanted to create a national archive, a Library Royal. Although he did not get royal backing, Dee acquired and preserved a number of old texts; he also wrote original papers on mathematical and scientific subjects. At the same time, he appears to have kept in touch with Elizabeth, and may have acted as her eyes and ears in Bonner's court. Certainly when she became Queen, Elizabeth called upon Dee's skills, though he would later leave England to travel widely – teaching, learning and collecting.[13]

For Elizabeth's coronation date, Dee chose 15 January 1559 (Jupiter was in Aquarius, giving a ruler crowned on that day impartiality, independence and tolerance; Mars was in Scorpio, giving the ruler passion and commitment).

In anticipation of the event, Elizabeth moved by barge from Whitehall to the Tower on 12 January. On 14 January, she made her formal entrance into the City of London and on to Westminster. She wore a dress of gold tissue and a mantle of gold cloth lined with ermine. Crowds thronged the streets, where tableaux showing Elizabeth as the natural heir of Edward IV, Henry VII and Henry VIII were displayed, depicting her as the bringer of peace, harmony and prosperity through the Protestant religion. That evening there was a fireworks display.

Elizabeth's coronation took place on Sunday 15 January 1559, in Westminster Abbey. First came 1,000 members of her household mounted on horseback, followed by the Queen in an open litter decked with gold brocade, surrounded by her footmen and Gentlemen Pensioners. Behind her litter came Robert Dudley, mounted and leading her white hackney. Then came the Lord Chamberlain and the Lords of the Privy Chamber. At the gate to the city were effigies of Henry VII (holding a red rose) and Elizabeth of York (holding a white rose), Henry VIII (holding both a red and a white rose) and Anne Boleyn, as well as a Queen that represented Elizabeth herself.

After the coronation ceremony, a great banquet was held in Westminster Hall, where each course was announced by nobles riding into the hall on horses. Elizabeth retired to bed at 1.00 a.m. completely exhausted. The next day it was planned she would attend a joust, but the combination of the previous day's exhaustion and a heavy cold caused the event to be cancelled.

As Elizabeth settled into forming her Council, busy minds were already occupied with her potential marriage. Among her Councillors, at least one felt that he had a greater role to play than just a political one. Almost at once, Henry Fitzalan, 12th Earl of Arundel, let it be known that he was a willing suitor for the Queen's hand in marriage. He reasoned that, after the unpopularity of Mary's foreign marriage to Philip of Spain, Elizabeth would want an English husband. With Edward Courtenay no longer a

125

contender (he had died in exile in Italy), who better than one of the country's most senior and well-connected noblemen? One, moreover, who had a family line that could be traced back to William d'Aubigny, the first Earl of Arundel? Only time and Fitzalan's efforts would tell, it seemed.

In July 1559, Elizabeth set out on her first progress (the visits that she made to towns and aristocratic homes in southern England). Going first to her own property in Dartford in Kent, and then onto Cobham Hall, home of her friend Lord William Cobham, who later became an ambassador to the Low Countries, a Knight of the Garter and a Privy Councillor, she continued on her travels, ending up at Nonsuch in Surrey, which had been built by Henry VIII, but was now Henry Fitzalan's property.

On Sunday night, Fitzalan held a banquet, a masque (a court pageant) and a concert in the new Queen's honour. On Monday, she watched coursing from a stand in the park, after which the children of St Paul's performed a play, which was followed by another banquet. When Elizabeth left Nonsuch, Fitzalan gave the Queen not just the usual gift of a few pieces of gold, silver or gilded plate, but an entire cabinet full. But would Elizabeth be so easily impressed by such measures?

Although Fitzalan was a 47-year-old widower who had married twice, he might have proved a suitable candidate had he not been a staunch Catholic and also unimaginative and physically unprepossessing. Ambassador de Feria was pleased to report to Spain that he didn't hold out much hope for Fitzalan's suit: 'Arundel has been going about in high glee for some time and is very smart … but I did not lose hope, as the Earl is a flighty man of small ability.'[14]

As would become clear as more time passed, Elizabeth set her sights high, demanding youth, intelligence and a high degree of physical beauty in any man whom she favoured. Within a relatively short time, Fitzalan realized that his suit would be unsuccessful.

Elizabeth, already accustomed to being a focus for offers of marriage, had frequently stated that she had no wish to marry. She made light-hearted reference to marrying on occasions such as in 1560 when she visited the 75-year-old William Paulet, 1st Marquis of Winchester, a skilled and experienced politician married to Lady Elizabeth Seymour (the sister of Queen Jane Seymour), saying, 'by my troth, if my Lord Treasurer were but a young man, I could find it in my heart to have him for a husband before any man in England.'[15] As Elizabeth was still young, most of those around her believed that the Queen would eventually give in and choose a husband. It was considered inconceivable that she would wish to remain a maid and never marry.[16]

127

With the coronation completed and Elizabeth now lawfully Queen, she was faced with a number of urgent problems. In February 1559, she held her first official Parliament in which three critical issues were raised. The first was to create a 'uniform order of religion', finally settling the sensitive religious question after the violently turbulent years of Henry VIII, Edward VI and, particularly, Mary I. The second was to review statutes 'contrary or hurtful to the commonwealth', that is, to end the war with France that Mary's Spanish husband, Philip II, had foisted on the English people. The third was the question of the succession: both Edward VI and Mary I had died without heirs, and if Elizabeth should die in the same state, there could well be civil war as rival factions fought to place their candidate on the throne.

Another major problem that took several years to sort out was the currency, which had been thoroughly debased under Edward

VI and Mary I. As a step to lower the costs of the Court, in her first six months Elizabeth reduced the Crown's expenditure from £267,000 to £108,000.[17] She sent Sir Thomas Gresham, a financial expert, to the Netherlands to arrange to repair English credit, which he carried out with considerable success. The debased coinage was eventually recalled and new money reissued, making English currency once more respected in the European money markets. This was a major achievement that re-established England's supremacy as a trading nation.

On the question of religion, Elizabeth sought a pragmatic solution that would address Protestant concerns but avoid offending Catholics. She legislated for a Protestant church with the monarch at its head, but refused her father's title of Head of the Church, which, it was argued, could only be held by a man (since men could not be ruled by a woman in matters of religious doctrine). In a masterly act of compromise, Elizabeth agreed to become 'Supreme Governor as well in spiritual and ecclesiastical causes as temporal'.[18]

A Royal Commission passed the Act of Supremacy in which the authority of the Pope was solemnly renounced and the whole government of the church vested in the Queen, her heirs and successors. An important clause enabled them to delegate their authority to commissioners of their own appointment.[19] The Act of Uniformity was also passed, which made compliance with Protestant worship compulsory and allowed the Queen to appoint all bishops.[20]

As for the matter of succession, a marriage leading to a lawful heir was the most expected outcome. Almost as swift to pay his court as Henry Fitzalan was Philip II of Spain, Elizabeth's erstwhile brother-in-law. In his wish to marry Elizabeth, apart from his distinctly lustful feelings for the young and attractive lady, Philip wanted to retain influence in this strategically important country. Moreover Philip was prepared to do pretty much anything to keep England out of French hands – and France already had its eye on England and the throne.

When Mary I died, Henri II of France had announced that, as Elizabeth was illegitimate, the throne of England now belonged to Mary, Queen of Scots, who was married to his eldest son, the Dauphin François. According to this reasoning, the Queen of Scotland, who would be the next Queen of France, was also now Queen of England. Scotland, a country that bordered England, would provide any invading French army with an admirable starting point for an invasion.

Philip sent his envoy, Ambassador de Feria, to begin marriage negotiations with Elizabeth within days of her accession. Elizabeth was fascinated by the negotiations, holding several meetings with de Feria, who assumed that as the King of Spain had offered his hand, Elizabeth would accept. Philip had spelled out to his ambassador that by offering for the Queen of England he was rendering 'this service to God … [I]t will be evident that I am serving the Lord in marrying her and that she has been converted by my act.'[21]

Elizabeth had other ideas. She hedged the subject by coquetting and flirting, pointing out that her people would not approve of her taking a foreign husband, especially one of whom they already had experience, moreover one who had abandoned her half-sister. Surely he would do the same with Elizabeth? She also reminded Philip that the Pope would never allow him to marry her unless she became a Catholic, and this was extremely unlikely to happen.

129

While de Feria had his doubts about Elizabeth's sincerity towards Philip, especially when he realized that other ambassadors were approaching her and her Councillors with their own marriage offers, the other ambassadors seemed to feel that Spain would walk away with the prize. Michiel Surian, Venetian Ambassador to the Court of Philip II, wrote from Brussels, 'As to what the Count de Feria is negotiating with regard to the marriage of Miladi Elizabeth, I am unable to write anything authentic, but the whole Court is full of the King's intention to have her for himself ...'[22]

Elizabeth's Council also expressed doubts as to Philip's suitability as King of England, however. They raised concerns about his religious intolerance, his poor treatment of Mary, his profligacy, Spain's severe financial difficulties, and its war with France, which England did not want to get further dragged into. Moreover, there were legal complications: if Elizabeth was permitted to marry her sister's husband, that would mean that her father (Henry VIII) was legally allowed to marry his brother Arthur's wife, Catherine of Aragon, and that would mean that the divorce and therefore Henry's subsequent marriage to Anne Boleyn were both illegal and Elizabeth herself illegitimate.

Any of these points would have been enough to give Elizabeth the excuse to step back from Philip's offer. Presented to her as a case against marriage by her Councillors, they were irrefutable. She could now flirt, negotiate and procrastinate, confident of being 'forced' to withdraw by her Council if matters became too serious.

Philip himself seemed to have a better understanding of the situation and soon realized that Elizabeth had no intention of accepting him. In April 1559, he reversed course and arranged to marry Henri II's daughter, the 14-year-old Princess Elisabeth de Valois, as part of his peace negotiations with the King of France. He had previously arranged that his only son, Prince Carlos, marry

Elisabeth de Valois, however, Carlos's mental state was deteriorating, so Philip decided to marry her instead.

Elizabeth I teased Philip a little over the suddenness of his change of heart. On 7 April 1559, de Feria met with the Queen, who took him to task over the news that Philip was planning to marry the French princess. He reported how she chided him: 'Your Majesty, she said, could not have been so much in love with her as I had represented, if you could not wait four months for her.'[23]

Despite having been vociferously against the match, now the English were furious at the slight to their Queen. Obscene ballads were written and circulated that were highly insulting to the unfaithful Spanish King.

❧

This was not the end of Philip's involvement in Elizabeth's marital status, however. Even if Philip could not marry her himself, England was too great a prize to let go. Two of his cousins, the sons of his paternal uncle Ferdinand I (1503–64, Holy Roman Emperor 1558–64), would be suitable candidates, Ferdinand and Charles, Archdukes of Austria. However, Ferdinand, though 'high spirited and lusty', was an uncompromising Catholic and was rumoured to have a morganatic wife (a wife of inferior status). Furthermore, Ferdinand was against the match and his inflexible religious beliefs made him ineligible to the English.

His younger brother, the 19-year-old Charles, was more flexible. Elizabeth expressed interest; was he a soldier, did he ride and dance? She enquired about what he looked like, if he was well educated, and whether he had been noted to have loved any woman and, in which case, what kind?[24]

Charles was described as being 'of sanguine complexion, and, for a man, beautiful and well-faced, well-shaped, small in the waist and well and broad breasted; he seems in his clothes well thighed and well-legged.'[25]

The Imperial Ambassador Count von Helfenstein also sent back glowing reports to Ferdinand I on the Queen as a potential wife for his son and on the enthusiasm of her Council for the match.[26] The formal proposal of marriage from Ferdinand I on behalf of his son was brought to England in May 1559 by Baron Caspar von Breuner. He joined forces with the Spanish Ambassador Don Alvaro de Quadra, Bishop of Aquila, who introduced him to the Court. At first, everyone thought von Breuner was offering the hand of Ferdinand I himself, but de Quadra made it clear that the offer was for the younger, more adaptable Charles.

Elizabeth seemed pleased and said that the proposal should go before her Council, but she would prefer to see a man before she considered marrying him. De Quadra found this an unreasonable request, but Elizabeth was adamant. She would rather be a nun, she said, than 'marry without knowing with whom and on the faith of portrait painters'. De Quadra knew the Emperor would never agree to Charles coming to England at the Queen's suggestion and she must have known, as he did, that the Archduke Charles would not be presented to the Queen like merchandise on approval.[27] By autumn 1559, Elizabeth had written to Ferdinand I that she was not considering marriage, but that she was honoured by Charles's interest.[28]

Concerned that the alternative to an alliance through marriage might be invasion and conquest, certain English nobles were well aware of the advantages of Charles becoming King Consort. Sir Thomas Chaloner, the English Ambassador to Spain, gave Cecil his opinion: 'In mine opinion, be it said to you only, the affinity is great and honourable; the amity necessary to stop and cool many enterprises. Ye need not fear his [Charles's] greatness should overrule you. He is not a Philip, but better for us than a Philip.'[29]

England was, in addition, still weak after the rule of Edward VI and Mary I. It would take all Elizabeth's diplomatic skill to play this high-stake game, holding out the hope of marriage to ward off the threat of invasion in the knowledge that England would be hard put to defend itself against a determined enemy.

Matters were complicated by Ambassador de Feria's frustration with the Queen. Whereas he had enjoyed direct access to Mary I, Elizabeth insisted that all communications should first go through her advisers Cecil and Parry, well-known Protestants and also men whom de Feria detested.

De Feria continued to aid Philip in his increasingly frustrating efforts to sort out a suitable husband for the young Queen. It would be no easy task. De Feria warned Philip, 'She is incomparably more feared than her sister was. She gives her orders and has her own way as absolutely as her father did.'[30]

In a report to de Quadra, warning him of the difficulty of negotiating marriage with Elizabeth, de Feria wrote, 'Your Lordship will see what a pretty business it is to deal with her … I think she must have a hundred thousand devils in her body, notwithstanding that she is for ever telling me that she longs to be a nun and to pass her time in a cell praying.'[31]

Elizabeth's other suitors included 33-year-old Adolf, Duke of Holstein-Gottorp, brother of Christian III (King of Denmark and Norway 1534–59). Unusually among the Queen's marriage candidates, the Duke actually visited England. Adolf was handsome, Protestant, wealthy and professed to be deeply in love with Elizabeth.

Although she had formed a liking for him, it appears that Elizabeth did not share his desire to get married. In the end, Elizabeth let him down gently and with great diplomacy, and he was able to return home after a magnificent reception with every sign that he still enjoyed her favour, as well as with splendid presents and the Order of the Garter.[32] On his return home, the Duke married Christine, daughter of Philip I, Landgrave of Hesse, who would bear him 10 children, 5 sons and 5 daughters; something of a blow to Elizabeth's Council, who desired to see her produce healthy English heirs.

Another, less welcome, suitor was Crown Prince Eric of Sweden. He had been wooing Elizabeth since before her accession, with no success. Now that she was Queen he renewed his efforts, sending his brother, Duke John of Finland, to act as his emissary in September 1559. He was 'very courteous and princely, and well spoken in the Latin tongue', and Elizabeth seemed to like him – so much so that there was some talk that she might marry John instead of Eric. Cecil allowed himself one brief moment of despair at his royal mistress's antics, 'How he shall speed, God knoweth and not I.'[33]

Flirting with his brother apart, Elizabeth tried hard to discourage this most persistent of suitors, writing to Eric in February 1560:

> We are grieved that we cannot gratify your Serene Highness with the same kind of affection ... but, as often we have testified both in words and writing, that we have never yet conceived a feeling of that kind of affection towards anyone ... we do not conceive in our heart to take a husband, but highly commend this single life, and hope that your Serene Highness will no longer spend time in waiting for us.[34]

Eric, on hearing that Duke John had begun to woo Elizabeth on his own behalf, recalled his brother. He sent a new Ambassador, Nicholas Guildenstiern, who came with treasure to present to the Queen – 18 large piebald horses and two shiploads of 'gifts' – and a message 'that he would quickly follow in person, to lay his heart at her feet.'[35]

In the knowledge that Elizabeth had accepted the gifts and that the soon-to-be King was reputed to be very handsome, there were rumours that Elizabeth was about to accept him. Broadsheets were published in anticipation of the event, showing portraits of the two side by side. Cecil was forced to make the Lord Mayor stop these publications, emphasizing that while the Queen was not 'miscontented', she could not allow her image to be joined in the same paper with any 'King, or with any other prince, that is known to have made any request for marriage to her Majesty.'[36]

In case Eric should actually make good on his promise to come to England, plans were drawn up for his reception, bearing in mind that she was a 'maid' and therefore certain formalities would need to be omitted out of honour and courtesy.[37]

For a further two years, the kingdom planned and waited as Eric threatened to come to England to woo her in person and bombarded her with expensive gifts. Eventually he realized that she would never succumb to his blandishments and his attentions ceased. Some years later, he would marry his low-born mistress, Karin Mansdotter.

Meanwhile, new diplomatic channels, and thus new marital possibilities, were opening up. After intense negotiations, in April 1559, England signed the Treaty of Cateau-Cambrésis with France and Spain. The main thrust of this treaty was to broker a peace between Spain and France with a return to pre-war borders. For England, the only failure of the negotiations was to achieve the immediate return of Calais, about which Elizabeth was obsessive. The French offered to return Calais after eight years or pay a forfeit of 500,000 crowns, but everyone doubted their intention of fulfilling this condition. As part of the peace negotiations, Cecil began discussions with Sir William Maitland of Lethington and his colleague, William Kirkaldy of the Grange, to separate Scotland from France with the aim of getting French troops out of Scotland.

One part of the plan was that the 22-year-old James Hamilton, 3rd Earl of Arran, should be called back from France to try to seal an Anglo–Scottish alliance. His father was the heir to the Scottish throne after Mary, Queen of Scots. Sir James Croft wrote to Cecil that the Scottish nobility were bent on Protestant independence from Catholic France, that Hamilton was to be recalled, and that a marriage for him was being considered 'you know where'.[38]

Kirkaldy wrote back, cryptically and pointedly, to say that Elizabeth might want to wait before she made any immediate plans for her marriage. Nonetheless, it was certainly in England's interests to unite the island under Protestant rule, removing the French threat from its northern border, and it was felt that many Scots would support the marriage of Elizabeth with Hamilton.

In any case, it appears that the young Scot had English help to escape from France in early 1559. As Hamilton was an open supporter of the French Protestants (the Huguenots), Henri II tried to have him arrested, but he managed to flee to safety in Geneva. On 16 July, Elizabeth sent the diplomat Sir Harry Killigrew to bring Hamilton to England, but he had already set out, arriving in disguise before Killigrew could even deliver his message.

On arrival, Hamilton met the Queen and Cecil, staying at the latter's house in Cannon Row. By this stage, there was no longer any talk of marriage. It is possible that Hamilton may already have been showing signs of the mental illness that would later claim him: in 1562 he was judged insane and handed into the care of his brother. Whatever the reason, Hamilton was secretly sent on his way back to Scotland in August to support the Protestant nobles.

On 10 July 1559, Henri II died from injuries sustained during a joust when a lance splintered and a sliver of wood pierced his helmet and went into his brain through his eye. This made Mary, Queen of Scots the Queen Consort of France by virtue of her 15-year-old husband, François II (King of France 1559–60), ascending to the throne. As Mary's power grew, Scotland posed an ever greater threat to England. Not only was Mary a Catholic and allied with France, she also had a claim to the English throne. It was rumoured that there might be an active plot to use Scotland as a staging post for an invasion of England.

Tensions between the countries increased. When Jacques de Savoy, Duc de Nemours, mentioned that he was thinking of wooing Elizabeth, the Constable de Montmorency responded, 'Do you not know that the Queen-dolphin [Mary, Queen of Scots] has right and title to England?'[39] At a joust celebrating the betrothal in July 1559 of Emmanuel Philibert of Savoy to Margaret of France, Duchess of Berry, Scottish heralds showed Mary, Queen of Scots' arms including the quartered arms of England.

The English protested, but the French argued that it was only fair – Elizabeth still took the official (if symbolic) title of Queen of France (dating back to the claims of Edward III). Privately, Henri II had thought England, France and Scotland could be united under his son François and his daughter-in-law Mary, Queen of Scots. The new King, François II, would come to be perceived as less of a

137

threat since he had to face rival religious and political factions in France before taking any serious interest in Elizabeth's throne.

Meanwhile, an English nobleman who thought he might catch the fancy of the Queen was Sir William Pickering, one of the young men who had congregated around the late Henry Howard, Earl of Surrey, who was executed on charges of treason by Henry VIII in 1547. At the time of Wyatt's rebellion, Pickering had been involved in the plot against Mary I and was forced to flee abroad. He joined the embassy to Emperor Charles V in Brussels.

He and Elizabeth were old friends, and he came to London to see her in May 1559. The 43-year-old Pickering, a lusty, handsome, intellectual, single gentleman, was welcomed by Elizabeth. To everyone's interest, the couple spent many hours together alone, and he was given rooms in the palace. Ambassador de Feria commented that Elizabeth saw him secretly just two days after his arrival and that 'yesterday he came to the palace publicly and remained with her four or five hours. In London they are giving twenty-five to a hundred that he will be King.'[40] Historian William Camden described Pickering as '... a man of good family though little wealth, and who had obtained reputation by the cultivation of letters, by the elegance of his manners and by his embassies to France and Germany ...'[41]

Not everyone was pleased with Pickering. He began to behave as if he was already royalty, inviting people to his house and leaving them so that he could dine alone with musicians playing. On one occasion he was about to enter the Privy Chamber, which was open only to those of noble title (as a knight he was only entitled to be in the Presence Chamber outside), and Henry Fitzalan, 12th Earl of Arundel, took him to task. Pickering called him 'an impudent, discourteous knave'.[42] However, Pickering's suit of Elizabeth would end as all her others had: as a friend, but not a husband.

138

With all these suits coming to nothing, the question arises how Elizabeth managed to placate the Council, who saw her marriage as a political necessity.

When Elizabeth took the throne early in 1559, the Commons had presented the Queen with an address requesting that she marry as a matter of urgency. Her reply was a masterful fudge; she would consider marriage, but not if it compromised national or religious interests. She stated:

> … I will never in that matter conclude anything that shall be prejudicial to the realm, for the weal, good, and safety whereof I will never shame to spend my life. And whomsoever my chance shall be to light upon, I trust he shall be as careful for the realm and you – I will not say, as myself, because I cannot so certainly determine of any other – but at the leastways, by my goodwill and desire, he shall be such as shall be as careful for the preservation of the realm and you as myself.[43]

139

She then went on to reassure them that a suitable successor could be found regardless of whether she had an heir, and that, in any case, a Queen's offspring was no guarantee of a 'fit governor'. She also took care to underline her virginity: '… in the end this shall be for me sufficient: that a marble stone shall declare that a Queen, having reigned such a time, lived and died a virgin …'[44]

One can only speculate if Elizabeth made this claim to publicly bolster her moral character, or if she truly was a virgin at this stage. Perhaps, if not, she felt that abstinence would restore her 'pure' state. It is reported that one of her favourite prayers included the lines:

'… grant that I may continually have care and regard not to sully nor to abase this Thy holy image restored in me through Jesus Christ, but instead keeping it pure and untainted by any carnal affection …'[45]

Elizabeth may have believed that abstinence was in some way a factor in her succeeding to the throne. If she had indeed had a physical affair with Thomas Seymour and borne a child, she might have seen her subsequent years of turmoil as some kind of punishment. Both her own experiences to this point and as an observer to her father's imbroglios may have caused her to arrive at the conclusion that the wisest path was to remain chaste in order to succeed as the Queen of England. Whether she saw this as God's will or her free choice, or whether it was just a public front masking a different private reality, is buried with Elizabeth herself.

140

The other irrefutable fact was that she was openly wary about giving up her independence by marrying. In a letter to Holy Roman Emperor Ferdinand I in June 1559, Elizabeth praised his son, her suitor, Charles, diplomatically acknowledging that it was a most honourable match, but stating, 'When however we reflect upon the question of this marriage and eagerly ask our heart, we find that we have no wish to give up solitude and our single life, but prefer with God's help to abide therein of our free determination.'[46]

Nonetheless, Elizabeth's advisers, as well as nobles around Europe, ignored her forthright assertions that she did not desire to marry, putting it down to politics and maidenly modesty. Throughout 1559, Elizabeth was besieged with suitors from England, Scotland, Spain, Sweden and Saxony. In October, William Cecil wrote to the statesman Ralph Sadler, 'I would to God her Majesty had one and the rest honourably satisfied.'[47]

But perhaps Elizabeth did have 'one' in mind – a particular suitor that occupied a place above all others in her heart.

6

The Great Love
1559–60

୬୨

One particular gentleman had emerged as a firm favourite of the Queen by 1559 – but far from being a king, prince or nobleman with an irreproachable pedigree, Robert Dudley, the man chosen by Elizabeth, was the descendant of convicted and executed traitors. Robert Dudley's grandfather, Edmund, had helped devise new ways of raising taxes under Henry VII's administration. When Henry VIII came to the throne, the young King's advisers arbitrarily selected Edmund and another officer to be scapegoats for Henry VII's heavy taxation policies. They were both executed on 17 August 1510. Following his father's death, six-year-old John Dudley, Edmund's eldest son, became the ward of royal official Sir Edward Guildford. This would be a springboard for his eventual rise to power.

John Dudley possessed extraordinary talents as both a soldier and administrator. As a favourite of Henry VIII, he was granted several positions and titles, but he became even more powerful under Edward VI, when he became Edward's first minister after ousting Edward Seymour from the position in 1549. In this position, he effectively ruled the country. In 1551, he was also made 1st Duke of Northumberland, but less than two years later, he fell rather spectacularly from grace, executed for high treason after plotting to place his daughter-in-law Lady Jane Grey on the throne after Edward VI's death. His abilities as a shrewd politician would become legendary. Sir Richard Moryson, Ambassador to the Court of Charles V, said that Dudley 'had such a head that he seldom went about anything but he conceived three or four purposes beforehand.'[1]

John Dudley married Sir Edward Guildford's daughter, Jane, with whom he had 11 children that survived infancy: 7 sons and 4 daughters. Robert Dudley was their fifth son, and according to historian William Camden, he shared his birth date, 7 September 1533, with Elizabeth I.[2] However, there are no existing records of Robert's actual birth date. Robert was placed in the household of Edward VI as one of the 'King's Children' – the young King's companions – and his father hoped that he and Edward would become friends. However, there is nothing to indicate that Edward felt more than mild friendship for Robert.

Robert's relationship with Elizabeth prior to her becoming Queen is largely the subject of conjecture. They were roughly the same age, and as members of the Royal Court, both were pupils of Roger Ascham, although they were probably never taught together. Ascham reported that whereas Elizabeth preferred history and languages, but Robert was more interested in mathematics, an interest that carried on into his adult life.[3]

In order to strengthen his own position, Robert's father negotiated politically or financially advantageous marriages for his children. In 1550, the 18-year-old Robert married Amy Robsart, who was 17 at the time. The couple had most probably met when Robert stayed in Wymondham as part of the force, under his father's command, that went North to put down Kett's rebellion.

Edward VI attended the marriage, which took place the following year, on 4 June 1550, at the royal palace in Sheen (Richmond, Surrey), as did the King's half-sister, Lady Elizabeth.

Although it was obvious to all present that the couple held each other in great affection, the marriage was also financially advantageous. Amy was the only legitimate child and heiress of Sir John Robsart, Lord of the Manor of Syderstone in Norfolk.

At that time, there were different schools of thought concerning marriage matches. Some argued in support of there being at least some affection between a couple, if not love, given that a marriage was for life. On the other hand, William Cecil would present the opposite case when drawing up a list of points for and against marriage in 1566 (the question in hand was Robert Dudley's suitability as a husband for Elizabeth). One point read *nuptiae carnales a laetitia incipient et in luctu terminantur*, meaning 'marriages of physical desire begin with happiness and end in grief'.[4]

After their marriage, Robert and Amy went to live in Norfolk, where he became Constable of the Castle. However, it was not John Dudley's plan to have his son live so far away from the centre of power for long. From 1551, Robert was given a series of Court posts, thanks largely to his father, including Chief Carver to the King, joint Commissioner for the Lord Lieutenant of Norfolk, and Master of the Royal Buckhounds.

By 1553, John Dudley, now 1st Duke of Northumberland, was at the zenith of his power and Robert was dividing his time between London and Syderstone, Norfolk, where he had been elected a Justice of the Peace and Member of Parliament. He also received lands near Yarmouth, as well as in Northamptonshire and Leicestershire, by grace of his father and also Edward VI. But the family's fortunes would change with the death of Edward VI in July 1553.

❧

As soon as the King died, John Dudley started to plot to cut Mary and Elizabeth out of the succession and secure the Crown for Lady

Jane Grey, who had recently married his son, Guildford. Mary and her supporters resisted, marching on the capital, and most of John Dudley's men deserted him for Mary's side, leaving John and Robert to flee. They continued their campaign, with Robert taking part, but soon realized the futility of their struggle, as the rest of the Council supported Mary and proclaimed her Queen.

Although John Dudley pledged that he was the servant of the Council and, therefore, to Mary I, he and his sons were arrested and taken to the Tower of London. On 18 August, John Dudley was tried for treason, along with his eldest son, John, 2nd Earl of Warwick, and both were found guilty.

Despite the ruthless reputation she would later acquire for her religious persecutions, Mary I was surprisingly lenient with the Dudleys. She seized the lands given to Robert by his father and Edward VI, but John Dudley was the only one to be executed on 22 August 1553 on Tower Hill. Even Jane Grey and her husband Guildford Dudley were spared, remaining prisoners in the Tower.

Unfortunately for Jane Grey, Thomas Wyatt's rebellion against Mary I in January 1554 led the Queen to reassess her position. Mary's advisers won out, arguing that as long as Lady Jane Grey lived she would always be a focus for discontent and, therefore, a threat to Mary. On 12 February 1554, Jane and Guildford were subsequently executed. The other Dudley brothers, John, Ambrose, Robert and Henry, remained prisoners in the Tower.

Romantic history has it that Elizabeth and Robert were imprisoned in the Tower together, where they met secretly and fell in love. In reality, from March to May 1554 Elizabeth was held in the Bell Tower, while the Dudley brothers were in the Beauchamp Tower from July 1553 to October 1554, the next tower along on the west wall. While Elizabeth was allowed to walk along the wide roof gutter between the two towers, she was easily observed from a

144

row of houses that faced Tower Green. Furthermore, Elizabeth was always attended by four guards, so it is unlikely that she could have seen or communicated with any of the Dudleys, let alone met Robert in secret.

In any case, there is no evidence to indicate that she would have wanted to at that time. As far as she was concerned, the Dudleys' plotting, had it been successful, would also have deprived her of the throne – and possibly might have resulted in her death – so it is unlikely that she would have regarded them sympathetically. There are contemporary accounts of Elizabeth receiving notes and posies from an admirer, but it is more probable that these were from Edward Courtenay, who was also imprisoned in the Tower at the time, for his father's implication in a Roman Catholic uprising, and who was also viewed by some as a possible husband for Elizabeth.

During the Dudleys' incarceration, their mother, Jane, appealed to the Queen for clemency for her sons, 'gifting' her few remaining jewels and expensive items of clothing to those of the Queen's ladies-in-waiting who might be persuaded to speak to Mary I about her sons' release. After Jane's death in January 1555, her friends, including Mary's husband, Philip of Spain, continued to make her case, with the result that in October, John, Ambrose, Robert and Henry were released.

While Robert returned to Amy and their estates, in 1556, he joined his brothers, Ambrose and Henry, as part of the English army fighting in France on behalf of Spain – England and Spain were allied through Mary's marriage to Philip. Their service to the Crown went some way towards the rehabilitation of the Dudley family fortunes, and in March 1557, Philip sent Robert back to London with some dispatches for Mary.[5] The Queen welcomed the messages and rewarded the messenger and his brothers. Ambrose, the eldest surviving Dudley, was restored to the title of

Viscount Lisle. Robert's confiscated lands were returned. He returned to the war, and in August 1557, was Master of Ordinance at the Battle of St Quentin, in which his 22-year-old brother Henry was tragically killed in the fighting.

During these years, Robert would probably have had little opportunity to meet with Elizabeth. However, a rumour, recounted in the State papers as well as in the letters of Hubert Languet, a French diplomat, suggests that they were in contact and were on quite friendly terms. Reportedly, a jeweller named Dymock, who was visiting the Swedish Court in 1562, was asked by the King of Sweden why Robert was such a favourite. He replied, 'When she was but Lady Elizabeth ... in her trouble he did sell away a good piece of his land to aid her, which divers supposed to be the cause the Queen so favoured him.'[6] It is perhaps odd that neither Elizabeth nor Robert mentioned this as a reason for their friendship, but Elizabeth's debts after Mary I cast her off, combined with Robert's diplomatic astuteness, make the story plausible.

By 1558, Robert was living the life of a minor member of the nobility, although he appears to have had financial problems himself. Certainly, neither he nor Amy resided at Syderstone any longer; in fact it may have been too dilapidated to live in. With Robert primarily at Court in London, Amy moved around, staying with family and friends in comfortable houses, attended by a number of servants and accompanied by chests loaded with her personal possessions. So it was that Amy was living with friends, William Hyde and his wife Elizabeth, at Throcking, near Bishops Stortford, Hertfordshire, when Robert rode out on a 'snow-white horse'[7] to meet Elizabeth, the new Queen, at Hatfield, in November 1558, after Mary I's death.

Robert showed to his best advantage on horseback. He was muscular, tall and long-legged, but more importantly, he was a very skilled horseman, a talent that Elizabeth prized. On ascending the throne, Elizabeth made him her Master of the Queen's Horses. In this post, he was responsible for the riding horses, pack-horses and mules belonging to the Queen and her household. The role also demanded that he remain in close attendance to the Queen. Robert held this post until he died. Although he was awarded other posts and positions, he attached great importance to this first sign of the Queen's favour.

On 23 November 1558, Elizabeth left Hatfield for London, stopping at Charterhouse, the home of Sir Edward North, Baron North of Kirtling, whose son, Roger, was a close friend of Robert's. On 28 November, she left in procession for London, riding in a chariot as far as Cripplegate, and from there she made her way on horseback. In front of her rode the Lord Mayor, carrying the sceptre, and the Garter King-at-Arms; behind her came William Herbert, 1st Earl of Pembroke, with the sword of state, and the Sergeant-at-Arms as her bodyguard. She was dressed in a habit of violet velvet and rode a white horse. Riding behind her came Robert, on a black horse, making his first appearance in his new role.

If the sight of this famous jouster on horseback was not enough, Elizabeth could also see Robert to great advantage on the tennis court. In Tudor times, the show of masculine beauty, skill and strength in tennis was considered very attractive, as evidenced by the vivid description of the young Henry VIII coming off the tennis court after a strenuous game, damp with sweat, his shirt clinging to the musculature of his body, his face delightfully flushed, his chest heaving for breath. Similarly there were reports that the Queen often came to see Robert play, as this account, made after 1564, when Robert became the Earl of Leicester, indicates: '… de Quadra complained that the Queen had failed to attend an important meeting … on the grounds that she was

147

indisposed, but in fact had gone to watch Leicester playing tennis.'[8]

Robert also excelled as a dancer, and Elizabeth loved dancing. Venetian Ambassador Giovanni Michiel wrote in 1557, 'The Queen's daily amusements are musical performances and other entertainments and she takes marvellous pleasure in seeing people dance.' A further letter dated February 1559 showed that Elizabeth also liked to participate: 'Last evening … at the dance the Queen performed her part, the Duke of Norfolk [Thomas Howard] being her partner, in superb array.'[9]

Rumours began to circulate about the Queen's relationship with Robert Dudley. In April 1559, Spanish Ambassador de Feria wrote to Philip II, making his doubts known that the Queen would ever accept the pending suit of Ferdinand, Archduke of Austria, as the current gossip was that she was in love with 'Lord Robert', a married man:

> During the last few days Lord Robert has come so much into favour that he does whatever he likes with affairs and it is even said that her Majesty visits him in his chamber day and night. People talk of this so freely that they go so far as to say that his wife [Amy Robsart] has a malady in one of her breasts and the Queen is only waiting for her to die to marry Lord Robert. I can assure your Majesty that matters have reached such a pass that I have been brought to consider whether it would be well to approach Lord Robert on your Majesty's behalf, promising him your help and favour and coming to terms with him.[10]

Signs of the Queen's affection for Robert – and his for her – continued to grow more pronounced. On 23 April 1559, St

George's Day, Robert Dudley was elected Knight of the Garter, a surprisingly high honour, normally limited to only the most esteemed nobles. The Venetian Ambassador to Brussels received a report that Robert was 'a very handsome young man towards whom in various ways the Queen evinces much affection and inclination that many persons believe that if his wife, who has been ailing for some time, were perchance to die, the Queen might easily take him for her husband.' Robert himself seemed a willing partner in this developing intimacy.[11]

The foreign ambassadors at Elizabeth's Court focussed on any possible relationships that the Queen might have, concerned as they were by the crucial question of who might father the next monarch of England. While they believed that Elizabeth might consider an English husband, it seemed beyond the imagination of most that she would select Robert Dudley from a choice of suitors that included great princes and nobles.

The question of whether Elizabeth was fertile was also of considerable interest to them. In 1559, Ambassador de Feria wrote to Philip, 'For a certain reason they have recently given me, I understand she will not bear children.'[12] The Scottish Ambassador Sir James Melville had heard the same thing, probably surmised from reports that Elizabeth had erratic periods. This information would have come from chambermaids and laundresses who were paid a modest fee for their firsthand accounts, a valuable source of information for the vast number of foreign diplomats who wished to be able to report on the state of Elizabeth's health and fecundity to their royal paymasters.

In 1559, the Venetian Ambassador reported, 'Before leaving London, her Majesty was blooded from one foot and from one arm, but what her indisposition is, is not known. Many persons say things I should not dare to write [that the bleeding was to compensate for her lack of periods], but they say that on arriving at Greenwich she was as cheerful as ever she was.'[13]

Despite these reports of missed periods and Elizabeth's poor menstruation cycle, there is no record that the Queen's doctors believed Elizabeth was unable to have children.

◆

Apart from the fact that Robert Dudley was already married, a major stumbling block to any marriage plans was his rank. Although it was not unknown for a high-born noblewoman, even a member of the royal family, to marry a gentleman of more humble birth, this was normally a second or third marriage, after she had passed childbearing age. These ladies were usually independent and wealthy and free to please themselves, having fulfilled their family's expectations. Anne Seymour (née Stanhope), the Dowager Duchess of Somerset, for example, married her steward after the death of her first husband, Edward Seymour; Katherine Willoughby d'Eresby, Dowager Duchess of Suffolk, married her gentleman usher after the Duke of Suffolk's death; Lettice Knollys, after two marriages to noblemen, married her deceased husband's servant; and Frances Grey (née Brandon), Dowager Duchess of Suffolk and the daughter of Henry VIII's sister, Mary Tudor, took for her second husband her secretary and Master of Horses, a man also 16 years her junior. The Victorian author Lucy Aikin commented that on hearing of Frances Grey's marriage Elizabeth reportedly remarked, 'What, has she married her horse keeper?' to which William Cecil replied, 'Yes, madam, and she says your majesty would like to do so too.'[14] While this makes for a good story, in fact Frances's second marriage took place in 1554, and Robert was not made Elizabeth's Master of Horses until 1558.

150

In any case, none of these precedents were queens of childbearing age – the same could not be said of Elizabeth, whose heir would have a claim to the throne.

The Venetian Ambassador reported to the Doge in May, 'My Lord Robert Dudley is in very great favour and very intimate with her Majesty. In this subject I ought to report the opinion of many, but I doubt whether my letter may not miscarry ... wherefore it is better to keep silence than to speak ill.'[15]

The Ambassador, realizing quite correctly that his letters might be intercepted, was unwilling to openly state what everyone in the diplomatic community was thinking: that Elizabeth and Robert were having a physical relationship. Even the vast army of servants could not watch the Queen night and day, and gossip indicated that the couple had managed to steal time together alone. Given that they were both young, healthy and attractive, speculation was rife that they were secret lovers.

It is true that Elizabeth and Robert would have had few opportunities to be alone, but how difficult must it have been? At Court, the Queen's household had around 1,000 domestic servants working 'below stairs'. Around 500 to 600 people had access to the upstairs public rooms, while 80 to 100 had access to the Privy Chambers. On a more intimate level, Elizabeth had 3 or 4 Ladies of the Bedchamber, up to 12 Maids of the Privy Chamber, about 6 Maids of Honour and a Mistress of Maids (Kat Ashley was given this position when Elizabeth became Queen).

From the time she rose until the time she went to sleep, Elizabeth was almost continuously in someone's company. Her ladies-in-waiting, Councillors and guards had to be close enough to respond, should the Queen call. When dealing with business, she was attended by secretaries and clerks; when being entertained, she was surrounded by musicians, singers and dancers.

As the question of her chastity was of supreme interest to the suitors for her hand, the foreign diplomats strove to get information from her intimate circle of servants. Baron von Breuner, who was sent by Ferdinand I to negotiate a possible marriage between his son and Elizabeth, wrote on 6 August 1559:

> I have employed as my agent Francois Borth, who is on very friendly terms with all the ladies of the bedchamber and all other persons who have been about the Queen and have brought her up since childhood [Kat Ashley, Blanche Parry, Thomas Parry, etc]. They all swear by all that is holy that her Majesty has most certainly never been forgetful of her honour. And yet it is not without significance that her Majesty's Master of Horse, my lord Robert, is preferred by the Queen above all others, and that her Majesty shows her liking for him more markedly than is consistent with her reputation and dignity.[16]

Sir Thomas Chaloner, the English Ambassador to the Imperial Court in Brussels, wrote a letter to William Cecil warning that in diplomatic circles the Queen's relationship with Robert was subject to much lewd speculation, which he believed was scandalous and unfounded.[17]

Whatever the nature of their physical relationship, Robert believed that Elizabeth wanted to marry him. However, he had a lot of competition. He would need to make sure that no one else made a proposal that she might accept, and the only people Robert could count on for support were his family and a few close friends. In September 1559, Robert came up with a scheme to deal with the one suitor whom he believed he had cause to fear – Charles, Archduke of Austria, who was close to being an ideal candidate. The 19-year-old Charles was good-looking, strong, an enthusiastic horseman, a soldier, a Catholic who was tolerant of Protestants, the son of the Holy Roman Emperor and cousin of the King of Spain. His family were known to produce many healthy children (later, when Charles married Maria of Bavaria in 1571, they went on to have seven children).

Robert set out to disrupt the negotiations. Aided by his sister Mary Sidney, he began to mislead de Quadra, the newest Spanish Ambassador, supplying him with false information. On 7 September, de Quadra reported that Mary Sidney had told him that it was time to speak to the Queen about the Archduke: '… She said I must not mind what the Queen said, it was not the custom here for ladies to give their consent till they were teased into it.'

De Quadra then consulted Robert, who agreed that Elizabeth would accept Charles, as she needed the alliance. De Quadra tried to push the Queen into a formal agreement to marry Charles, but reported that when he pressed her, she seemed frightened and protested, over and over again, that she would 'not to be bound'. De Quadra was surprised at her vehemence: 'I do not believe that Lady Sidney and Lord Robert could be mistaken, and the latter says he never thought the Queen would go so far.'[18] Of course, Robert and his sister would have known that the more Elizabeth was pushed on the matter, the harder she would resist.

In October 1559, one of the least welcome of Elizabeth's marriage proposals arrived with Duke John of Finland, who had come to win the Queen for his brother, Crown Prince Eric of Sweden. While Robert may have been concerned in the beginning, he soon realized that he had nothing to worry about as it soone became apparent that this suitor had little chance of success.

For Elizabeth, however, the situation was stressful. This is well illustrated by a jousting tournament that was held in November 1559 at which Robert Dudley and Henry Carey, 1st Baron Hunsdon, another of Elizabeth's nobles, took on all-comers. As the Queen watched her beloved joust, she sat between Duke John of Finland on one side and von Breuner, representing Archduke Charles, on the other. According to de Quadra, 'The King of Sweden's son [Duke John], who is here, is fit to kill the Emperor's ambassador [von Breuner], because he said his father was only a clown who had stolen his kingdom ... The matter has reached such a point that the Queen is careful they should not meet in the palace to avoid their slashing each other in her presence.'[19]

The histrionic behaviour of the bizarre Swedes made for a good story, but for many, the fact that the Queen might have set her heart on Robert was already a matter of great concern, particularly the fact that he had a wife. The very existence of Amy was undeniably an obstacle to a marriage between Robert and Elizabeth – if one was indeed being considered – and by late 1559, rumours were circulating that Elizabeth and Robert were only waiting for Amy to die from her long-standing illness in order for them to marry. De Quadra, who was still smarting over Robert's interference in the negotiations over Archduke Charles, wrote to Philip II on 13 November 1559 that he had heard, '... veracious news that Lord Robert has sent to poison his wife.' Elizabeth, he had heard, was only pretending to consider marrying Prince Eric and Archduke Charles 'until this wicked deed is consummated'.[20]

Despite the rumours, there is no evidence that Robert had abandoned or neglected his wife; nor is there anything to suggest that he treated Amy harshly. While she was living with the Hydes at Throcking, he visited Amy quite frequently. They, the Hydes, their servants and friends spent pleasant evenings together playing cards or dicing, so much so that Robert, short of cash as always, sometimes had to borrow money from Mr Hyde to make bets as they played.[21]

Back at Court, Robert was faced with open opposition from noblemen determined to stop any pretensions he might have of marrying the Queen. In late 1559, Thomas Howard, 4th Duke of Norfolk, a 23-year-old gentleman who was England's Premier Duke and who himself nursed an ambition to be Elizabeth's husband, threatened Robert's life. De Quadra was pleased to report to Philip, 'I think this hatred of the Lord Robert will continue as the Duke and the rest of them cannot put up with his being King.'[22]

On 18 November, de Quadra again wrote to Philip, 'He [Robert] has been warned there is a plot to kill him, which I quite believe, for not a man in the realm can suffer the idea of his being King.'[23] Robert also feuded with Henry Fitzalan, 12th Earl of Arundel, whose advances had been rejected by the Queen. He, too, objected to the knight stepping into a position that should have been reserved for a duke or an earl. Fitzalan's servant would later state that although he felt the matter of Elizabeth's marriage should be up to the Queen and that Robert was 'as meet a man as any in England', he prayed God that 'all men may take it well, that there might rise no trouble thereof'.[24] Rumours of plots to kill Robert Dudley reached such a point that he is said to have worn chain mail under his clothes.[25]

Members of Elizabeth's own inner circle also commented on Robert. Kat Ashley, who always endeavoured to protect her much-loved Elizabeth, was mindful of the danger of rumours to a woman's reputation. She tried to warn Elizabeth to be careful. Late in 1559, Ambassador von Breuner wrote to Ferdinand I that Elizabeth had responded to Kat Ashley's warnings by defending Robert: 'She [Elizabeth] hoped she had given no one just cause to associate her name with that of her equerry or of any other man. But, she said, in this world, she had had so much sorrow and so little joy! If she showed herself gracious to her Master of Horse, he deserved it, for his honourable nature and dealing.'[26] Von Breuner himself judged their relationship to be one based on innocent love.[27]

Meanwhile, at least one observer took to heart Elizabeth's long-held conviction that she had no intention of marrying. Roger Ascham, who had known her from childhood, wrote to his friend Sturm in early 1560: 'I told you rightly ... that in the whole ordinance of her life she resembled not Phaedra, but Hippolyta ... for by nature and not by the counsels of others, she is thus averse and abstinent from marriage. When I know any thing for certain, I will write to you as soon as possible; in the mean time I have no hopes to give you respecting the King of Sweden.'[28]

156

In May 1560, William Cecil left Court to head negotiations for making peace with Scotland. The French Mary of Guise was acting Regent in Scotland for her daughter Mary, Queen of Scots, who was in France with her husband, François II. Mary of Guise, keen to maintain Scotland's links with France, was ill and believed to be dying, which would make discussions between the English and Scottish Councils easier.

Even in the midst of these political negotiations, Elizabeth's marriage was not far from the statesman's mind. Cecil wrote a private report of the proceedings to Elizabeth from Edinburgh, ending his letter, 'So most humbly of Almighty God I do require that it may please Him to direct your Majesty's heart to make a choice of a husband that may be father to your posterity ...'[29]

The next month he wrote again, ending with his 'continual prayer, that God would direct your heart to procure a father for your children.'[30] Cecil would have accepted almost any prince, but he prayed most sincerely that the father of England's future monarch should not be Sir Robert Dudley.

The Treaty of Edinburgh, which Cecil negotiated was, at least, a success for England. Scotland would be governed by a Council of 11 members, 9 chosen by the Scottish lords and 7 by Mary, Queen of Scots. All French forces were to be withdrawn to France and their fortifications at Leith, Dunbar and Eyemouth were to be dismantled. In addition, the Queen of Scots would stop using the English royal arms and would recognize Elizabeth as Queen of England. Cecil had achieved all his demands.

However, as for his and the other Councillors' prayers regarding Elizabeth's marriage, they appeared to have no effect. Elizabeth continued to favour Robert. It was said that while Cecil was in Scotland, the Queen hardly left the Court and that Robert was always with her to keep her away from his rivals. Certainly, as Master of the Horse he was with her daily. With the vigilant Cecil away, the rumours increased that Elizabeth and Robert were having a physical relationship. This is also the most likely time for Elizabeth to have become pregnant. If this was the case, the child conceived of this affair would have been born sometime between January and April 1561.

When Cecil returned to England, far from being praised by the Queen, he was met by a storm of complaints. Why had he not insisted that the negotiations include the return of Calais? This was one of her priorities, and she had been persuaded by someone that Cecil had failed by not making this a condition of the treaty.

Cecil suspected that Robert had a hand in plying the Queen with notions of recovering Calais which, as any sensible politician knew, was lost forever. Cecil knew that Robert had enjoyed Elizabeth's full attention during his absence and suspected that he might have wanted to turn the triumph of a man he saw as a rival for the Queen's appreciation into a failure in her eyes. Cecil became depressed at what he felt were uncalled-for attacks on him by the Queen and threatened to resign.

The situation was becoming increasingly heated. Elizabeth and Robert's alleged affair was the talk of the Royal Courts of Europe. In England, too, the rumours were gaining ground among the people. In the late summer of 1560, 'Mother' Anne Dowe (Dove), aged 68, appeared before the bench on charges of slandering the Queen by claiming Elizabeth was pregnant. She asserted that in June she had heard from an owner of a house in Rochford that Robert had given Elizabeth an expensive petticoat costing 20 nobles. Mother Dowe had replied that the Queen could have bought one for herself. Several days later, she repeated the story of Robert giving the Queen the expensive petticoat to an acquaintance, who replied, 'Thinkst thou it was a petticoat? No, no, he gave her a child, I warrant thee.' She then told the tailor that Elizabeth and Robert had been playing 'legerdemain' (sleight of hand, later known as hanky-panky), to which he retorted 'That is not so!' Mother Dowe replied, 'Is, for he hath given her a child.' The tailor countered, 'What, she hath no child yet!' to which Mother Dowe replied, 'No, if she hath not, he hath put one to the making.'[31]

Mother Dowe was imprisoned for indiscreet assertions. Her claims were somewhat undermined by the fact that the other parties to these conversations said she had been drinking. However, they show the extent of the rumours about Elizabeth and Robert's intimate associations at the time, and the suspicions that the Queen may indeed have been pregnant.

Scarcely a month later, in September 1560, the dramatic and tragic death of Amy Robsart, Robert's wife, would bring the rumours to a fever pitch, marking a turning point in Elizabeth's relationship with Robert Dudley.

7

The Amy Robsart Scandal, 1560–63

By 1558, Amy was staying in the house of William Hyde at Throcking, as her estate in Syderstone was now uninhabitable. Robert's accounts indicate that messengers frequently delivered communications between husband and wife, and that he visited her regularly.[1]

Early in 1559, the account entries indicate that Robert's servants rode to Mr Hyde's house 'for my lady', delivering gifts, clothes, money and messages from Robert to his wife. The deliveries included venison and spices, all exotic and expensive at the time and flavours that Robert would have grown accustomed to in Court cuisine such as cinnamon, saffron (said at the time to be worth its weight in gold), mace, nutmeg, pepper or ginger.[2] The fact that they were delivered to coincide with one of Robert's visits to the Hydes may indicate that perhaps their diet was not as refined as he might have liked.

One of Amy's few surviving letters was written on 7 August 1559, to John Flowerdew, a neighbour and friend to Robert and Amy in Norfolk (his son William was married to Amy's half-sister, Frances Appleyard). In the letter, written from Hayes Court near Chislehurst in Kent, the home of Amy's mother's family, Amy asks John Flowerdew to shear and sell some wool at once, even at a loss, as Robert needed money to settle a debt. Flowerdew agreed, but wanted confirmation that Robert was happy for this to be done. Amy admitted that he hadn't actually agreed: 'I forgot to move my Lord thereof before his departing, he being sore troubled with weighty affairs, and I not being altogether in quiet for his sudden departing.'[3]

It appears that Robert had been with her at Hayes and had been upset when he left. Amy insisted that Robert's wish was for the wool to be sold and emphasized the urgency: '... my Lord so earnestly desired me at his departing to see those poor men satisfied as though it had been a matter depending upon life; whereof I force not to sustain a little loss thereby, to satisfy my Lord's desires, and so to send that money ... to whom my Lord hath given order for the payment thereof.'[4]

Since so few letters from Amy survive, this particular one is often shown to illustrate that she had no head for business and that Robert and Amy had parted on bad terms. Another interpretation might be that Amy was confident to make decisions and fulfil Robert's requests on his behalf. Their parting was, according to Amy, somewhat emotional. He was 'sore troubled with weighty affairs', among them possibly the question of Elizabeth's other suitors, including the very eligible Charles, Archduke of Austria.[5]

By 1559, Elizabeth had given Robert land in Yorkshire, as well as the manor of Kew. She had also made him Lieutenant of the Castle and Forest of Windsor, and given him a licence to export woollen cloth free of duty. He had yet to buy a 'home' estate and settle his wife, most probably because his fortunes were only just being restored. While from 1550 to 1553 Robert had been an up-and-coming gentleman, receiving gifts of land and well-paid posts at Court, after his imprisonment and conviction as a traitor, he was deprived of most of his lands and was reduced to surviving on the revenue from the estates given to him as part of Amy's dowry. Robert's fortunes only changed after 1558, when Elizabeth became Queen.

ANNA·BOLINA ANG·RECINA

*Previous page:
Elizabeth the
Queen, dressed in
coronation robes
(c.1559–1600).*

*Elizabeth's parents:
Anne Boleyn (left),
her mother, the
second wife of
Henry VIII
(below).*

ANNO DÑI · · 1 5 4 4 ·

ADI MARI
THE MOST
INGE HENRI

THE AGE OF

DOVGHTER TO
VERTVOVS PRINCE
THE EIGHT

XXVIII YERES

Left: Elizabeth's half-sister Mary (Mary I), aged 28. Mary's mother was Catherine of Aragon, Henry VIII's first wife

Below: Catherine Parr, Henry VIII's sixth wife, who later married Thomas Seymour. Many people believed that Elizabeth had an affair with Seymour.

THARINE. PARRE

Thomas Seymour, Catherine Parr's husband, was accused of behaving indecently towards the Princess Elizabeth. Seymour is one of the men with whom Elizabeth may have had children.

*Robert Dudley, Earl of Leicester,
was Elizabeth's great love — and another
possible father of her children.*

Thomas Parrie.

Right: Thomas Parry was Elizabeth's cofferer. Parry gave evidence against Thomas Seymour at the enquiry into his behaviour in 1549.

Below: Charles, Duke of Angouleme, was one of Elizabeth's suitors.

Left: William Cecil, Lord Burghley, was Elizabeth's principal adviser.

Below: Sir Francis Bacon, who may have been the love child of Elizabeth and Robert Dudley.

Robert Devereux,
Earl of Essex, was a great favourite of the Queen
– and may have been Elizabeth's son.

In the time before he was appointed to a Court post, Robert would have lived on what he could make out of his rents, flocks and crops. He would not have been able to afford to lease or buy an estate nearer to London or to afford serious expenditure on his lands. It is probable that having Amy live with friends was the best option financially for them both, allowing Robert to rent the manor houses to bring in extra revenue.

While living in such households as those of William Hyde, Sir Richard Verney and Sir Anthony Forster still required some outlay, it was nothing like the sums that were needed for Amy to run her own household. To keep even a small manor house running depended on a staff of servants who had to be fed and clothed. This required a large budget. Later in the year, when Robert was appointed to the Queen's Court, his expenses would have, if anything, increased, as he had to show himself to advantage among the royals and nobles, as well as to attract the Queen's attention.

Amy's health could have been another reason why the Dudleys did not settle in their own home. As early as April 1559, Spanish Ambassador de Feria was reporting to Philip that Amy had 'a malady in one of her breasts'. In the same month, Paolo Tiepolo, the Venetian Ambassador, reported in the same context that Robert's wife had been ailing for some time.[6] Amy could have had cancer, an illness that was believed to be incurable, and both Amy and those close to her might have feared that she would die at any time. Amy's maid, Mrs Pirto, also testified at the inquest into Amy's death that her mistress suffered from severe depression, leading her to admit the possibility that Amy had considered suicide.

If Amy was ill or suffering from depression, she would have been unable to carry out the duties of running her own household. In this case, by putting her in the safe hands of friends, where she would not have to carry out the stressful duties of a lady of the manor, Robert may have been ensuring that she suffered from as little pressure as possible. Of course, from an outsider's point of view, such as that of the foreign ambassadors, among others, who were disapproving of Robert's relationship with the Queen, they might have interpreted Robert's actions rather more sinisterly, as part of a greater plan to get rid of Amy in order to marry the Queen. Some speculated that Amy was not, in fact, ill and that the entire story had been devised as a cover for Robert when he killed her. Certainly by late 1559, ambassadors such as de Quadra were openly accusing Robert of plotting to murder his wife, and Robert was most probably aware of these rumours.[7]

In September 1559, Amy went to stay with Sir Richard Verney, one of Robert's friends, at Compton Verney in Warwickshire. Two months later, she had moved again, this time to the household of Robert's treasurer and friend, Sir Anthony Forster, at Cumnor Place in North Berkshire. This move brought Amy closer to Robert – the house was about 30 miles from Windsor, where he had lodgings.

The Forsters were an established Shropshire family with three sons and two daughters. Cumnor Place was a well-built two-storey former monastic building of four wings built around a courtyard. It would have had large, impressive glass windows, panelling, wooden floors, a park and gardens, and included every creature comfort. Before Forster took up the lease, it had belonged to Dr George Owen, whose relation, Mrs Owen, stayed on as part of the lease. She lived in one part of the house, Sir Anthony and his family in another and a third part was turned over for Amy's use; it was here that she resided along with her servants, including Mrs Pirto and her attendant, William Huggins (or Hogan). Amy also had a footman and perhaps other staff, as in

1559 she received pairs of hose for three of 'those that waiteth on my lady'.[8] Another lady, a widow named Mrs Odingsells, was also a guest in the house. She was most probably Edith Odingsells, whose sister, Alice, was married to Forster.

Amy would spend the coming months settled in this comfortable manor house, surrounded by people who wished her well, and supplied by her husband with such fineries as sewing silk for her embroidery and a looking-glass. The last letter that survives from Amy is to her tailor, dated 24 August 1560, about a new dress. The tone of the letter is cheerful and shows Amy looking forward to the pleasure of a new gown, made in the russet colour (a reddish brown) that she seemed to favour.[9] She seemed in good spirits.

163

Just two weeks later, on Sunday, 8 September 1560, tragedy struck. Amy was found lying dead at the foot of the stairs in the hall. On the day, Amy reportedly insisted that everyone in the house attend a local fair at Abingdon, although Mrs Owen and Mrs Odingsells both declined (the Forsters are not mentioned), the latter stating that she would prefer to go the following day when the gentry, rather than the commoners, would be there.

Amy was angry with the widow for refusing to go to the fair, but she could not order Mrs Odingsells to do her bidding. She did insist that all her servants spend the day at the fair, however. Amy had dinner with Mrs Owen later that evening, after which they parted company – and that was the last that anyone saw of her until the servants, on returning that evening, found Amy lying dead at the foot of the staircase, her neck broken.[10]

When Robert received news of his wife's death, he immediately sent word to his household officer Thomas Blount, who he had sent to Cumnor, instructing him to find out what had happened. Robert understood that the news of Amy's death would throw suspicion on him.[11]

He asked Blount to conduct an open inquiry to learn the truth, composed of a jury of 'discreet and substantial men' who would be seen as honest. Robert also requested that Blount send him his 'true conceit and opinion of the matter, whether it happened by evil chance or villainy ...', adding a postscript that he had also requested that his wife's half-brother, John, as well as others close to Amy be present so that they could keep an eye on matters.[12] Amy's other half-brother, Arthur, was also sent for to ensure that Robert could not be later accused of a cover-up.

Robert acted quickly, with an eye to his own interests. His feelings for Amy were now largely irrelevant: he needed to minimize the damage that his wife's unnatural death might have on his chances of marrying Elizabeth. It was important that he remain in London, partly to be near the Court and partly to stem any accusations that he had rushed to Cumnor to orchestrate a cover-up or to intimidate the jury at the inquest. He counted on Blount to handle things at Cumnor without interfering personally. He was insistent that the jury should be composed of local men of good standing, even if they were hostile towards Forster or himself, as this would count for their impartiality. He knew that there had to be a full and honest appraisal of events, resulting in a finding that Amy's death had been an accident, in order for him to be free to marry Elizabeth after a suitable period of mourning.

As instructed by Robert, Blount stopped at Abingdon and spoke to the landlord of the inn to gauge the immediate reaction of the local people to the tragedy. The general feeling seemed to be that Amy's death had been accidental. Although there may have been some talk that it might have been murder, Forster was considered so honest by the local people that this speculation was not given much credence. Others thought it was suspicious that Amy had insisted on sending everyone to the fair on the day, which led them to conclude that Amy might have died by her own hand.

Blount asked the inn landlord if she had been suicidal, as the servants had reported to him that she had been depressed: 'No, good Mr Blount, do not so judge my words; if you should so gather I am sorry I said as much.'[13] Blount hoped it was an accident, but seemed to fear it was suicide, as he implied when he wrote to Robert, 'My Lord ... The tales I do hear of her make me think she had a strange mind as I will tell you at my coming.'[14]

Robert himself went to great lengths in his letters to Blount never to mention the possibility of suicide. On 12 September, he wrote, '... if it fall out a chance or misfortune, then so to say; and, if it appear a villainy as God forbid so mischievous or wicked a body should live, then to find it so.'[15] He made no mention of a third possible verdict, self-termination. This was not to be mentioned or considered, possibly because it was the one that Robert most feared was true.

There would have been a good deal of evidence to support a verdict of suicide and this might have been better for Robert, but he did all he could to protect his dead wife from this conclusion, which was considered a grave sin. If she had taken her own life, she would have been denied a Christian burial and would have been laid to rest in unhallowed ground, although her rank would have saved her from the fate of being buried at a crossroads with a stake through her heart. In any case, her soul would still be damned for eternity.

With all this in mind, Robert and Amy's intimates would have grasped at the notion of an accidental death with almost frantic single-mindedness, since the alternative, as they saw it, was too hideous to contemplate. A verdict of suicide might also have been damaging to Robert, as his opponents would claim he had driven her to it. The best possible outcome was a verdict that Amy had been ill and had accidentally fallen. As the Cumnor house has since been demolished, it is unknown whether this is a realistic explanation for Amy's death. The records refer to a 'pair of stairs': that is, a short flight to a small landing, then a second short flight to an upstairs landing. The bottom set of stairs was reported to have 8 steps; even if there were more, the whole number was unlikely to exceed 14 treads.

If Amy had planned to take her own life, throwing herself down such narrow, short stairs would have been more likely to result in injury than death. They would be suitable for an attempt that was essentially a cry for help, but in that instance it would be important for someone to find her quickly, in case she really did hurt herself. Ordering her servants to leave the house would tend to support the idea of a deliberate suicide attempt, however, the design of the staircase tends to preclude this as a convincing explanation. An accidental fall would be plausible, but in that case, how would Amy's neck have broken on a short flight of stairs?

Another possible explanation for Amy's death emerged through research conducted in the 20th century, which would support a theory of accidental death. If Amy did indeed have advanced untreated breast cancer, she might have developed brittleness in her bones that possibly resulted in a spontaneous break. Professor Ian Aird, in 1956, demonstrated that breast cancer can cause secondary deposits in the bones, making them brittle (the deposits occurred in 50 percent of fatal cases studied; 6 percent of these showed deposits in the spine). If in a fall down a flight of stairs, as Aird explains, '... that part of the spine which lies in the neck suffers ... the affected person gets spontaneously a broken neck. Such a fracture is more likely to occur in stepping downstairs than in walking on the level.'[16] Only an examination of Amy's skeletal remains would be able to confirm or refute such a hypothesis, however.

After his wife's sudden death, Robert retired from Court to his house at Kew. He awaited news of the inquest from Blount. His mind was set somewhat at rest when Blount informed him that, in his opinion, the death had been a tragic accident: '... I have almost nothing that can make me so much as think that any man should be the doer thereof, as, when I think your lordship's wife before all other women should have such a chance, the circumstances and as many things as I can learn doth persuade me that only misfortune hath done it and nothing else.'[17]

After weighing up all the testimony and evidence, the jury formally determined a verdict of accidental death. The foreman wrote to Robert to let him know, who in turn wrote to Blount, stating that the verdict 'doth very much satisfy and quiet me.'[18]

And so the matter would have rested had not the Spanish Ambassador intervened. In a dispatch to Philip dated 11 September 1560, de Quadra (after meeting with Cecil, who was disgruntled with Robert at the time), stated that after promising him that he would keep anything he told him secret, Cecil had told him that he was going to withdraw from the Queen's service and that he perceived that the Queen was facing ruin over her 'intimacy with Lord Robert'. Cecil also claimed that the realm would not tolerate Elizabeth's marriage to Robert:

> ... He told me the Queen cared nothing for foreign princes.
> She did not believe she stood in any need of their support.

167

She was deeply in debt, taking no thought how to clear herself, and she had ruined her credit in the city. Last of all he said that they were thinking of destroying Lord Robert's wife. They had given out that she was ill, but she was not ill at all; she was very well and taking care not to be poisoned. God, he trusted, would never permit such a crime to be accomplished or so wretched a conspiracy to prosper.[19]

De Quadra's letter, dated 11 September, also stated that he had come to Windsor five days before (the 6th), and that on the next day (the 7th), Elizabeth had told him that Amy was dead, or 'nearly so' and had asked him not to say anything about it. He continued:

... Certainly this business is most shameful and scandalous, and withal I am not sure whether she will marry the man at once, or even if she will marry at all, as I do not think she has her mind sufficiently fixed. Since writing the above, I hear the Queen has published the death of Robert's wife and said in Italian, *Si ha rotto il collo.* 'She must have fallen down a staircase.'[20]

This letter was a blow to Robert, and also to Elizabeth. If it were to be fully believed, Cecil had as good as said that Amy was about to be murdered, and that not just Robert was implicated in such a plot, but the Queen as well.

Similarly, if de Quadra's letter was accurate and Elizabeth had, in fact, informed him that Amy was dead or 'nearly so' on 7 September, this would have been the day before it actually happened (the death occurred 8 September and news reached Windsor on 9 September). This odd behaviour was compounded by the Queen asking him not to mention what she had said to anyone. The report seemed to lay bare a plan drawn up by the Queen and her lover to murder his wife, leaving them free to marry.

However, the letter is not as incriminating as it first seems. The story that Robert and Elizabeth were waiting for his inconvenient wife to die and that Robert would eventually use poison to kill her was an old one and often repeated. In fact, poison was the one thing never mentioned in connection with Amy's death.

The remarks made by Cecil are more of a puzzle. He was quite capable of using the ambassador as a means of transmitting his opinion to the Queen, but is highly unlikely to have said anything that reflected badly on her. Given the use of 'spin' in modern-day politics, it is possible to imagine that Cecil might have spoken to de Quadra in secrecy expressly to make sure the latter did, in fact, convey the information to Philip. Cecil may have felt it was diplomatically wise to complain about Robert and the negative impact on England if he and Elizabeth were to marry. As for the Queen's remark about Amy being dead 'or nearly so', Elizabeth could well have been referring to Amy's terminal illness and adding, rather sadly, that it would be better not to talk about it.

This letter confirms one thing: that in September 1560 Amy's death was now expected to happen at any time. On 17 September, Robert's brother-in-law, Henry Hastings, 3rd Earl of Huntingdon, wrote him a letter in which he added a brief postscript: '... As I ended my letter I understood by letters the death of my lady your wife. I doubt not but long before this time you have considered what a happy hour is it which bringeth man from sorrow, to joy, from mortality to immortality, from care and trouble to rest and quietness and that the Lord above worketh all for the best to them that love him ...'[21] The very fact that Hastings felt he could add his condolences at the end of a mundane letter, as well as their tone, suggest that Amy's death was not only expected, but perhaps even welcomed as an end to her 'care and trouble'.

Evidence seems to suggest that those close to Amy were waiting for her ordeal to end. She had been settled at Cumnor for nine months and seemed content. She was close enough to London that Robert could visit or send messengers and was under the watchful eye of Lady Anne Forster, Mrs Odingsells, Mrs Owen and Amy's ever-present maid, Mrs Pirto. All that was needed to allow Robert and Elizabeth to marry and produce an heir to the English throne was for Amy to die naturally, surrounded by friends, family and physicians, without a word of scandal. Yet, in the end the manner of Amy's death left the whole affair open to conjecture, enabling the already circulating rumours of a murderous plot to flourish at Elizabeth's Court.

If Amy was murdered, the most logical question to ask would be who would have benefited from the timing and manner of her death? It is hard to argue that Robert and Elizabeth did. Had Amy lived a few weeks or months longer and died of natural causes, Robert would have had a real chance of becoming King of England. They had no reason to rush; Elizabeth had successfully held off her various suitors for two years and showed few signs of giving in to any one of them. She and Robert had waited so long; a little longer would not have mattered.

Furthermore, if Robert had genuinely wanted his wife out of the way, he had another option. He and Amy had no children and, with her ill health, were not likely to. A lack of children was a lawful reason for divorce at that time, and it was held to be the wife's fault unless she could prove otherwise. If Robert had wanted his freedom at any cost, he could have divorced Amy at any time.

Later writers, wishing to denigrate Robert, often refer to his imagined penchant for killing his enemies with poison. If Robert had wanted to kill his wife, poison would, indeed, have done the trick. Small doses, ending with a sufficiently large one, would have caused Amy's death in a way that mimicked a natural illness. But Robert would not have benefitted from Amy suffering a suspicious and unnatural death. Thus, if the timing, method and result of Amy's death all acted against Robert, is it possible that someone else might have had a motive to kill her in such a way as to tarnish Robert, making it impossible for Elizabeth to marry him?

There were certainly members of the Privy Council who feared what would happen if Robert became king consort, including William Cecil, Henry Fitzalan, Thomas Howard and Thomas Radclyffe, 3rd Earl of Sussex. The timing would fit this hypothesis. Amy was in the final stages of her illness and any day might die in her bed, freeing Robert to woo the Queen in earnest. It was crucial that she die in a way that pointed the finger at her husband, but without the investigation of an open murder that would risk the true perpetrator being discovered.

If Amy's death was the result of this type of plot, the plan worked perfectly. It could have been suicide, or an accident, or murder. In the end, the verdict was accidental death; however, the rumours of murder were damaging enough, spreading through England and the Royal Courts of Europe in a matter of days. If it could not be proved, it also could not be disproved. Robert's reputation was irretrievably blemished: with Amy's tragic death, the chance of Elizabeth and Robert marrying died as well.

The trouble with trying to identify a murderer among the English nobles is that so many of them might have had a motive. William Cecil, who, after falling out with the Queen over the Scottish negotiations, stood to lose his position in her Court and

171

possibly lose his life in the Tower, was certainly doing everything he could to prevent a marriage between Robert and Elizabeth. Then there was Thomas Radclyffe, a member of the Court who was vehemently opposed to Robert, yet who, after Amy's death, stated that he would love and serve whoever Elizabeth married. Had he engineered the death and its aftermath, he could utter such sanctimonious sentiments, secure in the knowledge that the husband would certainly not be Robert. Similarly, cousins Thomas Howard and Henry Fitzalan both hated Robert and they could have acted together in a Catholic-led conspiracy to end Robert's chances of marrying the Queen.

However, it is hard to see how any noble or alliance of nobles could have managed such a plot without discovery. Although none of them would have committed the deed himself, no matter how carefully a plot is laid, there is always the risk of being caught. If one of the nobles arranged it, he would have used a servant, friend or co-conspirator, although any of these options carried the risk of someone turning informer. There were no successful plots against Elizabeth during her lifetime because her intelligence service was extremely vigilant and one of the plotters usually betrayed the plan, wittingly or unwittingly.

Nevertheless, Amy's actions on the day might actually support the theory that she was the victim of a murder plot designed to look like an accident. She seemed to go to great lengths to make sure that everyone in Cumnor Place was out on that particular day, and when Mrs Owen and Mrs Odingsells declined, her angry outburst against Mrs Odingsells appears to have resulted in them not dining together. That meant Amy only had one dinner companion, and when she left the room to go down the stairs she was on her own. One reason for Amy to wish to be alone was that she was expecting a visitor.

A hypothetical scenario is that Amy was approached by a messenger, telling her there was a plot against her husband. This messenger may have arranged to come to the house on the evening of 8 September to bring Amy letters that she could send to Robert to warn him of the danger. However, as the messenger was afraid of being seen, could Amy arrange to be on her own that night? There was a fair in Abingdon and she could send her servants and friends there, saying she felt unwell and would not be joining them. At a prearranged time she could place a lighted candle in a window; the messenger would wait outside the house and creep in when he saw the light to meet Amy at the door at the bottom of the staircase. It would have been a simple job to snap her neck, arrange her artistically at the foot of the stairs and leave by the same way. According to information garnered for the enquiry, the hood of her robe had suspiciously not been 'disarranged': that is, was still over her head, which would be unlikely in an accidental fall down a staircase.

173

The tableau was perfect. If Amy's death was deemed a suicide, Robert would be blamed for neglecting his ill wife and breaking her heart through his flirtations with Elizabeth. If the verdict was accidental death, Robert could be accused or at least suspected of a cover-up. If it was determined a murder, any investigation would centre on those at Court who hated or disliked Robert or, more satisfactorily, on Robert himself. Even without a firm conviction, the process would be time-consuming and enormously embarrassing for Robert.

Could one of the European Royal Courts have been responsible for plotting the murder? In 1560, Robert had one main rival for the Queen's hand – Charles, Archduke of Austria. His foreign diplomats at the time believed that only Robert stood between a marriage between Charles and Elizabeth. Surely, if Robert were out of the running, Elizabeth would come to her senses and agree to marry him? The plot could have been hatched in Spain (which was part of the Holy Roman Empire ruled by Charles's brother, Ferdinand I), well away from Cecil and his burgeoning secret service. The messenger would have had to speak English, but if he were in the employ of the Spanish he could have been onboard ship and on his way to Spain the day after the crime, before word reached Robert and the Court that Amy was dead.

Any investigation would falter if the planners and the perpetrator were out of the country. All that was necessary for their plan to succeed was that Robert should fall under suspicion, regardless of the outcome of any enquiry. The contents and timing of the letter from de Quadra to Philip would fit perfectly into the framework of a plan arranging the murder of Amy while making it look like an accident. The letter was very efficient in fuelling rumours that Robert had murdered his wife, supported by apparent 'evidence' supplied by Elizabeth and Cecil.

❧

After the determination of the inquest, with Amy's reputation safe from the taint of suicide, Robert was free to arrange a grand funeral and burial for his 28-year-old wife. On 20 September, her body was brought to Oxford, where her coffin rested in Worcester College. She was buried two days later in St Mary's Church, Oxford. The funeral was suitably magnificent, with the church draped in black cloth, and fine apparel for Amy as well as the heralds attending the funeral procession. Money was no object, with '… the exchange of one hundred pounds of white money into gold, which was sent to Oxford for the charges of the burial'.[22]

Lady Margery Norris, a cousin of Alice, Anthony Forster's wife, was the chief mourner at Amy's funeral. She was accompanied by Sir Richard Blount, a close friend of Robert's. Robert himself did not attend, as was the practice at the time. Custom held that a lady should act as chief mourner at another lady's funeral, and the husband was not expected to be present. It is not safe to assume that guilt or remorse kept Robert away.

Exiled from the Court under a cloud of suspicion and rancour, Robert was grateful to his few supporters. Elizabeth's Ambassador to the French Court, Sir Nicholas Throckmorton, wrote a tender letter to his friend:

> I understand of the cruel mischance late happened to my lady your late bedfellow, to your discomfort ... I will no further condole with your Lordship thereby to renew your grief, but only say that as we be all mortal ... so is she gone before whither we must all follow to a place of more assurance and more quiet than can be found in this vale.[23]

175

Support also came from less likely sources. His previous rival William Cecil came to visit him. Although they had been in opposition, each striving to replace the other in the Queen's counsel, Cecil was now supportive of his colleague. Robert wrote to Cecil, 'I thank you much for your being here. And the great friendship you have showed towards me I shall not forget ... I pray you let me hear from you what you think best for me to do ... I beseech you sir, forget not to offer up the humble sacrifice you promised me.'[24] The 'humble sacrifice' is presumably a deferential petition to the Queen, requesting permission to return to Court.

For her part, Elizabeth seemed to show suitable respect for Amy's passing; a letter to Thomas Radclyffe, dated 6 October 1560 described Hampton Court as being 'stuffed with mourners (yea many of the better sort in degree) for the Lord Robert's wife'.[25]

Although many statesmen and diplomats believed Robert was innocent and that Amy's death had been a tragic accident, others didn't. Robert's foreboding of rumours and conspiracy theories turned out to be accurate. By October, a month after Amy's death, Sir Nicholas Throckmorton wrote to his English colleagues about the gossip openly circulating in France that she had been murdered.[26] In letters to Robert and Cecil, he gave his opinion of what would result if Robert married Elizabeth at that time, '… the Queen our Sovereign discredited, condemned and neglected; our country ruined, undone and made prey.'[27] The scandal was threatening to engulf political relations with European powers.

Throckmorton sent his secretary, Robert Jones, back to report to the English Court. In November, Jones arrived at Greenwich and reported to Cecil that Mary, Queen of Scots had said, 'The Queen of England is going to marry the Master of her Horses, who has killed his wife to make room for her.'[28] On 27 November, Jones told Elizabeth the same thing and reported that her reputation was being tarnished by the whole affair.

Elizabeth laughed, replying that the verdict had cleared Robert, who had been at Court when the death occurred and that none of his people had been at Cumnor. In Jones's report of the conversation, he described the Queen as looking tired and ill, 'surely the matter of my Lord Robert doth perplex her.'[29] In December, Throckmorton wrote that the rumours were still persisting. Cecil wrote back, 'I know surely that my Lord Robert himself hath more fear than hope, and so doth the Queen give him cause.'[30] Cecil hoped that since Elizabeth was not obviously about to marry Robert, the rumours would eventually die out from lack of substance.

In fact, despite the passage of time, the rumours implicating Robert in Amy's death would endure long after events. In 1567, seven years after Amy's death, John Appleyard, her half-brother, fell out with Robert. Although he had received several posts through Robert's influence, including Sheriff of Norfolk and Suffolk (in 1559, before Amy died), he claimed he had received only 'fair promises' and had not been rewarded by his brother-in-law as well as he imagined he should be.

He claimed that Robert's followers had blackened his name for the offence of suggesting that his sister's case be reopened, as he believed she had been murdered. He even asserted that 'he had for the Earl's sake covered the murder of his sister'. He would be imprisoned for his accusations, charged with being part of a plot to discredit Robert fabricated by Thomas Howard and Thomas Radclyffe, among others. On Appleyard's release he submitted to the Court that he accepted that Amy's death had, indeed, been an accident.[31]

Many years later, in a vitriolic attack on Robert Dudley called *Leicester's Commonwealth*, published in 1584, the author recorded what purported to be an account of Robert's life, but was, in fact, more of a character assassination. The text claimed that 'this was my Lord's good fortune to have his wife die at that time when it was like to turn most to his profit'.[32]

This false version of events became accepted as common knowledge and repeated in future publications, sometimes with additional scurrilous anecdotes. For example, in the *Flores Calvinistici*, published in the Netherlands in 1586, the author added the invention that Amy was 'destroyed by a small nail thrust gradually into her head'. Future historians sometimes included quotations from *Leicester's Commonwealth*, usually on the principle that there was no smoke without fire, despite the lack of proof for the purported facts.

Certainly just after Amy's death, at the end of 1560, Elizabeth had reason to be concerned. She was well aware of public opinion

177

at home and abroad. A full year before, in December 1559, Baron von Breuner, in his last report to Ferdinand I about Elizabeth's marriage plans, had resignedly written that she would marry where she liked, 'But herein she errs, for if she marry the said my Lord Robert, she will incur so much enmity that she may one evening lay herself down as Queen of England and rise the next morning as plain Mistress Elizabeth.'[33]

The conflict she must have felt between her desire to demonstrate her affection for Robert as well as her belief in his innocence and her understanding of the need to appease public opinion led to some contradictory behaviour.

In November 1560, two months after Amy's death, she had papers drawn up that would finally give Robert a title: 1st Earl of Leicester. However, Elizabeth decided she could not grant him this reward at such a time. When she was due to sign them, she cut the papers up with a knife, saying in explanation that the Dudleys had been traitors for three generations.

Robert was furious, but Elizabeth reportedly patted him on the cheek, telling him, 'No, no! The bear and ragged staff [Robert Dudley's coat of arms] are not so easily overthrown.'[34] However, Elizabeth also passed him over for another promotion in December, when Sir John Parry, Master of the Wards, died. Robert had hopes of being awarded this extremely lucrative appointment. Elizabeth gave it to Cecil instead.

❧

Wider events were also having an impact on Elizabeth's political decisions and marriage prospects. The King of France, François II, died in December 1560, leaving the 18-year-old Mary, Queen of Scots a widow and no longer Queen of France. She was now Elizabeth's rival for marriage proposals from European royalty, and would soon return to rule Scotland. At the time, Scotland was torn between Catholic and Protestant factions, and the latter feared the Catholic Mary's reign.

In December, a marriage was again proposed, this time formally, between Elizabeth and the Protestant James Hamilton, 3rd Earl of Arran, who was next in line for the Scottish crown after Mary. The Queen, ever diplomatic, praised Hamilton, but said she 'was not disposed to marry'.[35] This decision is in seeming contradiction to the fact that Elizabeth supported the Protestant rebels in Scotland and was wary of Mary, Queen of Scots, who had a claim to the English throne (they were cousins, descended from Henry VII). If Elizabeth should die childless, Mary was next in line to be Queen of England.

William Cecil hoped that Elizabeth would see reason and accept a husband, responding, 'Well, God sent our mistress a husband and by time a son, that we may hope our posterity shall have a masculine succession. The matter is too big for weak folk and too deep for simple. The Queen's Majesty knoweth of it, and so I will end.[36]

In early 1561, the former Crown Prince and now King of Sweden, Eric XIV (King of Sweden 1560–68), also renewed his offer of marriage. The Swedish Court asked the English royal jeweller Dymock to come to Sweden with 'jewels and patterns of jewels drawn on parchment' and, to feel out the territory, took the opportunity to ask Dymock about the rumours that Elizabeth planned to marry Robert. Dymock reassured them, saying he had met with Kat Ashley, who he said had related to him that the Queen had said she would rather not marry, and certainly not Robert.

He continued, claiming that despite Robert giving the Queen an extravagant gift in the expectation of a title (probably a dukedom, to make him a more fitting consort for the Queen) and

179

a large sum of money, he had in fact received no title and a small gift of land. Dymock told the Swedes that some of the Lords would surely support Eric's suit and that he should push forward. He even claimed that Robert would also be in favour of a marriage between Eric and Elizabeth, especially if Robert were given the hand of Eric's sister, Princess Cecilia, with a suitably large dowry.[37] Eric appears to have taken much of this at face value since he continued his unwelcome wooing. He would also make an unsuccessful marriage proposal to Mary, Queen of Scots.

In reality, Robert had no intention of reducing his pressure on Elizabeth to marry him, despite the evolving political outlook and his own changed fortunes. By January 1561, he had come up with a new scheme to persuade Elizabeth to overcome her fears and make him her husband. Ambassador de Quadra wrote to Philip II that Sir Henry Sidney, Robert's brother-in-law, had approached him to tell him that the Queen was wishful to marry Robert, and suggested that if Philip supported the idea, Robert would become 'like one of your own vassals'.[38]

As an extra bargaining point, Sidney remarked that Elizabeth was tired of the ranting of the extreme Protestant preachers, and that this might be a time to negotiate with her over how the state religion could develop in future. De Quadra, looking ahead, finished:

> I have no doubt that if there is any way to cure the bad spirit of the Queen, both as regards religion and your Majesty's interests, it is by means of this marriage, at least while her desire for it lasts … The general opinion, confirmed by certain physicians, is that this woman is unhealthy, and it is believed she will not have children, although there is no lack of people who say she has already had some, but of this I have seen no trace and do not believe it. This being so,

perhaps some step may be taken in your Majesty's interests towards declaring, as the Queen's successor after her death, whoever may be most desirable to your Majesty.[39]

In February, Robert spoke directly to de Quadra, confirming what Sidney had said. De Quadra agreed to speak to the Queen, who told him she was indeed fond of Robert and that her subjects preferred that she marry an Englishman, although she had not definitely made her mind up to marry Robert – or anyone. Provocatively, she added in confidence that she would like to make de Quadra her confessor, as she had a secret she would like to tell him.

What she wished to divulge will rest forever unknown as de Quadra and Philip did not trust Elizabeth, who they felt prevaricated for her own political purposes. Philip told de Quadra: '... her words are so little to be depended upon ... she has no intention of fulfilling what she says and only wishes to use your authority for her own designs and intentions.'[40]

Could the secret have been that she was already married to Robert or perhaps even pregnant? The idea was not a stranger to public gossip: in the same month, on 27 February 1561, Thomas Burley was on trial on charges of slandering Elizabeth by saying, 'Lord Robert did swive [have penetrative sex with] the Queen.'[41]

Several months later, on 30 June 1561, Robert organized a banquet for the Queen, followed by a river party. Elizabeth, Robert and de Quadra were together on a barge, watching the other boats loaded with her courtiers. The mood was joyful, with singing and music, laughing and joking. Robert suggested that since de Quadra was a bishop, he should marry Robert and Elizabeth there and then. As de Quadra reported, 'They went so far with their jokes that Lord Robert told her that, if she liked, I could be the minister to perform the act of marriage and she, nothing loath to hear it,

181

said she was not sure whether I knew enough English.'[42] De Quadra tried to join in with the spirit of the moment and replied that if she got rid of her Protestant advisers and restored Catholicism, he would be delighted to marry them whenever they liked.

However, the laughter seems to have faded by July, when Elizabeth went on a progress to Essex and Suffolk. She was said to be irritable and to look pale, 'like one lately come out of childbed'.[43] Apart from how she might have been feeling physically, she would have been aware that Mary, Queen of Scots would be imminently arriving in Scotland, and, as a young widow, she was an attractive marriage prospect. Elizabeth would have to play her cards carefully. She knew that foreign kings might reason that by wedding Mary they could rule Scotland, and could then conquer England in her name. In the face of competition from her cousin to the north, Elizabeth needed to exert all her charm and diplomatic skill to maintain European interest in her as a possible choice for marriage.

The summer of 1561 was also disastrous for one of Elizabeth's possible heirs, Lady Catherine Grey, the younger sister of Lady Jane Grey. As the granddaughter of Henry VIII's sister Mary Tudor, she had a potentially legitimate claim to the throne. She had already suffered a fall from grace when her sister Jane was overthrown, resulting in Catherine being cast out and her first marriage annulled. Mary I had made Catherine and another sister, Mary, Ladies of the Privy Chamber, but Elizabeth, who did not much like the sisters, had demoted them to the lesser rank of Ladies of the Presence Chamber. Catherine was angered, as she saw herself as Elizabeth's legal heir and thought her rank should be higher.

In 1561, the relations between Elizabeth and Catherine worsened dramatically. At the end of 1560, Catherine had clandestinely married the son of Edward Seymour, 1st Duke of Somerset (Edward VI's former Protector who had been executed for treason, and who had been partly responsible for the execution of his brother Thomas Seymour). Catherine married Edward Seymour, 1st Earl of Hertford, without asking the Queen's permission, which was a penal offence. By the summer of 1561, she found herself pregnant. To make matters worse, she had lost the deed of jointure (a document detailing the financial arrangements of husband and wife), so she had no official proof of the secret marriage, which would make the child illegitimate.

Desperate, Catherine sought the help of Robert, who was her brother-in-law. As she was on the summer progress with the Royal Court, she crept into his bedroom one night, the only time she could find him alone, woke him and told him all, begging him to intercede with Elizabeth for her. The next morning, Robert told the Queen, who was furious. Not only had Catherine married without notifying her, she had no official evidence of the marriage, and Elizabeth did not approve of her choice of husband. She was also with child, something that was potentially dangerous to Elizabeth as it could make Catherine the focus of a rebellion to oust Elizabeth, who had no heir, from power. Elizabeth sent her to the Tower, where Edward Seymour would later join her.

Robert continued to try to gain leverage in his pursuit of the Queen, but Elizabeth seemed to have hardened in her attitude towards marrying him, at least publicly. The scandal over his wife's death may have cast a long shadow. Robert Kyle, an Englishman acting for Eric XIV of Sweden, wrote to the Swedish King on 27 July that Robert had threatened to have him imprisoned for putting the King's marriage proposal before the Queen. Kyle's letter reported that Elizabeth proceeded to humiliate Robert in front of her nobles, maintaining that 'Lord Robert had plain answer from the Queen's mouth in the Chamber of Presence, all the nobility being there, that she would never marry him, nor none so mean as he, with a great rage and great checks and taunts to such as travailed for him, seeing they went about to dishonour her.'[44] Robert, his pride wounded, asked permission to go abroad, which was granted. He left the Court in high dudgeon, presumably hoping that Elizabeth would soon beg him to return.

⤴

In France, there was renewed interest in Elizabeth's marital status. Stricken by religious conflicts, France had agreed to withdraw its troops from Scotland in the Treaty of Edinburgh that Cecil had negotiated. Scotland itself was torn between Catholic and Protestant factions. All the Royal Courts angled to try to gain the best possible position, and one arm of French foreign policy was alliance through marriage.

In August 1561, Mary, Queen of Scots arrived back in Scotland, escorted by three of her uncles, including François de Lorraine, Chevalier de Guise, the Admiral and Commander-in-Chief of the French Navy. He was an exciting and extremely handsome gentleman. The three noblemen decided to pay a visit to the English Court before returning to France. Reportedly, Elizabeth enjoyed a most pleasant flirtation with François.

Later in the year, a former French suitor reappeared, Jacques de Savoy, Duc de Nemours; he wanted to send his brother, the Cardinal of Ferrara, to England to ask for Elizabeth's hand. His suit foundered when it became clear that the Cardinal's main aim was to use the question of marriage as a means to discuss England returning to the Catholic fold. Elizabeth refused him entry to England on the basis that she would happily accept his visit as a royal messenger, but 'not as the Bishop of Rome's minister'.[45]

By autumn 1561, Robert's plans to win Elizabeth's hand were in disarray. It was clear he could not rely wholly on Spanish support to persuade Elizabeth to marry him. He contacted the Huguenot Henri de Navarre, the cousin of 10-year-old Charles IX (King of France 1560–74), and offered English support for the Huguenots in the French Wars of Religion in turn for Henri's support for Robert's marriage to Elizabeth. Henri refused to commit himself.

Throckmorton, the English Ambassador in Paris, was furious that Robert had acted independently and in a manner against official policy, but Robert did not care; his hopes were renewed as Elizabeth was granting him gifts that showed he was still in her favour. In February 1562, he was made Constable of Windsor Castle, and later, Constable and Steward of Warwick Castle. He was also finally allowed to inherit the estates of his deceased uncle.

Then, in June 1562, more rumours began to surface, this time about Elizabeth's marriage to Robert. William Cecil had managed to turn one of de Quadra's servants, Borghese Venturini, into a spy. Venturini made a report to him about the dispatches de Quadra had sent to Philip, which alleged '... that the Queen was married to Lord Robert before only two or three witnesses ...' and that Venturini had heard de Quadra say '... that the Queen was secretly married to Lord Robert, of which he had informed the King of Spain.'[46]

According to Venturini, another of de Quadra's dispatches reported that the Queen herself had told the Ambassador that, on coming back from William Herbert, Lord Pembroke's house one afternoon, her ladies had asked if they should kiss Robert's hand after they kissed hers, if he was now her consort? 'She told them, no, and they must not believe everything they heard.'[47]

Presented with this information by Cecil and accused of acting inappropriately, de Quadra was quite annoyed, not least because he'd been striving for years to convince Elizabeth to marry. He told the Council, 'I do not think, considering what others say of the Queen, that I should be doing her any injury in writing to his

Majesty [Philip II] that she was married, which in fact I never have written, and I am sorry I cannot do so with truth.'[48]

This gossip, though vehemently denied, revealed the Spanish involvement in Robert's plans and put paid to his ability to use Spanish influence to gain the Queen's hand. As Elizabeth reduced her contact with de Quadra to almost none, Robert now made his support of the French Huguenots public, offering them his backing, doubtless expecting their support for his marriage with Elizabeth in return. His brother-in-law, Sir Henry Sidney, joined Sir Nicholas Throckmorton in Paris to try to broker a peace between the Catholic and Protestant factions and may have also lobbied the French Protestant faction on Robert's behalf.

Robert also used English politics to help gain support for marrying Elizabeth. In the summer of 1562, Mary, Queen of Scots requested a royal meeting in York in order to try to persuade Elizabeth to name her as the formal, legal heir to the English throne. As Mary had refused to ratify the Treaty of Edinburgh (which acknowledged Elizabeth as lawful Queen of England) on her return from France, the Council voted against Elizabeth going to such a meeting. Robert, however, was firmly in favour. He reasoned that if Elizabeth named the Catholic Mary as heiress, then the Protestant Lords would be forced to support him as the Queen's husband in their urgency to get her married and to create a Tudor heir in the line of succession.

However, concerns about the broader political context won out. At the time, in France, the Catholic House of Guise (Mary's relatives) were attacking the Protestant Huguenots. The Council felt that if François, Duc de Guise was successful in defeating the Huguenots, he might try to attack England on Mary's behalf. Elizabeth and her Council decided that England should give limited support to the Huguenots and that a meeting with Mary was impossible. The question of Elizabeth's heir would have to wait. Or had it already been dealt with? Did Elizabeth already have a child, albeit an illegitimate one? Were Robert's efforts to gain Elizabeth's hand a way of making a secret liaison an official one? The rumours persisted. In June 1562, testimony was given in a Wiltshire court recounting the following conversation: 'It is said my Lord Robert is fled out of the realm ... It is told me he hath the Queen with child, and therefore he is fled.'[49]

Whatever the truth of the gossip, the only type of heir that counted was a lawful one, and the fears of the English Council on the urgency of this need were soon to be aggravated.

❧

In 10 October 1562, Elizabeth became ill at Hampton Court after taking a relaxing bath and a long walk. For a week she lay in bed, getting weaker and less responsive. As she did not appear to be recovering, her cousin, Henry Carey, 1st Baron Hunsdon, arranged for Dr Burcot, a German physician, to visit her. In spite of the lack of any spots or rash, he immediately diagnosed smallpox, a very serious illness that often resulted in death. When he told Elizabeth the news, she furiously ordered him to leave.

With the Queen seriously ill and little idea of how to treat her, a panic ensued as to who should succeed her if she should die. An heir had to be acknowledged and ready to assume the throne. The Council was split on who should be nominated: the candidates included Catherine Grey (the granddaughter of Mary Tudor); the Catholic Margaret Douglas, Countess of Lennox (the daughter of Margaret Tudor); and Henry Hastings, 3rd Earl of Huntingdon, known as the Puritan Earl (he was descended from the brother of Edward IV and Richard III). No one recommended Mary, Queen of Scots – the Catholic votes went to Lady Margaret Douglas, who was the mother of two healthy sons.

However, Elizabeth still refused to name a successor. When the Council came to the gravely ill Queen's bedchamber, she asked them to name Robert the Protector of the Realm, to make him a noble and to pay him £20,000 a year. According to a Spanish account of the scene, she said that 'although she loved and had always loved Lord Robert dearly, as God was her witness, nothing improper had ever passed between them.'[50]

She further asked that Robert's body-servant, Tamworth, who slept in his bedchamber, should be given £500 a year for life. She commended her cousin, Henry Carey, 1st Baron Hunsdon, to the Council, and also praised her household members. She became so agitated and delirious that the Councillors agreed to all her demands in order to calm her.

Elizabeth's statement about Robert that 'nothing improper had ever passed between them' has long intrigued historians. She appears to be saying that they had never had a sexual relationship. On the other hand, she could also have made this statement with a clear conscience if they had gone through a form of pre-marriage, the *de futuro*, in which the couple say 'I will', rather than 'I do', or a *de praesenti* marriage, in which vows are exchanged in front of witnesses. These were both religiously and legally acceptable marriages, which would have permitted the couple to have officially sanctioned sexual relations.

If such a marriage did take place, it probably would have been in the summer of 1560, in the months before Amy Robsart died. With his wife dying from a terminal illness, Robert and Elizabeth may have gone through the marriage ceremony in front of a few chosen witnesses, which would have made their relationship legitimate in the eyes of the Church. They would have imagined that a second, formal, public ceremony would take place after Amy's death, but any consequences of their actions, such as a pregnancy, would make the child legitimate since it had been lawfully conceived.

Henry VIII had behaved in a similar manner with Elizabeth's own mother, Anne Boleyn. In anticipation of divorcing Catherine of Aragon, he had married Anne in January 1533, several months before his divorce became final in April, and in May Henry and Anne were publicly proclaimed to be legally married. This had been in part to protect any child conceived: Elizabeth was born in September. If Robert and Elizabeth also chose a secret ceremony, any sexual activity would be lawful and natural, which would enable Elizabeth to make what she feared was her deathbed vow in all honesty.

Another possibility is that Elizabeth and Robert were having a sexual relationship that did not include vaginal penetration, although this would obviously preclude the possibility of a secret pregnancy or child. This would allow Elizabeth to state publicly that she was a virgin, which would have been technically true. In Tudor England, although anal sex was illegal, it was sometimes used as a form of birth control.

It is notable that most of Elizabeth's statements on her sexual status tended to be worded in such a way that they referred to her as Queen, neatly sidestepping anything that happened prior to 1558, including her relationship with Thomas Seymour.

Elizabeth's sickbed wishes never had to be carried out. She began to get better after Dr Burcot was persuaded to return, grumbling and complaining at her rudeness. He wrapped the patient in red cloth, laid her on a mattress before the fire and gave her a potion to drink. She began to cry when spots appeared on her hands, but the doctor asked her brusquely if it were better to have spots or to die. The treatment worked, and within a month Elizabeth recovered, her face unmarked by smallpox scars.

189

However, Lady Mary Sidney, Robert's sister, who had nursed her throughout her illness, fell ill and was badly pockmarked; she left Court and never returned. Elizabeth never forgot her courage and nobility, and remained her friend for the rest of her life.

By 20 October 1562, Elizabeth was able to resume her duties. She named two new members to her Council, Thomas Howard, 4th Duke of Norfolk – and Sir Robert Dudley. On November 26, she approached Robert in Windsor Park, where he was having a shooting match. Elizabeth, who had come to watch with several of her ladies, was dressed as a maid, with her hair loose and wearing informal robes. She told Robert that he was in her debt as she had 'passed the pikes' for his sake.[51] The phrase literally meant that she had passed through some deadly danger, which could have referred to her bout with smallpox. But why 'for his sake'? Could it have referred to her going through the trauma of childbirth?

Following the Queen's brush with death, Parliament was frantic about the question of the succession. They presented her with a petition, begging her to marry or to name a successor. She obfuscated, stating that even if she did not desire marriage as 'a private woman', as a Queen she realized she had certain duties and would not rule it out.[52] Given this, she would not be pressed to name a successor, as she might yet produce an heir by birth.

Her Councillors wouldn't give in. January 1563 started with yet another broadside to persuade Elizabeth of the vital importance of marrying and having a child. When she attended services at Westminster Abbey, the Dean of St Pauls preached about Elizabeth's lack of an heir and her duty to get one: 'For as the marriage of Queen Mary [to Philip of Spain] was a terrible plague to all England, the want of your marriage and issue is like to prove as great a plague … If your parents had been of your mind, where had you been then? Or what had become of us now?'[53]

The Queen was furious that once again she was being lectured on a matter that she considered her personal and private concern. It did not bode well for the next sitting of Parliament, at which the issue would come up again.[54]

Cecil realized the futility of acting in this manner, but the government continued its campaign. In April 1563, the Lord Keeper of the Great Seal, Sir Nicholas Bacon, made a submission to the Queen on behalf of Parliament, begging her to marry and beget an heir; this time he emphasized the joy of motherhood: 'If your Highness could conceive to imagine the comfort, surety and delight that should happen to yourself by beholding an imp of your own ... it would, I am assured, sufficiently satisfy to remove all manner of lets, impediments and scruples.'[55]

Bacon might have done better if he had studied Elizabeth's previous remarks on the subject of children. From her own experience, families were not necessarily a source of 'comfort and delight'. She knew that princes, and especially princesses, could have their rank stripped away and find their status in doubt. As she had told a Scottish diplomat in 1561, '... some [say] that this marriage was unlawful, some that one was a bastard, some other, to and fro, as they favoured or misliked. So many doubts of marriage was in all hands that I stand aw[e] myself to enter into marriage fearing the controversy.'[56]

She knew, too, that a ruler had cause to fear their heir and also knew that a blood tie was no guarantee of love and fidelity: 'Princes cannot like their children, those that should succeed unto them.'[57] Furthermore, there was no guarantee that an heir would follow her policies, as she had stated in 1559 in an address to Parliament: 'although I be never so careful of your well doings, and mind ever so to be, yet may my issue grow out of kind, and become perhaps ungracious.'[58] Not to mention that if, indeed, she had borne a child

191

by Thomas Seymour or Robert Dudley, she already knew the pains and terrors of childbirth.

To strengthen her argument, Elizabeth raised the fear of civil war, telling her Council that although she might be old, '… God would send her children as he did to St Elizabeth, and they had better consider well what they were asking, as, if she declared a successor, it would cost much blood to England.'[59] It was not impossible to foresee a situation arising in which the country could be torn apart by different factions supporting the Queen, her successor, or other candidates to the throne.

If she named either Catherine or Mary Grey as heir, there would be disgruntled Protestants who supported Henry Hastings, never mind the reaction of Catholics. If she named Mary, Queen of Scots, there would be Catholics who supported Lady Margaret Douglas, as well as an extreme Protestant backlash that could well risk her reign. The wisest move was the one she chose: to offer possibilities, but no certainties. She summed up her position, 'So long as I live, I shall be Queen of England. When I am dead, they shall succeed that have the most right.'[60]

Catherine Grey was taken out of the running. She had been sent to the Tower with her son and unrecognized husband, Edward Seymour, but he had bribed their warders to enable them to visit each other in secret; when Catherine fell pregnant and gave birth to a second son in February 1563, the heirless Queen was furious. A second commission was set up and a formal declaration made that the marriage between Catherine and Edward had never taken place, making their two sons bastards and resulting in Edward having to pay a fine of 15,000 marks for having seduced a virgin of royal blood and having 'ravished her a second time'.[61]

The couple were separated, with Catherine sent to her uncle, and Edward Seymour remaining in the Tower. This did not seem to dissuade those who supported Catherine and her sons as heirs for the throne. Later in the year, a Member of Parliament named John Hales published a pamphlet with the support of Catherine, her uncle Sir John, Edward Seymour and his mother Anne Seymour, the Dowager Duchess of Somerset, which made an argument for Catherine Grey as heiress. It claimed that her marriage was legitimate, making her sons lawfully born male heirs, direct descendants of Henry VII, pure English and Protestant.

Viewing this development as a conspiracy, Elizabeth reacted harshly. Hales was incarcerated in the Fleet prison for six months, and Catherine was removed from her uncle's care and spent the rest of her life in captivity (she would die in 1568, at the age of 27), moving from house to house. She never saw her husband again.

Cecil, who had been a favourer of Lady Catherine's title to the Crown although he refused to be enlisted in any campaign in her support, recognized the prudence of lying low and not offending the Queen. He did, however, hope that the matter would force Elizabeth's hand in finally choosing a husband: 'God give her Majesty by this chance a disposition to consider hereof, that either by her marriage or by some common order, we poor subjects may know where to lean and adventure our lives with contention of our consciences.'[62]

Cecil's attitude towards Robert had changed and they had achieved a relationship bordering on friendship. Both seemed to find each other a more valuable ally than enemy. Cecil wrote to Sir Thomas Smith, the Queen's Ambassador in Paris, 'I must confess myself to be much beholden to his Lordship [Robert] and for my part I do endeavour myself in good earnestness to merit well of him.'[63] But Cecil's support did not have the result Robert wished for, and he found himself part of an extraordinary plan hatched up by Elizabeth in the spring of 1563.

∾

In March, the Scottish Secretary of State, William Maitland of Lethington, came to London to sound Elizabeth out on who Mary, Queen of Scots' next husband should be, as well as to try to persuade the Queen to formally recognize Mary as her heir. As it turned out, Elizabeth had an idea on both these topics. To everyone's amazement, Elizabeth's suggestion of a husband for Mary was Lord Robert Dudley!

He was, she said, a model of everything that was manly, noble and fine. Ambassador de Quadra, writing to Philip, reported that Maitland had told him that Elizabeth had said it was a pity Ambrose Dudley did not have his brother's physical perfection, courtly manners and intellectual capacity so they could each marry one of the brothers. Maitland, presumably not sure if Elizabeth was joking or not, responded that, as Robert was so much to her taste, the Scottish Queen could not deprive Elizabeth of such a jewel; she should marry Robert herself so that '... when it should please God to call her to himself, she could leave the Queen of Scots heiress both to her kingdom and her husband.'[64]

Thomas Randolph, the English Ambassador to Scotland, had the unenviable task of trying to persuade Mary that this union was a good idea. He passed on Elizabeth's own thoughts that '... being determined to end her life in virginity, she wished that the queen her sister should marry him.'[65]

Mary, who had made derogatory remarks about Elizabeth and her 'Horse-Master' before, was now faced with the lure of being recognized as heir to the English throne if Robert were her consort, and did a quick U-turn, at least officially. She denied she had ever spoken rudely about Elizabeth or Robert and thought the idea had considerable merit. However, having persuaded Mary to consider the match, Randolph now found that Robert would not agree. Randolph reported back, 'Now that I have got this Queen's goodwill to marry where I would have her, I cannot get the man to take her for whom I was a suitor.'[66]

Robert was in a difficult position – he still had hopes of marrying Elizabeth, and knew that if he showed the slightest desire to wed Mary, Elizabeth would turn on him for betraying her, yet if he publicly refused outright to consider the match, she would label him as disloyal to the Crown.

There were also foreign policy reasons to maintain the offer for as long as possible. While Mary was considering marrying Robert, she would not accept the courtship of anyone else. Mary had let it be known that she was interested in Carlos, Prince of Asturias, the only son of Philip II. Although the young man was known to be mentally ill to the point of violence, he might become the future King of Spain, so Mary was prepared to overlook this. Philip, hoping that his recent marriage to the French Élisabeth de Valois would provide him with another son, was less enthusiastic about such a match.

Mary also considered marrying her brother-in-law, Charles IX of France, but his mother, Catherine de Medici, Regent for the King, stopped this in its tracks. She disliked Mary and had no intention of handing overall control of the country back to the House of Guise (Mary's relatives), who would have removed Catherine de Medici from power.

Another young gentleman Mary was considering as a consort was the 18-year-old Henry Stuart, Lord Darnley, a descendant of James II (King of Scotland 1437–60). Darnley had a valid claim to the succession to the Scottish throne as his mother was the half-sister of James V of Scotland and his father was James's second cousin. He was made more attractive by the fact that he also had a claim to the English throne through his mother, who was the daughter of Henry VIII's elder sister, Margaret Tudor. A match between Darnley and Mary, Queen of Scots would provide the strongest claim both to the throne of Scotland and that of England.

It was therefore in Elizabeth's interests to prevent Mary from making any formal marriage alliance with Prince Carlos, Henry Stuart or anyone else. Whether in earnest, as a diplomatic ploy, or as a blind for her own relationship with Robert, she maintained her support for Mary marrying her favourite suitor.

At the same time, she showered gifts on Robert, including land and important posts. His brother, Ambrose, was given the Order of the Garter for his valiant, if unsuccessful, service in France. Robert himself was made High Steward of Cambridge and High Steward of Windsor. He was awarded lands in Lancashire, Yorkshire, Rutland, Surrey, Carmarthen, Cardigan and Brecknock, as well as the finest and best of all estates, the magnificent Kenilworth Castle in Warwickshire. A year later, in 1564, Elizabeth would finally give him the earldom that would raise his rank to one more suitable for marrying a Queen, investing him with the titles of Earl of Leicester and Baron Denbigh. Whether or not the scandal over Amy Robsart's death had prevented Elizabeth from marrying Robert, it seemed that now that several years had passed, she felt she could renew her political patronage. In the years to come, Robert would remain deeply involved in Elizabeth's political and private life.

For all the political intrigue and Elizabeth's evasiveness over marrying, in the five years that she had been Queen, England had begun to recover her strength and status. It was a far different country to the one she had inherited. Elizabeth had achieved the admiration of her people in what was seen as her unflinching loyalty to the English nation.

8

Politics or Love?
1564–82

B y 1564, against all odds, Elizabeth had reached the age of 31 without yet committing to marriage. However, for England the intricate balance of power in Europe was raising some concerns. Philip II of Spain was now married to Elisabeth de Valois, the sister of Charles IX, the King of France, who was also a close friend of Mary, Queen of Scots (a member of the French Catholic House of Guise). For her part, the widowed Queen of Scots was herself a problem; Mary was considering Carlos, Philip's son, as a possible husband; his cousin, Charles, Archduke of Austria, was another contender for her hand. With a Catholic alliance of England's most powerful neighbours a grave reality, Elizabeth's ministers were worried. However, Charles IX's mother, Catherine de Medici, fearing that such alliances might lead the Guises to hold too much power in France, suggested that her 15-year-old son might marry Elizabeth instead.

Elizabeth, in public at least, seemed delighted with the idea; in private, she revealed otherwise. As King of the great nation of France, Charles IX would be unable to spend more than a fraction of the year with her in England. Moreover, he was far too young for her, less than half her age. Elizabeth was even heard to refer to herself as 'old'.

De La Mothe Fénelon, the French Ambassador, tried to flatter Elizabeth into submission: '… all the world stood amazed at the wrong she did to the grand endowments that God had given her of beauty, wisdom, virtue and exalted station, by refusing to leave fair posterity to succeed her ... If such a marriage could happen, then would commence the most illustrious lineage that had been known for the last thousand years.'[1]

When Sir Thomas Smith, the English Ambassador to France, met with Charles IX and his mother, he raised the issue of the disparity in their ages. The King told him that he found no fault with Elizabeth and wished her 'as well content with me as I am with her age.'[2] Charles IX wished negotiations to proceed at once, but Sir Thomas tried to slow things down.

'If the King had three or four years more, and had seen the Queen's Majesty, and were fallen in love with her, then I would not marvel at this haste.'

'Why, I do love her indeed,' the youthful King replied, and when the Ambassador suggested, perhaps unkindly, that in his foolish youth Charles had yet to discover what love was, Catherine de Medici stated, 'This is no foolish love.'[3]

Back in London, Elizabeth reiterated that people would find the difference in their ages incongruous. In any case, she stated, her people had made it clear that they would prefer her to marry an Englishman, although who this might be Elizabeth kept to herself. In reference to Robert, she said, '... as to the Earl of Leicester, I have always loved his virtues. But the aspirations towards honour and greatness which are in me, cannot suffer him as a companion and a husband.'

De Fois, the French envoy, replied that his King would be happy if she married an Englishman, but would consider it an insult if she were to marry another European prince. Elizabeth agreed that she might be considering an English husband, but restated, 'I will never concede to a husband any share in my power.'[4]

While Elizabeth was reassuring de Fois that she was looking for an English husband, plans were afoot to find a suitable foreign prince to be her consort. The death of Emperor Ferdinand I in July 1564 had meant that an alliance of the Holy Roman Empire with England against France and Scotland now seemed an attractive political option, and the possible idea of a marital union between Elizabeth and Charles, Archduke of Austria, was resurrected.

Elizabeth knew that this was also a useful ploy to prevent a marriage between Charles and Mary, Queen of Scots. Cecil enclosed a letter to Sir Thomas Smith along with Elizabeth's message of formal condolence to the new Emperor Maximilian II (Holy Roman Emperor 1564–76) on the death of his father, stating that Elizabeth's message might be an expression of her intention to marry the Archduke.[5]

Dr Christopher Mundt, Cecil's intermediary at the Imperial Court, wrote in August 1564, that the matter was 'most vital to the whole Christian world', and that despite the Queen's virtuous modesty in not wanting to be seen seeking a husband, it was important to ensure a perpetual succession'. Cecil replied in September:

> With regard to her Majesty's inclinations on the subject of her marriage, he [Cecil] can with certainty say nothing; than that he perceives that she would rather marry a foreign than a native prince, and that the more distinguished the suitor is by birth, power, and personal attractions, the better hope he will have of success. Moreover, he cannot deny that the nobleman who, with them, excites considerable expectation, to wit Lord Robert, is worthy to become the husband of the Queen. The fact of his being her Majesty's subject, however, will prove a serious objection to him in her estimation. Nevertheless, his virtues and his excellent and

heroic gifts of mind and body have so endeared him to the
Queen, that she could not regard her own brother with
greater affection. From which they who do not know the
Queen intimately, conjecture that he will be her future
husband. He, however, sees and understands that she merely
takes delight in his virtues and rare qualities, and that
nothing is more discussed in their conversation than that
which is most consistent with virtues, and furthest removed
from all unworthy sentiments.[6]

Despite such reassurances, Maximilian II, Archduke Charles's
brother, warned his Ambassador not to 'suffer himself to be led by
the nose'.[7] The discussions continued.

Knowing the Queen's liking for handsome, well-made men,
Cecil wrote to ask Mundt, was it true that Archduke Charles had
a bent neck? Mundt answered in all honesty that it was. But,
'Alexander the Great had his neck bent towards the left side; would
that our man may be his imitator in magnanimity and bravery. His
body is elegant and middle size, more well grown and robust than
the Spanish Prince.' This was damning the marriage candidate
with faint praise – Prince Carlos of Spain had one shoulder higher
than the other and legs of uneven length. As a boy he was short and
thin, and as an adult he could not be described as robust or healthy.

Robert was involved in intrigues of his own, plotting to prevent
Elizabeth's marriage to Archduke Charles. He could not bear for
her to choose someone else as her husband. He still retained his
unique position of influence with the Queen, but there were
obvious strains in their relationship.

In August, they argued when one of Robert's followers was not
allowed access to the Queen's rooms. Robert had shouted at the
man who had turned away his colleague, threatening that he would

lose his job. Elizabeth angrily put Robert firmly in his place: 'God's death, my Lord! I have wished you well, but my favour is not so locked up for you that others shall not participate thereof ... I will have here but one mistress and no master.'[8]

To further underline her independence, Elizabeth started flirting with Sir Thomas Heneage, Treasurer of the Privy Chamber. Robert reacted jealously, to which Elizabeth responded in verse that this wasn't a very attractive trait:

> *No crooked leg, no bleared eye,*
> *No part deformèd out of kind,*
> *Nor yet so ugly half can be*
> *As is the inward, suspicious mind.*[9]

Heneage was seen by some as a natural competitor to Robert for the Queen's favour. Cecil had remarked on an apparent change in affection in a letter to Sir Thomas Smith in October, 'There are sundry rumours ... that my Lord of Leicester should not have so great favour as he had; ... that Mr Heneage should be in very good favour with her Majesty and so misliked by my Lord of Leicester.'[10]

Heneage was the same age as the Queen and a graduate of Queen's College, Cambridge. He had been Steward at Hatfield before becoming a Gentleman of the Privy Chamber. He was married to Anne Poyntz, who was from a prominent West Country family. He and his wife had one child, a daughter named Elizabeth, who was born in 1556. Nonetheless, Robert was still considered as the Queen's closest associate, even though Elizabeth had put into motion a proposed marriage between him and Mary, Queen of Scots, to which both parties seemed lukewarm at best.

Sir James Melville, the Scottish Ambassador, visited Elizabeth in 1564, in part to try to arrange a meeting between her and Mary.

They touched briefly on Lord Robert, whom the Queen referred to as 'her brother and best friend, whom she would have married herself had she minded to take a husband.'[11] Melville records that:

> She [Elizabeth] took me to her bed-chamber and opened a little desk, wherein were divers little pictures wrapt within paper, and their names written with her own hand upon the papers. Upon the first that she took up was written, 'My lord's picture'. I held the candle, and pressed to see that picture so named. She was loath to let me see it; at length my importunity prevailed for a sight thereof and found it to be the Earl of Leicester's picture. I desired that I might have it to carry home to my Queen; which she refused, alleging she had but one picture of his. I said again that she had the original, for he was at the farthest part of the chamber, speaking with secretary Cecil ... She showed me also a fair ruby, as great as a tennis-ball. I desired that she would either send it or else my Lord of Leicester's picture, as a token unto the Queen [Mary]. She said, if the queen would follow her counsel, that she would in process of time get them both, and all she had.[12]

Melville seemed to have the measure of Elizabeth, understanding her resistance to marriage: 'I know your stately stomach. You think, if you were married, you would be but Queen of England, and now you are King and Queen both – you may not suffer a commander.'[13]

When Melville finally left the Court, Robert was his escort. He told Melville to report to Mary that he was not so presumptuous that he would ask for her hand. He claimed it had all been a plot, 'a wily move of Mr Secretary Cecil, designed to ruin him with both Queens.'[14]

Robert was not ready to give up on Elizabeth yet. He wrote to Cecil in October, asking again for his support in winning over the Queen. He knew that Cecil was endeavouring to try to marry her to a foreign prince, but stated: 'I will now tell you plainly that I am a claimant for the hand of the queen, and it seems to me that she looks upon no one with favour but myself.'[15]

He requested that Cecil cease his other attempts to marry off Elizabeth and concentrate on promoting Robert's case, promising to reward Cecil with 'further elevation'. Cecil passed Robert's hopes on to Elizabeth, who promised Robert he should have his answer by Christmas. When the end of the year arrived, Elizabeth wavered, as always, and failed to keep her promise.

These events brought an end to talk of Mary, Queen of Scots and Robert's marriage – in any case, neither had seemed keen to pursue the idea. In reality, Mary was considering a prospect she felt was more suitable, her cousin Henry Stuart, Lord Darnley, whose name had been raised as a potential husband several years earlier by his mother, Margaret Douglas, Countess of Lennox. At that time, other candidates, Elizabeth's opposition to the idea (he had a claim to the English throne as a grandson of Margaret Tudor) and Darnley's own youth had put paid to the idea. Now he was older and had grown into an outstandingly handsome young man.[16] His bloodline linked to Mary's would give the couple an almost unshakeable position as heirs to the English throne. In the end, Mary's decision was swayed by love. She married him, against all opposition, in July 1565, proclaiming him King of Scotland.

Although this alliance was arguably a threat to Elizabeth's throne, it also had positive repercussions. Mary was now unable to marry any of the available foreign princes or kings: such a marriage would have allied Scotland with strong European nations that could threaten England. Furthermore, the Queen of Scots' new

203

husband was considered to be an immature, shallow, selfish fool, and was unpopular with many of the Scottish nobles. There was much opposition to their union, and Elizabeth herself had not consented, so she did not feel bound to discuss the couple's position as heirs to the Crown of England. In addition, the marriage left Robert at her Court in England.

This did not stop Elizabeth from enjoying the company of other men at Court. In 1565, Thomas Butler, 10th Earl of Ormond ('The Black Earl'), became Elizabeth's favourite for a time. He was a charming and amusing Irishman who Elizabeth had known since childhood. They had met at the court of Edward VI, where Butler, like Robert, was one of the sons of nobles selected to be educated with the young King. He and Elizabeth had a further link as cousins, since Anne Boleyn's grandmother had been a Butler.

In honour of his dark, smouldering good looks, Elizabeth called him her 'black husband' and openly delighted in his company. At the time, Butler was separated from his first wife and he spent much time at the Court in England, and Elizabeth trusted his opinion and enjoyed his company. They would remain close friends over the years, with Butler building a Tudor castle in Ireland to be able to welcome the Queen, although she would never visit the country.

Elizabeth would bestow honours on him in later years and her favour of him sometimes gave rise to rumours about the nature of their relationship. When Butler willed an extraordinarily large inheritance to the eldest of his illegitimate sons, Piers, speculations arose that the son must have a very illustrious mother. Some claimed that it had been Thomas Butler, not Thomas Seymour, who had fathered a child to Elizabeth in 1548, and that the child had gone to his father's family in Ireland to be raised.

The year of 1565 also saw the first instance of Robert showing favour to someone other than the Queen. It was reported that he seemed to have a special fondness for Lettice Knollys, who was a maid of the Privy Chamber. At the time, the 22-year-old Lettice was married to Walter Devereux, 1st Earl of Essex, with whom she had two daughters. The Spanish Ambassador Guzman da Silva is alleged to have described her as one of the 'best-looking ladies of the court'.[17] The Queen was apparently displeased with this development, and Lettice left Court to return to her husband's home in Staffordshire. This would not be the end of Robert and Lettice's relationship, however.

~&

Meanwhile, developments to the North of the border were showing Mary, Queen of Scots' choice of husband to be a disaster. In less than a year, Mary and Darnley had come to dislike each other intensely. Thomas Randolph, the English Ambassador to Scotland, wrote to Cecil, 'I know now for certain that the Queen repenteth her marriage, that she hateth the King and all his kin '[18]

Darnley, who was drinking to excess, started rumours that the Queen's Italian secretary and musician, David Rizzio, was also her lover. As Mary was pregnant at the time, Rizzio was accused of being the father of her child. In March, Darnley and a group of Protestant nobles who supported him murdered Rizzio in Mary's presence.

In June, estranged from her husband, Mary gave birth to a son, James. There would be some attempts at reconciliation between the couple, but in early 1567, Darnley was murdered, an event that would lead to further problems for Mary. She faced rebellion from Protestant nobles and general suspicion about her next choice of husband, James Hepburn, 4th Earl of Bothwell, who had been implicated in the murder of Darnley. These events would contribute to Mary losing her throne in July 1567.

Although these developments carried political advantages for Elizabeth, they were unlikely to change her rather sceptical opinion of marriage. Parliament had again taken up the question in 1566, trying to get the Queen to agree to marry or settle the succession. Elizabeth responded angrily: Did she not govern well? she demanded, before storming out of the meeting. They tried, over the following days, to get a response and Elizabeth agreed to some concessions, but again flew into a temper, calling her Councillors various names from 'traitor' to 'swaggering soldier'.[19] When William Parr, 1st Marquis of Northampton, tried to speak, she told him he would be better to say nothing; his marital problems had taken an Act of Parliament to sort out. She turned on Robert himself, stating that of all people she had expected his support. When he responded that he was ready to die at her feet, Elizabeth retorted 'that had nothing to do with the matter'. She then ordered him to be put under house arrest.

When she had calmed down, Elizabeth finally agreed that she would marry as soon as was convenient and have children as soon as nature permitted, but reminded her government that despite being a woman, she had the courage of her father and would 'never be by violence constrained to do anything'.[20] As for the succession, she was painfully aware of the dangers to the country and herself of choosing the wrong heir, whose ambitions of power could imperil the kingdom.[21]

Elizabeth allowed negotiations for a possible marriage with Charles, Archduke of Austria, to continue. In June 1567, Thomas Radclyffe was sent to Emperor Maximilian II's Court with the Order of the Garter for the Emperor, along with a portrait of Elizabeth for his brother, Archduke Charles.

Radclyffe sent back a lengthy report describing Charles: auburn-haired, with a good complexion, cheerful, courteous, princely, with good hands and well-proportioned legs. He spoke his native German, as well as some Spanish, Italian and a little Latin. He was universally beloved, a most virtuous man and a valiant warrior, having led his father's armies against the Turks to keep the eastern borders safe. He loved riding, hunting and hawking, and also liked to study, particularly astronomy and cosmography. Radclyffe was impressed by the Archduke and commended him to the Queen, saying he would make 'a true husband, a loving companion, a wise councillor, and a faithful servant, and we shall have as virtuous a prince as ever ruled.'[22]

Religion remained the sticking point, however. Archduke Charles had told Radclyffe '... if I might have hope that her Majesty would bear with me for my conscience [as a Catholic] I know not that thing in the world I would refuse to do at her commandment. And surely I have from the beginning of the matter settled my heart upon her, and never thought of other wife, if she would think me worthy to be her husband.'[23] As to whether he might convert to Protestantism, Charles replied that he and his family had always been Catholic and the Queen would think very little of him if he casually tossed his religion away. He only asked that he be allowed to attend Catholic services in private.

When the Council met to discuss the matter, Radclyffe, who was in favour, was abroad; Thomas Howard, who was in favour, was ill, and so Cecil, who was also in favour, was outnumbered. Robert, who was against the union, emphasized the religious divide, and the Council voted not to support the marriage.

Elizabeth, now aged 34, seemed somewhat relieved – as no doubt was Robert. The Spanish Ambassador da Silva, writing to Philip II, saw the religious question as just another justification for Elizabeth to avoid marrying, stating that the Queen leaves 'herself always a loop hole to escape from'.[24] Archduke Charles would finally marry his niece, Maria Anna of Bavaria, in 1571, with whom he would go on to have 15 children. Elizabeth was said to be insulted by this match.

In November 1568, Elizabeth had one last chance with one of her earliest beaus, Philip II, when she was told of the death of Elisabeth de Valois, his French wife. Elizabeth sent her condolences, claiming that she and her Court would go into mourning with suitably sombre ceremonies in the dead Queen's honour.

In an exchange with French Ambassador de La Mothe Fénelon, she expressed surprise that Philip had not written to her with the news himself, then surmised that perhaps it would not be deemed decent to send 'letters to an unmarried girl, like her …'. De La Mothe rejoined, 'I thanked her and only added that the King of Spain was still young enough to take a fourth wife.'[25] This exchange must have amused both parties.

Shortly after, relations with Spain became tense when four Spanish ships forced to take shelter in the Port of London turned out to be carrying money for a campaign to subdue Protestants in the Netherlands. Elizabeth promptly seized the cash for 'safe-keeping'. The Spanish governor of the Netherlands was furious and impounded all English goods, while, in retaliation, Elizabeth seized all Spanish goods in England. De La Mothe told her not to worry about the impact this might have on her relations with Philip: '… the King of Spain, being once more a widower, and in search of a suitable consort, would not for the world offend an unmarried princess like her; neither, for the same cause, should she quarrel with him who was on that pursuit.'[26] Elizabeth replied that she did not doubt the friendship of Spain.

Relations with Scotland had reached another impasse. Mary, Queen of Scots, who had been forced to abdicate, had fled to England in 1568, where she was immediately imprisoned by

Elizabeth. Mary sought Elizabeth's support in regaining her throne. Although Elizabeth was cautious, she had been persuaded to the cause on the condition that Mary ratify the Treaty of Edinburgh.

In 1570, Cecil met with Mary's advisers to draw up a treaty between the two Queens. In the second Article it was stated that Elizabeth's issue should have preference to the succession. Mary changed the wording to 'lawful issue', presumably a snide reference to the rumours that Elizabeth and Robert had had a child out of wedlock. Elizabeth agreed, but returned the insult, remarking that Mary 'measured other folk's disposition by her own actions'.[27] In any case, the matter was moot, as Mary still refused to accept all of the conditions of the Edinburgh treaty.

209

❧

With the Queen now aged 37, another drawn-out courtship began. Tentative approaches were made by the English Council to French Ambassador de La Mothe regarding a possible French husband. The Council possibly suspected that the project was doomed to failure and simply saw it as a way to flatter the French or win political influence. Elizabeth's response to the matter seemed to be more one of resignation: 'I am an old woman and am ashamed to talk about a husband, were it not for the sake of an heir.'[28]

Whether the French believed Elizabeth was sincere, it was too good an opportunity to miss. If Elizabeth fell for the charms of a handsome young Frenchman and became pregnant, England and France could be brought together by the issue of that union. Charles IX and his mother, Catherine de Medici, offered Elizabeth the elder of the King's two brothers, the 19-year-old Henri, Duc d'Anjou. Elizabeth again claimed to be worried about the age difference, to which a perhaps defensive Robert replied, 'So much the better for you.'[29]

She suggested that Henri make a brief visit to England so they could meet. Although the meeting never occurred, it was perhaps just as well that this was the case. Officially, Henri was tall, slender and handsome, with beautiful eyes and hands, but according to other reports, he was obsessed with clothes, perfume and jewellery, as well as purchasing expensive jewels with which to seduce naïve young ladies. Henri, firmly under the influence of the Guise faction, reportedly felt it would be better to lead an army to conquer England than to marry an old lady with a sordid reputation. He was said to have called Elizabeth a *putain publique* (a 'common whore') and 'an old creature'.[30]

Perhaps inevitably his alleged comments reached Elizabeth's ears. Although the French Ambassador reassured the Queen that the Duke had never said such things, there was also the question of religion. Henri wanted assurances that he and his courtiers could freely worship in the Catholic religion, that he rule jointly as King and receive a pension of £60,000 a year for life. The English refused to allow the devout Henri his Catholic faith. When it appeared that the whole project would fail, Catherine de Medici then suggested her son, François, Duc d'Alençon, who was even younger, as he was 'a much less scrupulous fellow'.

When Elizabeth asked Cecil how tall François was, he replied: 'About as tall as I am.' She was heard to respond, 'About as tall as your grandson, you mean' – Cecil's grandson was six years old at the time.[31] As François was only 15 years old, 21 years younger than Elizabeth, small in stature, with a big nose and smallpox scars, the idea was quietly dropped for the time being.

Although the French King Charles IX had previously supported Mary, Queen of Scots, he now increasingly looked to England as an ally. In April 1572, France and England signed the Treaty of Blois, a pact of mutual defence. As Elizabeth had fallen

210

ill that month with a high fever (probably colic), once again came the panic that she might die without an heir. As she recovered – Robert and William Cecil, now 1st Baron Burghley, by her side throughout her illness – the pressure for a successor was back on the agenda. Once again, François was proposed as a husband. But in August, the St Bartholomew's Day massacre in France occurred, in which thousands of Protestants were slain in the French Wars of Religion. This marked a low point in France's relations with its Protestant neighbours. The marriage to François was put on hold, although he continued to write Elizabeth the wonderful and romantic love letters of a devoted suitor.

The Queen also had her admirers in the English Court. Sir Christopher Hatton was appointed captain of Elizabeth's bodyguard in 1572, and was also a Member of Parliament. Well-educated, handsome and accomplished, this elegant dancer was said to be Robert's main rival at the time. Stories circulated about Elizabeth and Hatton, including that he 'had more recourse to Her Majesty in her Privy Chamber than reason could suffer, if she were virtuous and well inclined as some noiseth her.'[32]

Over the years, he would be a favourite of Elizabeth's, owing his place at Court to his never-ending adoration of the Queen, which he recorded in letters and poems. He would write, 'Your heart is full of rare and royal faith, the writings of your hand do raise me to joy unspeakable.'[33] Like Robert, Hatton was always near her; she nicknamed Robert her 'Eyes', and Hatton her 'Lids'. Each man added a cipher to his letters to the Queen; Robert signed with ôô (eyes) and Hatton with ΔΔ. In 1573, ill with a kidney problem, Hatton would write to Elizabeth from a Dutch spa, 'to serve you is heaven, but to lack you is more than hell's torment … Your Lids that are so often bathed with tears for your sake. A more wise man may seek you, but a more faithful and worthy can never have you.'[34]

Hatton also sent Elizabeth a jewel shaped like a lover's knot, 'the kind she most likes, and she thinks can not be undone.'[35] He would remain a devoted follower of the Queen, the only one of her professed lovers who never married, maintaining that he never found anyone else more worthy of his love. He did, however, keep discreet mistresses a long way from Court, at least one of whom provided him with a daughter named Elizabeth.

In the early 1570s, the young Edward de Vere, 17th Earl of Oxford, had also become a courtier in the Queen's Court. As a child, he had been placed in Cecil's household as a royal ward, and he married Cecil's 15-year-old daughter in 1571. By 1573, he appeared to be emerging as a favourite of Elizabeth's. In May, the Court correspondent Gilbert Talbot, 7th Earl of Shrewsbury, wrote that de Vere had lately grown in great credit with the Queen, and '… were it not for his fickle head he would pass any of them shortly.'[36]

Although de Vere was the kind of handsome young nobleman who amused the Queen, there is some debate about the true nature of her affections. Some historians have suggested that de Vere was actually the son born of Elizabeth and Thomas Seymour, [37] while others claim that he and Elizabeth themselves had an affair and had an illegitimate child.[38] He did receive some patronage from Elizabeth over the years, including an annual pension of £1,000, despite flirting with Catholicism and mismanaging his estates. He would also become a leading patron of Elizabethan arts.

Elizabeth's were not the only dalliances going on at Court in 1573. At around the same time, Robert's attentions were taken by Douglass Howard, Baroness Sheffield. The affair seems to have started in earnest with the death of her husband in December 1568. Robert stated that he loved Douglass, but could not publicly marry because it would ruin his position with the Queen. Douglass would later give testimony that she had been his secret wife, entering into a contracted marriage with him. Whatever the truth of this, what is indisputable is that she bore Robert's son, Robert Dudley, in August 1574. Robert would take custody of the boy when Douglass later married in 1579, and cared for his education and upbringing. He also made provision in his will for his 'base son', who later unsuccessfully tried to establish his legitimacy in court.

In the same year, the Court was alive with rumours that Douglass's sister Frances Howard was also in love with Robert and that the sisters were 'at great wars' over his affections. Robert is also thought to have rekindled his affair with Lettice Knollys in 1573, when her husband Walter Devereux, 1st Earl of Essex, was sent to Ireland. Despite these romances, Elizabeth maintained her close friendship with Robert. Other favourites might share her affection, but only one man seemed to hold her heart. His gifts were always lavish and personal. In 1572, he gave her a gold bracelet set with diamonds and rubies and a tiny clock mounted in gold. Two years later, he gave her a fan of white feathers with a gold handle decorated with a bear (his arms) and a lion (hers).

213

❧

In September 1578, matters changed significantly for both Robert and Elizabeth when Robert married Lettice Knollys. Robert and Lettice's relationship had already been the subject of scandal in 1575, when her husband had returned to England and discovered their affair. When he died of dysentery in 1576, there were rumours that Robert had poisoned the man.

Initially, Robert did not inform the Queen of his marriage. Many months later, when Elizabeth discovered the news, she was devastated. Robert was sent away for a time, while his wife was banished from Court and forbidden to return during the Queen's lifetime. Elizabeth heartily disliked Lettice and never forgave her.

In the end, Robert and Lettice would have one child in 1581, Robert Dudley, Lord Denbigh, but he died at the age of three.

Thus it came to pass that in 1579, at the age of 46, Elizabeth was again considering a marriage to François, Duc d'Alençon, who was by now 24 years old. She had told her desperate Parliament that marriage was still an option, although not one she would embrace for her own sake: 'If I were a milkmaid with a pail on my arm whereby my private person might be little set by, I would not forsake that poor and single state to match with the greatest monarch.'[39] François would be the last of the Queen's suitors.

There were a number of political advantages to a marriage with François. He was the heir to the throne of France, which was currently occupied by his brother, Henri III, who had become King in 1574 when their brother Charles IX died. Henri, who had made insulting remarks about Elizabeth years before, was married but had no children. There were unproved rumours that he was a homosexual and liked to wear women's clothes, although it is also recorded that he had many mistresses. During Henri's reign, the French Wars of Religion between Catholics and the Protestant Huguenots continued to rage.

François' relationship with his brother was one of rivalry. In 1575–76, François had challenged Henri III's rule and offered protection to both Catholics and Protestants, suggesting that the latter should have the right of public worship of their religion. The brothers made their peace, to the extent that the following year François commanded the King's army against the Huguenots, but by 1578 he had again fallen from grace and was arrested. François escaped to Belgium, part of the provinces of the Netherlands.

In 1579, the northern part of these provinces formed the Union of Utrecht to break away from Spanish rule (the entire area had been part of the Holy Roman Empire), and François was invited to be the hereditary sovereign. The following year he would be named 'Defender of Belgic Liberty' of the northern provinces, opposing the Spanish in the Catholic southern provinces. François had the support of the English Crown, which preferred the option of neither Spain nor France ruling the Netherlands. Elizabeth's political interest in François was his wish to drive Spanish forces out of the country to gain a free and independent Netherlands. During the courtship, the two also grew very close.

In 1579, François sent his charming envoy Jean de Simier to begin wooing Elizabeth on his behalf. He was 'a most choice courtier, exquisitely skilled in love toys, pleasant conceits and court dalliances.'[40] Elizabeth nicknamed him the 'Monkey' (a play on his name 'Simier') and enjoyed the imagination he put into the courtship, including sneaking into her bedchamber to steal a night cap to send to François as a love token. Despite his efforts, negotiations stalled because of the Duke's demands – he wanted to be crowned King after they married, receive a pension of £60,000 a year, and have equal rights to the Queen in allocating gifts of Crown possessions.

215

The issue of Elizabeth's heir was paramount, however. Could she still bear a child at her age? This question was discussed at length by her Councillors.

In a memorandum, Cecil noted that there were precedents of noblewomen who had given birth when older than Elizabeth. He noted that the Queen seemed perfectly designed for childbearing, 'of the largest and goodliest stature of well-shaped women, with all limbs set and proportioned in the best sort ... nature cannot amend her shape in any part to make her more likely to conceive and bear children.'[41]

Doctors were consulted, and they concurred that Elizabeth conceiving a child was possible. Other observers disagreed, believing that Elizabeth's health excluded the possibility given the dangers of childbirth. François' mother herself, Catherine de Medici, sought a report on the Queen's childbearing prospects from an English doctor. The unnamed physician reported, '... if the King [François] marries I will answer for her having 10 children, and no one knows her temperament better than I do.'[42]

Over the years, foreign envoys and ambassadors had been reporting rumours across the spectrum, ranging from her being physically incapable of sex to her being sexually promiscuous and already a mother. Some claimed she had at least 13 illegitimate children and that 'she never went in progress but to be delivered', while others asserted that she was regularly 'cupped' (a warm cup placed over an incision in the skin to draw off a quantity of blood) to compensate for her lack of menstruation. However, Henri III's Ambassador to Elizabeth's Court wrote that he could state with truth that the stories of Elizabeth's affairs 'were sheer inventions of the malicious, and of the ambassadorial staffs, to put off those who would have found an alliance with her useful.'[43]

❧

Elizabeth decided that she wanted to see François, and it was arranged that he visit England. At the news, Robert Dudley became so 'ill' that he was obliged to retire from Court, and Elizabeth let him go, even though she was not yet aware that he had married Lettice Knollys. Instead she found out about Robert's betrayal after François' envoy Simier was shot at by a guard. He suspected that Robert had been involved, and in revenge told the Queen about the secret marriage. Elizabeth was beside herself with rage and would have sent Robert to the Tower had his act been illegal; instead he was banished to his estates at Wanstead with orders to stay there until further notice.

With Robert's actions no doubt a bitter blow, she wrote sweet letters to François, 'I confess there is no prince in the world to whom I would more willingly yield to be his, than to yourself, nor to whom I think myself more obliged, nor with whom I would pass the years of my life, both for your rare virtues and sweet nature ...'[44]

On 17 August, François, who was the only of the foreign princes to woo Elizabeth in person, arrived at Greenwich. He was an instant hit. Though small (under five feet) and not classically handsome, he was charming and exciting, and Elizabeth clearly found him attractive. Her French was excellent, so they could woo without an interpreter and were said to enjoy 'secret visits'. They spent 12 days together and their romance seems to have blossomed. After leaving, he sent her 'a little flower of gold with a frog thereon, and therein Monsieur, his physiognomy.'[45] She fondly nicknamed her suitor her 'frog'.

217

However, English public opinion was not in favour of the union. The persecution of Protestants in France and the ongoing religious civil war meant the French were not trusted. Despite François' concessions to Protestants, he himself was Catholic and his mother, Catherine de Medici, was the Dowager Queen of France. A barrister from Lincoln's Inn, John Stubbs, added fuel to the flames by writing and publishing *The Discovery of a Gaping Gulf wherein England is like to be swallowed by another French marriage, if the Lord forbid not the banns by letting her Majesty see the sin and punishment thereof.* He wrote that the Queen's age would put her in great danger should she become pregnant, and that no young man would wish to marry an older woman unless he had an ulterior motive. François could not be trusted.

In response, a letter signed by the most influential of the Queen's courtiers was sent to the Mayor of London, advising him that all copies of the book were to be seized and destroyed for slandering the Queen and the Duke, and upsetting the people of the realm. The pamphlet writer Stubbs and the bookseller that had distributed it were sentenced to have their right hands cut off on 3 November 1579. François tried to intervene to gain the two men a pardon, but Elizabeth refused to back down. Each man lost his hand, and therefore his livelihood.

The Privy Council was also divided on the question. Although Cecil supported the marriage, Robert Dudley, among other Councillors, was strongly opposed. However, her Council left the final decision to her. Negotiations for the engagement continued through 1580, with François making political concessions to keep them going.

In April 1581, the new French envoy, Pierre Clausse Seigneur de Marchaumont, was invited to knight Francis Drake with the Queen's sword on her behalf. Drake had recently returned from pillaging the Spanish treasure fleet in the West Indies. In the process, she dropped her garter and de Marchaumont begged to keep it for François. Elizabeth said she needed it to get back to the palace with her stockings in place, but he could have it later, which he did. Many assumed the marriage was as good as signed.

Later in the year, François returned to England and was again royally entertained. He wrote the Queen messages of love, stating his desire to be 'kissing and rekissing all that Your beautiful Majesty can think of' as well as to be 'in bed between the sheets in your beautiful arms'.[46] He had no doubt that their passion would soon engender a son 'made and forged by the little Frenchman who is and will be eternally your humble and very loving slave'.[47]

Elizabeth visited François in his bedchamber, as one scandalized correspondent wrote. 'There goes much babbling and the Queen doth not attend to other matters, but only to be together with the Duke in one chamber from morning to noon, and afterwards till two or three hours after sunset. I cannot tell what a devil they do.'[48] In October 1581, on the day she celebrated the anniversary of her accession, Elizabeth was with François at Whitehall. As they were strolling in the gallery, she kissed her suitor and gave him a ring from her finger. She informed the French Ambassador, 'You may write this to the King, that the Duke of Alençon shall be my husband.'[49]

The next day she called François in and told him that, on reflection, she would not be able to marry him. The nation was opposed to the wedding, and childbirth at her age would be risky. She loved him, she said, but the marriage was impossible. François was devastated. He stayed on at Court for a further three months in case the Queen changed her mind. In the end, he was given £10,000 with the promise of £50,000 more when he left England.

In early 1582, Elizabeth accompanied him to Canterbury, where they parted in tears. Whether the whole engagement had been political theatre to gain influence in Europe, vengeance against the recently married Robert, true love, or a combination of all of these is unknown. However, Elizabeth did seem genuinely fond of the Frenchman, as is shown in her poem to him titled 'On Monsieur's Departure':

> *I grieve, and dare not show my discontent;*
> *I love, and yet am forced to seem to hate;*
> *I dote, but dare not say I ever meant;*
> *I seem stark mute, yet inwardly do prate.*
> *I am, and am not – freeze, and yet I burn,*
> *Since from myself my other self I turn.*[50]

Elizabeth never saw her 'frog' again. He returned to the Netherlands, where he contracted an illness that may have been malaria during his unpopular military campaigns. He died of a fever in Paris on 10 June 1584. When Elizabeth was told, her Court was ordered into mourning and she is reported to have wept inconsolably.

◕

In the following years, the Queen would continue to have favourites, but the frenetic years of political and romantic intrigue came to a close with the end of her engagement with the French Duke. She had played her hand masterfully and tactfully, maintaining the hope of her suitors and with it, political alliances. The line of separation between political angling and her true feelings is impossible to ascertain. Was her pattern of entering into and later exiting out of every marriage proposal attributable to personal or political caution?

Now middle-aged, the Queen would use her avoidance of marriage to her advantage, to demonstrate that she was dedicated solely to the nation's interests. She was 'married' to her people. The last twenty years of her life would see the pinnacle of her reign, with her navy winning one of England's greatest victories in the defeat of the Spanish Armada, England's seafarers exploring the globe, and the nation's poets, playwrights and essayists ushering in a golden age of literature.

9

Gloriana, 1582–1603

❧

I n the early 1580s, England's fleets were a growing asset to its strength. Sir Francis Drake had circumnavigated the globe between 1577 and 1580, for which Elizabeth knighted him in 1581. Tensions were rising between England and Spain, with the two nations and navies vying for power in the Netherlands, France and the Caribbean – and anywhere else they could sway influence. Later in the decade the tensions would heighten into war.

There were also revolts against English rule in Ireland, where it was feared the Catholic population would conspire with Spain and give it a base from which to attack England. In Scotland, the teenage James VI (King of Scotland 1567–1625) did not always have a firm grip on power and was imprisoned for a period in 1582–83 by plotting Protestant earls, and Elizabeth still feared plots hatched by Catholics who were trying to put Mary, Queen of Scots on the English throne. Some of the greatest tests and victories of Elizabeth's reign were yet to come.

In 1581 Elizabeth had a new favourite, who reflected the renaissance spirit of the times. An adventurer, navigator, poet and soldier, Walter Raleigh (c.1552–1618) was nicknamed 'Water', which reflected the way his name sounded when he pronounced it in his Devonshire accent.

Raleigh had sailed to America in 1578, and then served as a captain in a company sent to Ireland to suppress an uprising. On his return to England in December 1581, he became a prominent member of the Court, where it is clear that he greatly pleased the Queen. Elizabeth gave him a lease on Durham House on the Strand so that he could remain close to her. In 1585, he was knighted, and in 1587 he was given the post of Captain of the Gentleman Pensioners, the Queen's bodyguard. During this period, the extremely handsome Raleigh was at the height of his favour with the Queen, and benefited from the honours and gifts she bestowed on him. However, he did not have any real political influence with the Council.

Raleigh and Elizabeth exchanged poems during their relationship. One of the earliest is reported to have occurred when Raleigh, a new arrival at Court, wrote on a window pane, 'Fain would I climb, yet fear I to fall,' and the Queen then added, 'If thy heart fails thee, climb not at all.'[1] On another occasion, Raleigh wrote Elizabeth a poem that began:

> *Fortune hath taken away my love,*
> *My life's joy and my soul's heaven above.*
> *Fortune hath taken thee away, my princess,*
> *My world's joy and my true fantasy's mistress …*

And Elizabeth replied:

> *Ah, silly Pug, wert thou so sore afraid?*
> *Mourn not, my Wat, nor be thou so dismayed.*
> *It passeth fickle Fortune's power and skill*
> *To force my heart to think thee any ill …*[2]

In 1587, Raleigh set off on an expedition to attempt to found the colony of Virginia in the New World and also spent time in Ireland during the years that followed. Despite his absence from Court, Raleigh continued to hold Elizabeth's affections until 1592, when he was abruptly recalled from one of his expeditions by the Queen after it was discovered that he had secretly married one of her ladies-in-waiting, Elizabeth Throckmorton, in 1591; she was five months pregnant. It was strictly forbidden for ladies-in-waiting to marry without the Queen's consent and Elizabeth Throckmorton was dismissed from Court, while Raleigh was sent to the Tower. After his release, he returned to his estates rather than to Court. Over the years he went up and down in the Queen's favour, but would never regain his previous standing.

Raleigh was never a rival to Robert Dudley, who returned Elizabeth's love until his death. He did, however, have a serious rival in Robert Devereux, 2nd Earl of Essex, who is discussed in more detail in the last chapter.

As rivals for the Queen's attentions, Devereux and Raleigh were often on bad terms. However, in 1584, the year in which Devereux arrived at Court, a rather pleasant picture emerges of life for Elizabeth, surrounded by those both formerly and presently devoted to her.

A German visitor, Lupold von Wedel, wrote of the Queen dining in state at Greenwich, dressed in black and silver and attended by, among others, 'my lord of Leicester, the Master of the Horse, who is said to have had a love affair with the Queen for a long time. Now he has a wife. Then there was the Lord High Treasurer and the Keeper of the Privy Purse, my lord Hertford [Edward Seymour, Catherine Grey's son], who they say of all Englishmen has the most right to the throne.'

He noted Sir Christopher Hatton as being another of the Queen's former lovers, and ended, 'All of them ... were handsome old gentlemen.'[3]

223

◔

In 1585, Elizabeth sent troops to the Netherlands to aid the Protestant Dutch rebels who were striving to throw off the rule of Philip II. Spain had been extending its influence there and in France, posing a greater threat to England.

The Netherlands force was under the command of Robert Dudley, but they disagreed on the expedition's strategy. She wanted to avoid direct confrontation with Spain and try to engage in negotiations, while he supported active military intervention and Dutch independence from Spain. As a result of Robert's military campaign, the Dutch Council of State offered him the post of Governor General of the United Provinces, which he duly accepted.

Elizabeth was furious with this direct contradiction of her wishes and made no attempt to control her anger. She wrote to Sir Thomas Hencage, his friend and her own representative in the Netherlands, saying that Robert had greatly offended her by going expressly against her orders. Elizabeth also wrote to Robert directly:

> How contemptuously we conceive ourselves to have been used by you, you shall by this bearer understand; whom we have expressly sent unto you to charge you withal. We could never have imagined, had we not seen it all out in experience, that a man raised up by ourself and extraordinarily favoured by us above any other subject of this land, would have in so contemptible a sort broken our commandment in a case that so greatly toucheth us in honour.[4]

Robert duly and humbly apologized to the Queen, saying her words had caused him such misery that he had fallen ill. It was an old but effective ploy that he had used over the years to show his repentance and regain the Queen's favour, and after a few months Elizabeth forgave him. Even direct disobedience could not truly come between them, it seemed. By August 1585, Elizabeth promised support to the Dutch in the Treaty of Nonsuch, an event that triggered the Anglo-Spanish War, a conflict that would continue for the next 19 years.

At the same time, Elizabeth was facing another threat closer to home. Mary, Queen of Scots, who had been in English custody for 18 years, had become involved in a plot to dispose of Elizabeth and have herself placed on the English throne. The plot was discovered while Mary was being held at Chartley Castle in Staffordshire under the strict surveillance of the Puritan Sir Amyas Paulet, who worked with Elizabeth's spymaster Francis Walsingham to monitor all Mary's communications. They intercepted letters containing details of the conspiracy, which involved six gentlemen assassinating Elizabeth, while a second group rescued Mary.

On discovering the plot, the Council arrested the conspirators and seized Mary's papers, thereby providing proof of her involvement. The Council met and pronounced a sentence of death, which needed Elizabeth's agreement. She procrastinated, wishing for any other outcome than the one facing her. It took the combined powers of Robert Dudley, William Cecil and Francis Walsingham to persuade Elizabeth that there was no alternative if she wanted to be safe from assassination.

On 4 December, the death warrant was drawn up, but Elizabeth still resisted signing it. Then in January, details of another plot against her emerged, giving Elizabeth, it seemed, no choice, but still she waited. Finally, on 1 February, Elizabeth approved the warrant. Worried that she might change her mind, Cecil had the warrant despatched immediately, and on 8 February

1587, Mary, Queen of Scots was beheaded at Fotheringhay Castle in Northamptonshire.

Elizabeth was heartbroken at her cousin's death, despite their mistrust of each other over the years. She was also worried about the consequences of the execution and how her European rivals might perceive it and consequently react. She told her Court that she had not meant the warrant to be served so quickly. The secretary who had carried it to Fotherhingay was arrested and imprisoned in the Tower.

The execution of Mary, Queen of Scots set off a sequence of events that would lead to Spain's attempted invasion of England. With Mary's death, Philip realized he could no longer rely on her to install a Catholic on the English throne. He acknowledged the Pope's decision to excommunicate Elizabeth and stated that he himself was heir to the throne on the grounds that firstly, Mary had named him her heir in her will, denying her Protestant son, James VI of Scotland, and, secondly, that he himself had a direct, lawful descent from the two daughters of John of Gaunt, the father of Henry IV: Philippa of Lancaster, Queen of Portugal, and Catherine of Lancaster, Queen of Castile. Philip wanted to conquer England, ending the problems that the island was causing him. Apart from conspiring with the Dutch Protestant rebels, during the 1580s England was also pursuing a policy of piracy against Spanish ships, attempting to plunder their treasure.

Just months after Mary's execution, Sir Francis Drake raided Cadiz, destroying a fleet of war ships. In response, Philip assembled an enormous fleet under the command of the Duke of Medina Sedonia and ordered his admiral to invade and conquer England, taking the Queen alive at all costs. This was not a reflection of his affection for her – instead, Philip planned to send the captive Queen to Rome where she would be triumphantly exhibited before being handed over to the Pope and his inquisitors for punishment.

These grandiose plans would, in the end, come to nothing. The giant Spanish Armada set out with 22 warships from the Spanish Royal Navy and 108 converted merchant vessels, but ended up limping back to Spain in a disastrous retreat after being harried by the English fleet and hit by storms. Elizabeth proved to be a rousing and fearless leader, planning to ride at the head of her army to wherever along the coast the enemy might seek to land, while her fleet went out to battle. Robert, in command of the ground forces, managed to dissuade her from this:

> Now for your person being the most dainty and sacred thing we have in this world to care for, a man must tremble when he thinks of it; specially finding your Majesty to have the princely courage to transport yourself to the utmost confines of your realm to meet your enemies, and to defend your subjects. I cannot, must dear Queen, consent to that, for upon your well doing consists all the safety of your whole kingdom and therefore preserve that above all.[5]

227

He recommended instead that Elizabeth address her troops at Tilbury on the Thames, where she gave a defiant and patriotic speech that has become one of the key moments in English history. Standing in front of her soldiers Elizabeth uttered some of her most famous words: 'I know I have the body but of a weak and feeble woman, but I have the heart and stomach of a king, and of a king of England too.'[6]

The defeat of the Spanish Armada in July 1588 heralded the highest point in Elizabeth's rule, and was a victory that lent England not only a strong sense of national pride, but also the sense that God was on the side of a Protestant victory against the Catholic enemy.

Elizabeth's moment of triumph at this great victory was soon overshadowed by great personal tragedy - the death of the Queen's great love, Robert Dudley. After the Armada was defeated, Robert, who had been the Lieutenant and Captain General of the Queen's Armies and Companies during the crisis, was lauded as a hero. His health had been poor, so he retired to take the waters at Buxton, and on his way there stopped off to visit friends in Rycote, where he wrote his last letter to Elizabeth. Later, on the Queen's death, it was found in a cabinet by her bed. It reads in part:

> At Rycote, August 29, I most humbly beseech your Majesty to pardon your poor old servant to be thus bold in sending to know how my gracious lady doth, and what ease of her late pain she finds, being the chiefest thing in this world I do pray for, for her to have good health and long life. For mine own poor case, I continue still your medicine, and find it amend, much better than with any other thing that hath been given me. Thus, hoping to find perfect cure at the bath, with the continuance of my wonted prayer for your Majesty's most happy preservation, I humbly kiss your foot, from your old lodging at Rycote, this Thursday morning, ready to take on my journey. By your Majesty's most faithful, obedient servant R Leycester.[7]

Six days after this letter, on 4 September 1588, Robert died at the age of 56. Elizabeth was devastated. Their mutual affection and trust had lasted until the end.

Soon after, others who had served the Queen since the beginning of her reign began to pass away. In 1590, Robert's brother Ambrose Dudley died, as well as the spymaster Francis Walsingham and Elizabeth's Household Controller Sir James Crofts. Then in 1591, Sir Christopher Hatton died at Ely Place in Hatton Gardens. Of her suitors, he alone had remained unmarried. Other deaths followed swiftly: Henry Carey, her most loyal cousin; Francis Knollys, her treasurer; Henry Hastings, a possible heir to the throne; and Elizabeth's beloved Blanche Parry, who was buried with the honours due to a baroness. Then, in August 1598, William Cecil fell ill, retiring to his house at Theobalds. As he lay dying, Elizabeth came to feed him broth with her own hand, chatting to take his mind off his ailment. With his death, she lost her first and best servant.

The last 15 years of Elizabeth's reign were not only peppered with personal losses, but with political difficulties. With the passing away of her old advisers and officials, a new generation was vying for control and her Privy Council suffered from factionalism, particularly between Robert Cecil, the son of her most trusted adviser, and the ambitious Robert Devereux, 2nd Earl of Essex. The conflicts with Spain and Ireland were costly and the kingdom's economy suffered. Repression against Catholics intensified. Elizabeth's popularity became slightly tarnished by all these factors, and her personal power and acuity weakened with age.

The Queen's health began to decline late in 1602. In February 1603, she received yet another blow – the death of Catherine Howard (*née* Carey), Countess of Nottingham, her cousin and one of her dearest friends – which left Elizabeth in a state of deep depression. In March, she fell ill and became extremely melancholic. Catherine Howard's brother, Robert Carey, came to Court and found a frail and sad Elizabeth seated on cushions on the floor, unable or unwilling to move. He recorded later that he heard 'forty or fifty great sighs … for in all my lifetime before, I

229

never knew her fetch a sigh, but when the Queen of Scots was beheaded.'[8]

Robert Cecil, trying to rouse Elizabeth, told her she must go to bed. The Queen replied, 'Little man, little man, the word *must* is not to be used to Princes.'[9] On 21 March, Catherine Howard's grieving widower, Charles Howard, 1st Earl of Nottingham, another valued old friend, was summoned. He persuaded her to retire to the comfort of her bed.

The end was slow and terrible. Elizabeth developed a throat infection that meant she could hardly talk, eat or drink. When Robert Cecil, obliged to plan the succession, asked her if James VI of Scotland was to succeed her, she simply lifted her hand in agreement. Elizabeth I died on 24 March 1603 at the age of 69 at Richmond Palace, with her old friend Archbishop Whitgift by her bedside. He knelt and prayed, staying with her through the last day. Some time after 2 a.m. she finally slipped away 'mildly like a lamb, easily like a ripe apple from the tree.'[10]

In the end, after all the years of wrangling with her government about the succession, the solution that was found was relatively trouble-free. As Elizabeth had no lawful heirs, James VI of Scotland had a strong claim by the line of Henry VIII's older sister, Margaret Tudor. If Elizabeth did have illegitimate children, none of them came forward to claim the throne and the transition went smoothly. James VI of Scotland took a second crown, becoming James I of England and Ireland.

Despite all the rumours and scandals over the years, the possible illegitimate child Elizabeth was suspected to have had with Robert Dudley did not become the next King of England – neither did any of the other children she was alleged to have borne out of wedlock.

230

Robert Dudley's
alleged child

Introduction

Robert Dudley's Alleged Child

ᔓ

T hroughout Elizabeth's long reign, the question of her heir was a matter of great concern and the cause of consternation both at home and abroad among her various Councillors, Europe's loyalty and aristocracy and her own favourites. Who would the Queen marry? And, if she failed to marry, who would be the next King or Queen of England?

Elizabeth, with characteristic stubbornness, resisted all attempts to marry or to name an heir. Even more frustratingly, over the years she wavered between steadfastly refusing to consider marriage and encouraging various members of the European royalty to pursue her, only to change her mind. Meanwhile, her Council feared that she would marry one of her favourites, Robert Dudley, for many years the most likely candidate. In the end, however, Elizabeth remained unmarried to the last, the Virgin Queen of legend.

For the first part of her reign, though, it seemed likely that Elizabeth would marry at some point and give birth to a legitimate heir. Why she chose not to do so is a matter of conjecture and has been the subject of a great many books, plays and films. One of the questions frequently raised is whether or not Elizabeth was able to have children. There certainly seems to be no firm evidence to support the idea that Elizabeth was incapable of conceiving. Indeed, throughout her life – even before she was Queen – there were rumours that she had had sexual liaisons with men such as Thomas Seymour and later Robert Dudley, and had given birth to an illegitimate child – possibly even children . Yet, if the rumours were true, why did she keep any child secret? It would not have been unprecedented for Elizabeth to disclose the existence of a child and for that child to be accepted as her heir. In 1571, her ministers even changed the wording of the Act of Succession, which had stated that the throne should go to the 'issue of her body lawfully to be begotten' to read 'the natural issue of her body'. This meant that any child whom the Queen acknowledged as her own, even one born outside wedlock, could potentially become the future King or Queen of England.

234

This decision no doubt resulted from the rumours at the time that Elizabeth had conceived a child with her favourite Robert Dudley during their inseparable years at Court when both were in their twenties or early thirties. In the same way as the child Elizabeth was reported to have had with Thomas Seymour, it could have been born in secret and placed with suitable foster parents.

But if this were the case, who would be the most likely candidate to be the offspring of Elizabeth and Robert? Looking at the evidence, four men stand out as possible contenders: Francis Bacon (1561–1626), Arthur Dudley (1561–?), John Harington (1560–1612) and Robert Devereux (1566–1601).

10

The Case of
Sir Francis Bacon

✢

ccording to the records of the time, Francis Bacon was born on 22 January 1561 at York House on the Strand in London, to Sir Nicholas Bacon and his second wife, Anne Cooke.

Sir Nicholas had graduated from Corpus Christi College, Cambridge and entered Gray's Inn (one of the Inns of Court); he was called to the Bar in 1533. During the Dissolution of the Monasteries under Henry VIII, Sir Nicholas acquired several estates, including Gorhambury near St Albans, which became the family seat. He held several posts under Edward VI, as Member of Parliament, Attorney of the Court of Wards and Liveries, and Treasurer of Gray's Inn. He was a highly skilled lawyer and a brilliant speaker. During the reign of Mary I, he lost his posts as he was a staunch Protestant, only to resume his career on the succession of Elizabeth I. The Queen immediately appointed him Lord Keeper of the Great Seal, a post in which he worked closely with his brother-in-law, William Cecil (they had married two of the learned and intelligent daughters of Sir Anthony Cooke). Francis was the youngest of all of Nicholas Bacon's children.

The date of Francis's conception tallies with the period during which Elizabeth and Robert Dudley were most rumoured to have engaged in a physical relationship – in anticipation of the imminent death of Robert's wife, Amy Robsart. If Elizabeth had conceived an illegitimate child, placing it within a family such as the Bacons, where there were children by two different mothers and family characteristics were less marked, would have been an inspired idea. Additionally, Sir Nicholas and Anne were suitable in so many other ways: he was a Protestant who had maintained his religion, as Elizabeth had done, even through the reign of Mary I, while his wife was one of Elizabeth's ladies-in-waiting and a fellow scholar in Greek, Latin, French and Italian. Conversely, however, the Bacon household was only a stone's throw from the royal palaces and the alleged foster parents were a daily part of Court life, which might not have been the best way to keep the true identity of such an important baby a secret.

Francis would have spent part of his childhood at York House, as well as at Gorhambury, where he may have attended the local grammar school at St Albans. He was an academically precocious child and was mainly schooled at home by different tutors. At the age of 12, he went to study at Cambridge with his brother Anthony, then aged 14. They went to Trinity College, where Francis, little more than a child, appears to have spoken out on various subjects, as he later wrote his opinion of the university: 'For the studies of men in these places are so confined and as it were imprisoned in the writings of certain authors, from whom if any man dissent he is straightway arraigned as a turbulent person and an innovator.'[1]

In 1576, Francis was placed in the care of Sir Amyas Paulet, the English Ambassador to France, so he could travel to Europe to extend his education. A French author, Pierre Amboise, wrote a biography of Francis, published in 1631, saying of his time abroad:

> ... Mr Bacon ... spent several years of his youth in travels,
> to polish his wit and form his judgement, by reference to the

practice of foreigners. France, Italy and Spain, being the countries of highest civilisation, were those to which this curiosity drew him. As he saw himself destined to hold in his hands one day the helm of the Kingdom, he did not look only at the scenery, and the clothes of the different peoples … but took note of the different types of government, the advantages and the faults of each, and of all things the understanding of which should fit a man to govern.[2]

Since both his father and his uncle, William Cecil, held posts of national importance, at the age of 15, Francis could have, with great reason, imagined himself in a similar position one day.

The travels, however, came to an end when Francis received word that his father, Sir Nicholas, had died on 20 February 1579. He immediately left France for England, but found that his father had already been buried in St Paul's Cathedral. Sir Nicholas's will was not kind to his youngest son: all his bequests went to his wife and to his other children. It has been suggested that Sir Nicholas was planning to make some other provision for Francis and that he died before he could do so. It has also been suggested that, if Francis was not his son, he had left his real parents to provide for the young man.

The first suggestion is possible; the second is almost certainly unlikely. A monarch would usually provide for an illegitimate child, in which case Sir Nicholas would have received additional grants of estates for the sole purpose of endowing them on the child, rather than leaving him penniless and drawing attention to his plight. A third possibility is that Sir Nicholas left nothing to Francis because he was hopeless with money. In later years, Francis would have serious problems with debt.

In lieu of a generous inheritance, in 1579, Francis entered Gray's Inn, aged 18. Within a year, he wrote to his uncle, William Cecil, asking him

237

to petition the Queen for an unnamed post. He emphasized his seriousness in his law studies and reminded Cecil that he had not been 'well left or befriended'. A second letter, written a month later, thanked Cecil in advance; he hoped to serve the Queen as his father had done, and was grateful for his uncle's support.

However, as it turned out, the post never materialized. Perhaps Cecil never used his influence to help his nephew, possibly because he viewed this brilliant young man as a potential rival to his own son, Robert Cecil; thus he could have deliberately suppressed Francis's attempts to advance himself in the royal service. Equally, Cecil may have been wary of the self-importance of the young man, who seemed convinced of his intellectual superiority. Such a man could be dangerous if he achieved a significant role in the political arena before he had gained some real experience of the workings of the Court. Possibly with this in mind, Cecil would later recommend Francis to the voters of Melcome Regis in Dorset, which town would duly return Francis as their Member of Parliament in 1584. A stint in Parliament would give Francis relevant experience and allow him to make his reputation with speeches and presentations.

In the meantime, Francis took up residence at Twickenham Park in 1580, in a house near Richmond Palace that belonged to his half-brother, Edward. Francis's brother, Anthony, who had been travelling in Europe supplying intelligence for the Privy Council, sent Francis a number of books and manuscripts that would support his literary work. In 1581, he helped Francis arrange a tour of France, Spain, Italy, Germany and Denmark to widen his knowledge. The tour lasted about a year and Francis returned home, having enjoyed the company of intellectuals all over Europe.

At this time, Francis was already pouring his energies into writing essays and books. He planned a series of four essays, of which at least two – 'In praise of Knowledge' and 'In praise of his Sovereign' – were published.[3] Francis was also interested in codes and ciphers (possibly because of his brother's work for the Privy Council), an interest that has led some researchers into his works to see each document as a minefield of codes, turning the simplest text into something wildly different.

In 1584, when Francis became a Member of Parliament, it was a period during which a number of Catholic plots to kill Elizabeth were being exposed. In November of that year, a Bill was presented to exclude from the succession to the throne anyone who was found to have been involved in a plot against Elizabeth, prompted mainly by Mary, Queen of Scots' actions. In February 1585, the MP William Parry was found guilty of taking part in such a plot, and was executed.

Francis wrote a lengthy report on the situation to the Queen, suggesting that more might be achieved if penalties against Catholics were relaxed, thus removing some of the cause of their discontent and the temptation to join in with any treasonable plots. He also reasoned that although Scotland and France were troublesome, the real enemy at that time was Spain. In 1589, he penned 'An Advertisement Touching the Controversy of the Church of England'. Neither seemed to gain the Queen's attention. This perhaps seems odd; even if Francis was the Queen's child and she remained reticent about drawing unwarranted attention to that fact, she could, at this time, have advanced him to a generous post on his obvious merits alone. The fact that she did not may suggest that she felt no particular special bond to this talented gentleman.

He wrote to Cecil in 1591 to lament the 'meanness of his estate' and felt he was wasting his time when he might be employed by the Crown in some significant post: '... I wax now somewhat ancient; one and thirty years is a great deal of sand in the hour-

239

glass ... I ever bear a mind, in some middle place that I could discharge, to serve her Majesty; not as a man born under Sol, that loveth honour; nor under Jupiter, that loveth business, for the contemplative planet carrieth me away wholly; but as a man born under an excellent Sovereign, that deserveth the dedication of all men's abilities ...'[4]

In 1592, Francis's brother Anthony returned from a spying mission in France after his arrest at Montauban on a charge of sodomy. Henri de Navarre, a personal friend, had interceded to get him released, and Anthony joined Francis in his lodgings in Gray's Inn. They worked and wrote together, while Francis waited for his political career to take off.

In February 1593, however, Francis made a serious error. Having endeavoured so hard to find favour with the Queen, he managed to offend her in a Parliamentary session. The members had been assembled to vote on a subsidy for the Defence of the Realm, and Cecil asked for an unprecedented triple subsidy. His son, Robert, made the request to the Commons to set the amount of the subsidy, which would then be ratified by the Lords.

Francis stood up and spoke. Cecil, he said, spoke on behalf of the Lords, but it was up to the Commons to set the amount of a subsidy. A vote was held and by 227 votes to 128 it was decided that the representatives of the Lords should withdraw and leave the matter to the Commons. That being done, according to the Parliamentary records:

Mr Francis Bacon assented to three subsidies, but not the payment under six years; and to this propounded three reasons, which he desired might be answered. 1. Impossibility or difficulty. 2. Danger and discontent. 3. A better manner of supply than subsidy. For impossibility, the poor man's rent is such they are not able to pay so much upon the present. The gentlemen must sell their plate and the farmers their brass pots ere this will be paid ...[5]

In the end, the Queen got her triple subsidy, but it was to be paid over six years, instead of the four she had originally wanted. Elizabeth was not amused.

Why Francis did this is a mystery. Perhaps he was genuinely concerned about the rights of the Commons being eroded by the Lords, as well as the burden on taxpayers. Another reason might be that, since the Queen had failed to reward him with a Court appointment he felt he had nothing to lose. On the other hand, he might have wanted to harass the Cecils, who he believed had failed to support him in his ambitions for a successful career in royal service. Or perhaps he simply imagined that his principled stand would make an impression on those who exerted influence at Court or would impress other MPs and set the foundation of a political power base.

The result of his actions was an immediate reprimand from William Cecil, leading Francis to write to him that he was sorry to find that his last speech in Parliament '... delivered in discharge of my conscience and duty to God and her Majesty and my country was offensive. If it were misconstrued, I would be glad to expound my words, to exclude any sense I meant not ...'[6]

Francis insisted that he had spoken as a matter of conscience, believing the tax would be unfair on the poor and had expected no profit from his actions. He was faithful to the Queen, he continued, and desired only to serve her. He begged Cecil to allow him to continue in his own good opinion '... and then to perform the part of an honest friend towards your poor servant and ally, in drawing your Majesty to accept of the sincerity and simplicity of my heart, and to bear with the rest, and restore me to her Majesty's favour.'[7]

The Queen made a good friend, but a bad enemy, and she saw Francis's intervention as an act of disloyalty. In 1593, the post of Attorney General fell vacant. Robert Devereux, 2nd Earl of Essex, who was friendly with the Bacon brothers, immediately recommended Francis for the post. His legal background made him an ideal candidate, and Devereux, who at the time was a firmly established favourite with Elizabeth, believed his wish would be the Queen's command.

However, there was another candidate in the running, Edward Coke, who was already Solicitor General and nine years older than Francis. He was an experienced practitioner in the Law Courts, whereas Francis was more interested in the theoretical side of law. Francis, realizing that he needed to placate the Queen, wrote to her that he was aware that his 'Majesty had taken some displeasure towards me' and 'I most humbly crave pardon of my boldness and plainness.'[8] As an apology, it left something to be desired. There was no sense of supplication, rather a justification of his having spoken his own mind.

It ended up being too little, too late. Even though Francis was allowed to attend the Court once more and Devereux reported that although Her Majesty had brought up Francis's subsidy speech again she seemed to have forgiven him, New Year came and went and the post of Attorney General remained vacant.

In March, the Queen made her decision – the new Attorney General was to be Edward Coke. This left his former post of Solicitor General vacant when he moved up, and both Devereux and Cecil recommended Francis for it. Devereux wrote to Francis, 'I find the Queen very reserved, staying herself from giving any kind of hope, yet not passionate against you till I grew passionate for you. Then she said that none thought you fit for the place but

242

my Lord Treasurer [Cecil] and myself.'[9] Francis was disappointed and bitter. He felt he had been led to an 'exquisite disgrace'. He would, he said, give up the Court, retire to Cambridge and return to his academic studies.

Matters were exacerbated by Francis's financial situation, which was dire. Anthony, his brother, had written to their mother asking if she would help pay Francis's debts. She had replied that although she loved him, she felt that he could not be trusted to manage his money and that he chose his friends unwisely as they exploited his largesse.[10] She would consider helping Francis if he were to give a full account of his debts and hand over control of his estates and finances to her to sort out on his behalf. Francis refused and, in the end, it was left to Anthony to raise the money to settle his debts. Between September 1593 and April 1594, Francis borrowed £358 from Anthony, who had to mortgage his estate to raise the money.

The post of Solicitor General remained unfilled. In 1594, a plot was discovered, supposedly to poison the Queen, but perhaps, in fact, to poison Don Antonio, a pretender to the throne of Portugal. The plotters, including the Queen's physician, Dr Lopez, were found guilty and executed. One of those most closely involved in the investigation of the charges was Devereux, with Francis as one of his chief assistants.

In the summer, a second plot was discovered and again Devereux and Francis were involved in the investigation and questioning of suspects. The Queen knew of their involvement and one of her favoured administrators, Sir Fulke Greville, told Francis that the Queen had spoken 'with very exceeding gracious inclination towards you ... So I will lay £100 to £50 that you shall be her Solicitor ...'[11]

Desperate now to catch the Queen's attention, Francis wrote a

243

memorandum on methods for ensuring her safety in light of the recent plots. In August the investigation was halted when the suspects started to confess, but as the role of Solicitor General was still vacant, no trial could be held. Francis's mother actually met with Robert Cecil to ask if the post could not be given to her son. Robert's reply was to remind her that the Queen often prevaricated; they would just have to wait.

Francis began to believe that he was the victim of a conspiracy to deny him advancement. He wrote a letter to Cecil in which he stated that he had received information from a friend who personally had nothing against the Cecils, that:

> ... from your servants, from your Lady, from some counsellors that hath served you in my business, he knew you wrought underhand against me ... as I reject this report, though the strangeness of my case might make me credulous, so I admit a conceit that the last messenger my Lord and yourself used dealt ill with your Honours ... for I am not ignorant of those little arts. Therefore I pray, trust not him again in my matter. [12]

Francis's letter managed to accuse Cecil of working against him, while insisting he gave such rumours no credence. In terms of his Court ambitions, he told Fulke Greville that he felt like '... a child following a bird, who when he is nearest flieth away and lighteth a little before, and then the child after it again, and so on ad infinitum ...'[13]

In October 1595, the new Solicitor General was appointed – not Francis but Sergeant-at-Law Fleming, soon to be Sir Thomas Fleming. An experienced and much admired lawyer, Fleming already had some influence at Court since his wife's father, Dr

Mark James, was the Queen's personal physician. Fleming was later confirmed in his post in 1603 by Elizabeth's successor, James I, and was knighted a year later. He would go on to become Lord Chief Justice of England in 1607.

At the time, Francis must have been devastated. Devereux, on the other hand, was furious. Years later when Francis wrote his recollection of the events, he recalled Devereux's response: 'Master Bacon, the Queen hath denied me you place for you ... you fare ill because you have chosen me for your mean and dependence; you have spent your time and thoughts in my matters; I die (these were his very words) if I do not somewhat towards your fortune; you shall not deny to accept a piece of land which I will bestow upon you.'[14]

After some persuasion, Francis agreed to accept the gift, telling Devereux that he would be faithful to him all his life in acknowledgement of what he owed him, and, should he ever become rich, he would give the equal value of this gift to one of Devereux's supporters who was likewise in need. He would be his 'homager', his liegeman, in return for the £1,000 that he was able to sell the land for.

In the same year, Anthony Bacon left his brother's lodgings in Gray's Inn and moved into Essex House, the home and base of Devereux, who by this time was building up a powerful group of nobles and was starting to disobey the Queen. Anthony acted as Devereux's secretary and ran his personal intelligence service, using his European experience and contacts to help him. He translated foreign communications, surveyed maps and invented and broke codes. Essex House also became a centre for Devereux's literary friends, who included Francis Bacon. Under Devereux's patronage, many talented poets, scholars, writers and artists of the time were given a place to meet, work and exchange ideas.

As the century came to a close, Devereux was heading slowly

and inexorably towards disaster, though. In 1596, intelligence reported a Spanish fleet, a second Armada, massing at Cadiz. Sir Francis Drake had died at Porto Bello in the Caribbean and the fleet was now led by Lord Howard of Effingham (Charles Howard, 1st Earl of Nottingham). Devereux, Sir Thomas Howard and Sir Walter Raleigh served under him. The force succeeded beyond even its own wildest dreams, successfully taking Cadiz in the process. The Queen's orders had been that they should destroy the fleet and return home since she had no need of a conquered Spanish city to garrison, provision and defend. While her officers agreed with her orders, Devereux protested, to no avail, and as they headed back to England, his suggestion that they remain at sea and try to intercept the treasure fleet due in from the West Indies was also ignored.

When the fleet arrived back, Devereux found himself held up as a hero to the people, but he received a different response from the Queen, who was angry with him. Elizabeth felt that while she had spent good money on the fleet, her forces had not taken advantage of the situation; they had failed to take any valuable prizes and had not even attempted to capture the treasure ships. Her ire was focused on Devereux – somewhat unjustly considering that he had shared her aims and had tried to persuade his colleagues to pursue them, but had been overruled. Devereux, in turn, was extremely angry with her response.

As one of his dearest friends, Francis wrote Devereux a lengthy letter, warning him that he could ill afford to offend the Queen. He was 'a man of nature not to be ruled', Francis said, and he did not have a great fortune fit for his position. He was also a soldier and popular with the people, and if the Queen truly took against him, she could ruin his life, keep him poor, and punish him and everyone and anyone who loved and supported him. Devereux should bear this in mind when dealing with Elizabeth, Francis warned. Giving in to her, as Robert Dudley or Christopher Hatton might have done, and asking no great favours was the best way to react. He should play down his military past, 'let that be a sleeping honour awhile', and he might regain the Queen's favour and be better able to serve himself and his followers.[15] It was good advice, but Devereux did not follow it.

In 1597, Francis published his first acknowledged work *Essays*, dedicated to his brother Anthony, and the *Meditationes Sacrae*. He also began to pursue Elizabeth, the granddaughter of William Cecil and the widow of Sir William Newport, the nephew and heir of Sir Christopher Hatton. Such a marriage would have solved the problem of his finances as Elizabeth was a very wealthy woman, but Francis was one of several suitors for her hand.

In September, matters came to ahead when Francis, arrested for debt while leaving the Tower after interrogating someone, was accused of trying to poison the Queen. He owed £300 to a goldsmith. He wrote to Sir Thomas Egerton, Lord Keeper of the Great Seal, and to Robert Cecil, who was Secretary of State, to try to get matters resolved, but in the meantime, his old rival Sir Edward Coke married the desirable widow, again pipping him to his desired post. If it was any consolation, the marriage would turn out to be a miserable union.

In that same year, Devereux was made Lieutenant-General and Admiral of a substantial fleet whose orders were to first go to Ferrol in Galicia and destroy the Spanish fleet harboured there, and then to proceed on to the Azores and intercept the Spanish treasure fleet. The project was a disaster from start to finish, however. The winds blew in the wrong direction, and when the ships finally left port they ran into a ferocious storm that drove most of them back. When they were finally refitted, it was decided that the fleet should go straight to the Azores. Devereux was in command, with Sir Walter Raleigh and Sir Thomas Howard acting as vice-admirals. Devereux and Raleigh argued, and while waiting for the treasure fleet, they managed to miss the bullion ships altogether. Another attempt to seize one of the islands and win a significant prize similarly failed, leaving the luckless fleet to limp back home in shame.

It seemed Devereux's luck had ended. In 1599, he led a further disastrous military campaign in Ireland, which destroyed his reputation and sent him spiralling on the path to his destruction. He was ordered to go north to Ulster and attack the forces of Hugh O'Neill, Earl of Tyrone; in fact he went south and lost several engagements. To compound matters, he knighted some of his followers, expressly against Elizabeth's orders, as only she could confer knighthood. Francis, who had always been a friend to Devereux, advised the Queen to bring him home, 'for to discontent him as you do and yet to put arms and power into his hands may be a kind of temptation to make him prove cumbersome and unruly.'[16] This advice proved premonitory. Elizabeth could no longer trust Devereux.

In September, far from attacking O'Neill, Devereux met with him to negotiate a truce and left Ireland against the Queen's orders. Two weeks later he was back in London with 200 soldiers. He rode out to Nonsuch Palace and surprised Elizabeth in her bedchamber before she had had time to dress or have her hair pinned up. She managed to placate him before having him confined to his rooms. The next day Francis arrived and managed to see his friend for a few minutes. Again, his advice was sound; Devereux should not present his negotiations with O'Neill as a victory – which they certainly were not. He should remain quiet and humble and say nothing to the Queen about returning to Ireland. In the end, however, his advice was irrelevant. Devereux did not meet with the Queen at all; instead he was sent to York House and Elizabeth began discussions with her Council as to how he should be treated.

The popular mob supported Devereux and thought he had been badly treated. Francis suggested that the Queen should make some small gesture in honour of his achievements to placate the people. Elizabeth knew the perils of being seen to give in to someone like Devereux, however, and this informed her decision. On 29 November 1599, charges were formally laid against Devereux without Francis in attendance, something that particularly annoyed the Queen. He defended himself, saying that he could not be present as he did not want to fuel the rumours, started by his enemies, accusing him of being instrumental in the charges laid against Devereux. As Devereux and the Queen were both popular, Francis was being painted as the villain behind the scenes.

Whether on the advice of Francis or not, the Queen decided that the charges should be heard by the Council in private to avoid further public outcry. However, with unfortunate timing for Devereux, the historian Sir John Hayward published *The First Part of the Life and Raigne of King Henrie IIII*. The subject was Henry IV, who had usurped the throne of Richard II, and the book was dedicated to Devereux. In it, Richard II was described as a bad ruler and the writer praised Henry IV for deposing him in the name of the people of England. The book also included a section featuring examples of rulers deposed for the good of the country.

Elizabeth passed the text to Francis, asking if he found the text treasonable. He replied, jokingly, that he did not, although he found some felonies there: '… the author had committed very apparent theft, for he had taken most of his sentences of Cornelius Tactitus …'[17] The Queen's reaction was to appoint Francis as one of the four Crown Counsels to present the case against Devereux, in particular the charge that Devereux had sponsored Sir John Hayward's book, giving 'occasion and countenance to a seditious pamphlet'.

Francis asked to be excused from this duty, but was denied. The hearing took place at York House on 5 June 1600. Devereux admitted to the charges that he had made a treaty with O'Neill rather than vanquishing him in battle, and that he had left Ireland without permission. The Council effectively found him guilty. As punishment, he was removed from certain Court posts and placed under house arrest.

Francis was asked by Elizabeth to prepare an account of the proceedings. When he read his report to the Queen, he was delighted when she indicated that she had been moved by the words of Devereux (as reported by Francis) and told him 'that she perceived old love would not easily be forgotten.'[18]

Francis began in earnest to try to rehabilitate his friend. He came up with the idea of creating two letters, one supposedly from his brother Anthony to Devereux, and the other, Devereux's reply, in which he could remorsefully show that he had been justly reprimanded and could be safely forgiven. Francis would then arrange for the Queen to 'accidentally' read the letters. This would make the contents seem more honest than a letter written directly to the Queen herself.

This ploy may have worked, as in July the house arrest was ended. Francis continued to help Devereux write to the Queen in a bid to regain her favour, even drafting letters for him to copy. In August, Devereux was freed completely, although he was forbidden to attend Court. While this was an improvement in his situation, he was denied a basic income and he began to despair. By October, Devereux's frustration was bordering on mad desperation and his behaviour became increasingly erratic. He lost his temper in public and insulted the Queen. The situation reached a point where even Francis was no longer able to help him. Devereux now crossed the line.

In early 1601, Devereux began to fortify his house and on Sunday, 8 February, he rose in rebellion against the Queen, marching into London with a party of noble followers. However, the popular support he had relied on completely failed to materialize and by 10 p.m, the whole affair was over. He was immediately proclaimed a traitor and was imprisoned in the Tower. When the rebels were interrogated, some swiftly turned on him, betraying Devereux's plans to seize the Queen, force her to dismiss those Councillors who he claimed were his enemies and make him some kind of Supreme Minister, her only adviser.

On 19 February, Devereux was brought to trial, where his defence was that he had only sought an audience with the Queen and that his enemies were working against him. This time, Francis, who had always stood by him in the past, said that the Earl's paranoia reminded him of a Greek character who wounded himself and then claimed it had been done by his enemies. When Devereux rejoined that Francis himself had previously sympathised with him, Francis agreed, saying he had 'spent more time in vain in studying how to make the Earl a good servant to the Queen and state, than he had done in anything else'.[19]

Francis must have known that Devereux was doomed and had no desire to fall with him, hoping instead to save some shred of credibility with the Queen. The outcome of the trial was a foregone conclusion. Devereux was condemned to death. He was beheaded on Tower Hill on 25 February 1601. Shortly after, in May 1601, Anthony Bacon died, and so Francis lost the two most important people in his life within a few months of each other.

Elizabeth never did shower Francis with the advancements he so badly wanted during her lifetime. When the Queen died in 1603, he hoped for more success under the new King, James I of England. Francis wrote a letter praising the King and hoping he might serve him as he had served his predecessor. Part of the letter reads, '... there is no subject of your Majesty's who loveth this island ... whose heart is not set on fire, not only to bring you peace-offerings ... but to sacrifice himself a burnt offering to your Majesty's service ...'[20] Those who believe that Francis was the son of Elizabeth and Robert Dudley interpret his words as an offer to destroy any pretension to the throne that he might have as the quasi-lawful son of the Queen. In reality, it reads rather more as him offering unqualified service to the King.

Francis did meet the King, but before James could make any moves in his favour or against, Francis was once again arrested for debt. This time his cousin, Robert Cecil, settled the bill and secured his release. He may also have provided him with the funds to purchase a knighthood, as Francis had written to him, 'I desire ... to marry with some convenient advancement ... I have found an alderman's daughter, an handsome maiden, to my liking.'[21] The young lady was 11 year old Alice Barnham, who was an heiress with a dowry of £6,000 in land and £300 a year in income. So Francis and Alice were betrothed, to marry when she came of age, and on 23 July 1603, two days before James I's coronation, Francis was knighted with 299 other gentlemen who had paid a suitable fee for the honour. The 45-year-old Francis would marry Alice on 10 May 1606 when she was just 14.

In June 1607, Francis was at last rewarded with the post of Solicitor General. Then in 1608, he published a retrospective history of the reign of Elizabeth I, *In Felicem Memoriam Elizabethae Reginae Angliae*. Those who believe Francis was Elizabeth's son point to a reference made in the book to Elizabeth being childless, like Alexander the Great and Julius Caesar. However, Alexander had a son, Alexander IV, who was born posthumously, while Caesar had a daughter, Julia, and an illegitimate son by Cleopatra, Ptolomy Caesarian, and was rumoured to be the real father of Marcus Junius Brutus. Given his knowledge of history and the classics, it is unlikely that Francis would have made such a basic mistake and that he was, indeed, suggesting that Elizabeth did have a child – although he did not make any reference to his or her identity.

In August 1610, Francis's mother, Anne, died. She had shown little affection for her son and towards the end of her life became a fanatical Puritan, obsessed with Catholic plots. In 1589 she had accused her eldest and favourite son, Anthony, of being a traitor, saying that he was plotting to kill her for her money. She believed that Anthony and Francis had Catholic friends who might lead them away from the path of True Religion, so she cursed Anthony and said that she wished he had died before his religious beliefs became corrupted. Anthony, the sweet peacemaker, must have been miserable to see his mother deteriorate to such a degree. For her funeral, Francis arranged for a sermon that she would have approved of, but, as he wrote to his fellow politician Sir Michael Hicks, 'Feast I make none.'[22]

253

In 1613, Francis was appointed the new Attorney General. At last he was in receipt of a respectable salary, which would be augmented by additional fees and bonuses that would finally give him a decent income. In 1616, he took out a lease on a house in London – Canonbury Tower in Islington. The site was likely to appeal historically to Francis; it had been an estate of the medieval Knights of St John of Jerusalem, and then belonged to the Priory of St Bartholomew. At the Dissolution it was given to Thomas Cromwell and then passed through several owners until, at the time Francis took out his lease, it was the property of Henry Howard, 1st Earl of Northampton.

The rooms were decorated with panelling and carving that some have interpreted to support theories that Francis was a

Freemason and a Rosicrucian. The first recorded English lodge of the Freemasons fraternal society (possibly descended from the medieval Guilds of Masons) was set up in the mid-1600s. The Rosicrucians were a mystical secret society founded in Germany in the early years of the 1600s whose symbol was a cross with a rose on it, which was also a symbol used by the Freemasons. The evidence presented for these theories is that Francis wrote *The New Atlantis*, published in 1627, about a utopian country led by an academic, scientific, monastic group called Solomon's House. As the name of Solomon and the notion of Solomon's Temple were linked to Freemasons and Rosicrucians, the hypothesis was that Francis was a member of these societies. However, the interpretation of the carvings may be open to question. Moreover, some of the decorations may have been in the house before Francis arrived, or added after he left (he lived at Canonbury for six years).

254

The year of 1616 brought long-awaited advancements for Francis, who found James I more appreciative of his talents than Elizabeth had been. He prosecuted the famous trial of the Earl and Countess of Somerset, Robert Carr and Frances Howard, for the murder of Sir Thomas Overbury in the Tower, and won the King's desired outcome: that the defendants plead guilty so they could be imprisoned and later discreetly released.

Francis also wrote a series of letters to James I's new favourite, Sir George Villiers, later 1st Duke of Buckingham, advising him of his duties and responsibilities, as well as warning him of potential dangers. An appreciative Villiers supported Francis as a candidate to replace the elderly Lord Ellesmere as Lord Chancellor, and in March, Ellesmere, already ill, decided to retire. Francis made him a single payment of £8,000 and stepped into the position with the agreement of all parties. He was now Lord Keeper of the Great Seal, the post his father, Sir Nicholas, had held. Francis finally held a position that would pay him a generous salary: perhaps £10,000 to 15,000 a year from the pay and perquisites.

Francis continued, for the most part, to stay in the King's favour, although he almost fell out with him and Villiers over an incident that occurred in 1617. The former Lord Chief Justice Sir Edward Coke, having lost the King's support, tried to regain it by offering his daughter, Frances, as a wife for Villiers' dissolute and slow-witted brother. When the young lady and her mother, Lady Hatton, objected, Coke kidnapped his daughter and tried to force her to marry. Francis, who thoroughly disliked Coke, sided with his wife, falling foul of Villiers, who wanted the wealthy heiress for a sister-in-law, as well as the King, who wanted his favoured Villiers to have his way.

Francis immediately backed down and later nobly refrained from gloating when Lady Hatton refused to make her daughter heiress to her fortune, thereby not benefiting the Villiers family as they had hoped, and Frances herself promptly left her husband and ran off with another man. Despite this, Francis was made Lord Chancellor in early 1618, and in May was created Baron Verulam.

Throughout this time, Francis continued writing essays, publishing *Novum Organum* in 1620, his textbook on the application of 'a new logic, teaching to invent and judge by deduction'.[23] He believed that Man could not move forward as long as he based his reasoning exclusively on his own prejudices, common folklore and previous knowledge. Starting from the beginning, everything should be re-examined and tested. His status as a philosopher and thinker was much admired by his contemporaries. The poet George Herbert in his poem 'The Temple', called Francis 'Truth's High Priest', 'Liberator of Science', and 'Master of what's real'.[24]

At Court, Francis advised, but stepped back when it seemed politic to do so. In February 1621, he received another sign of the

255

King's favour when he was created Viscount St Albans. However, his successes would be transformed to public disgrace a month later when a series of claims were made in Parliament that Francis had taken bribes. Since the salaries of public officials were low, it was not uncommon for them to embellish their income by taking fees and favours; it was quite in order to accept a 'gift' from a successful applicant after the fact. It was not, however, acceptable to receive a gift before a judgement, which was what Francis was accused of by two clients who had subsequently lost their cases.

Francis could not deny that irregularities had taken place. He appealed to the King in the hope he would save him, but James I was already facing opposition to favours he had issued to benefit Villiers. On the King's instruction, Francis surrendered the Great Seal and sent a letter of submission acknowledging the charges to the House of Lords. He confessed to corruption, responding to each of the 26 charges to indicate that most of them related to misunderstandings (for example, a gift had arrived on 1 January and had been recorded as a New Year present, not a gift relating to a case) or gifts given after a case had been decided. He was therefore confessing to a series of clerical errors, but not to actual bribery.

The Lords, some of whom held grudges against him, sentenced him to a fine of £40,000, imprisonment in the Tower at the King's pleasure, disqualification from any state post, from standing as a Member of Parliament, and from coming to the Royal Court. He was briefly imprisoned in the Tower and then returned to his childhood home. He was not to stay there for long; Villiers let it be known that he wanted York House, and Francis's pardon was delayed until he agreed to sell. Francis retired to Gorhambury.

For the rest of his life, Francis would devote his time to his academic work. He translated his earlier work *The Advancement of Learning (De Augmentis Scientiarum)* into Latin, revising and improving the text. He worked on his only fictional book *The New Atlantis*, with its utopian civilization of experimentation, learning and knowledge. He also started a major work, *Historia Naturalis*, and began working on a chapter on the history of life and death, which looked into the possibility of extending life.

In 1625, the year in which James I died and was succeeded by Charles I (King of England and Ireland 1625–49), Francis published a translation of the psalms from Latin to English, dedicated to the poet George Herbert. He also published a second book of essays, adding new ones to those published in 1612 and improving some of the existing ones. It is this selection that has enjoyed the most popularity over the centuries.

In this work, small insights into the man himself appear, as in the section 'Of Parents and Children', in which the childless Francis wrote, 'the noblest works and foundations have proceeded from childless men; which have thought to impress the images of their minds, where those of their bodies have failed.'[25] In 'Of Marriage and the Single Life', he noted that single men were more likely to undertake great adventures and to make the best friends and masters. A hint of longing from a man perhaps not happily married? He wrote movingly on the subject of friendship, but his feelings on love indicate that all might not have been well with his wife.[26]

By the end of 1625, he was seriously ill. In December, he wrote his final will, adding a codicil that cancelled his bequests to his wife. He stipulated that she should only have as much as the law allowed to a widow from her husband's estates. Four months after his death, Alice married her gentleman usher, Sir John Underhill.

Early in 1626, Francis was in London to attend Parliament, but was too sick to do so. He set off home for Gorhambury, but was taken ill on the way and stopped at the house of Thomas Howard, 21st Earl of Arundel, at Highgate, where he died on 9 April 1626, aged 65.

257

According to his wishes, he was buried quietly in the Church of St Michael's near St Albans, and it is here that a magnificent monumental statue of Francis stands. A second statue stands in the Chapel of Trinity College, Cambridge. He died with enormous debts; it seemed that he was as hopeless with money as his mother had warned.

Over the years Sir Francis Bacon has been the focus of much speculation. Some claim that he wrote the works published under the name of William Shakespeare, while others contend he had an even greater 'concealed literary career', writing under the names of John Lyly, George Peele, Stephen Gosson, Christopher Marlowe, Robert Greene, Thomas Lodge, Thomas Kyd and Thomas Nashe (playwrights), Edmund Spenser, Geoffrey Whitney and William Webbe (poets), Timothy Bright and Robert Burton (writers on melancholy). It is also claimed that he translated all or part of the King James Bible and penned the novel *Don Quixote*, published in 1605 under the name of Miguel de Cervantes.

And as for the evidence of Francis being the illegitimate child of Elizabeth I and Robert Dudley? Apart from researchers attempting to interpret the codes and ciphers that Francis so loved and concluding that they can be decoded to show 'that Francis was the elder son of a secret marriage between Queen Elizabeth and Lord Robert Dudley' there is no conclusive evidence. Elizabeth certainly did not grant him the favours that she showed to other members of the Court, and in fact seemed to impede his advancement. It is possible that this may have been a calculated diversion to avoid drawing attention to her parenthood, but apart from Francis's birth date there is little to indicate that he was the Queen's illegitimate son. But if Francis was not Elizabeth and Robert's son, who was?

11

The Case of Arthur Dudley

∿

I n June 1587, a boat was intercepted off the northern Spanish coast and a young Englishman was taken in for questioning, suspected of being a spy. He was sent to be interviewed at the house of Sir Francis Englefield, who had been a Catholic politician under Mary I and had fled to Spain under Elizabeth I's reign. What the captive had to say caused something of a stir, in Spain and later in England.

According to the young man, his name was Arthur Dudley. He was about 25 years old, which means he would have been born in about 1561. He had been brought up in a village near London in the household of Robert Southern, whose wife had been a servant to Kat Ashley. Arthur had lived as a normal member of the family until, at the age of five, he, alone among his brothers and sisters, was taken to London to be brought up as a gentleman. At the age of eight, Arthur was introduced to Sir John Ashley, Kat Ashley's husband and Elizabeth's senior gentleman attendant, who made Robert Southern his Deputy Controller of the Queen's household at Enfield. This is where the boy spent his summers, while in winter he stayed in London and received an upper-class education, with classes in Latin, French, Italian, fencing, music, dancing and law.

When Arthur was about 15, he told Ashley and Southern that he wished to go abroad to study, but his request was declined.

Arthur stole a purse of silver coins from Southern and headed for Milford Haven, hoping to be taken on board a ship for Spain, a country he had longed to visit. He ended up taking refuge in the house of George Devereux, the brother of Walter Devereux, 1st Earl of Essex; however, before he could get on a ship, Arthur was arrested by order of the local justices of the peace. The order for his detention had come from the Privy Council, which had instructed that Arthur was, under no circumstances, to be allowed to leave England. According to his interviewer Englefield's notes, 'This letter still remains in the castle of Llanfear, in the hands of George Devereux, and was seen and read by Richard Jones and John Ap Morgan, then magistrates of the town of Pembroke, who agreed that the respect thus shown to the lad by the Council proved him to be a different sort of person from what he had commonly been regarded.'[1]

Arthur was returned to London and taken to Pickering Place, where he was met by Sir Edward Wotton, the owner of the house; Sir Thomas Heneage, a favourite courtier of the Queen; and his guardian John Ashley, also close to the Queen, who all impressed on him that he must never do such a thing again. He was also told that it was Ashley, not Southern, who was paying for his education.

About four years later, after persistent pleading, Arthur was allowed to volunteer as a soldier to fight in the Netherlands under the protection of French Colonel de la Noue. In 1580, he was taken to de la Noue at Bruges in the care of a servant in the livery of Robert Dudley, 1st Earl of Leicester. De la Noue was later captured, and Arthur went on his own to France, returning to England for a brief time for additional funds.

Late in 1583, while still in France, Arthur received a letter from home, telling him that his father was ill and wished to see him before he died as he had something important to tell him. Arthur returned home and found Robert Southern at Evesham, where he had become an innkeeper. Before his death, he informed Arthur that he was not his father. He told him that in 1561, he had been sent for by Kat Ashley and ordered to go to Hampton Court. In a corridor leading to the Queen's private rooms, he met Lady 'Herington' (possibly Isabella Harington, one of Elizabeth's attendants), who gave him a newborn baby. He was told that the illegitimate child belonged to a lady at Court and its existence had to be concealed from the Queen. Southern took the infant to a mill at Molesey, where the miller's wife acted as a wet nurse for the baby. Later Southern took the boy to his home, about 60 miles from London, and brought him up as his own child in the place of one of the Southern children who had died in infancy. Arthur, Southern told him, was the baby in question.

Southern refused to say who Arthur's real parents were, and the young man left him in anger. He was called back by Mr Smyth, a local schoolmaster, and Southern finally agreed to reveal his parents' true identity as the young man had good reason to know. He claimed that Elizabeth I herself was Arthur's mother and Robert Dudley his father. In a state of understandable shock, Arthur fled to London, where he sought out Sir John Ashley. When he told Ashley and a Mr Drury (perhaps Sir Drew Drury, Gentleman Usher of the Privy Chamber and Lieutenant of the Tower) what Southern had told him, rather than deny it, the two gentlemen warned him to say nothing further about the matter. If he remained quiet, steps would be taken to provide for him in a fitting manner.

Their attitude and obvious agitation at his news persuaded Arthur that his newfound knowledge might be dangerous, and he returned to France as soon as possible. He went to the Jesuit College at Eu in Normandy, where he told the rector part of his story, but did not reveal everything. The rector recommended that he visit the Count of Eu, Henri, Duc de Guise, but Arthur went

261

instead to the Jesuit School in Paris, where he had heard there was an English priest, Father Thomas. Again, Arthur did not reveal the full story, fearing that the French might use the information against England if they found out his true identity. He wrote to Ashley, who never replied. He then wrote to Edward Stafford, the English Ambassador in Paris, telling him only that he had been the foster-child of Robert Southern 'whose memory she [Queen Elizabeth] had reason to have graven on her heart'.[2]

When it looked as if there was a possibility of war between France and England, Arthur set sail for home on a vessel belonging to a Mr Nicholson of Ratcliff. When they arrived at Gravesend, Arthur must have appeared suspicious to Nicholson, who threatened to have him arrested. Arthur wrote a letter to Robert Dudley and persuaded Nicholson to have it delivered; years later, Nicholson was proud to report that the great Earl of Leicester had thanked him most kindly for this service. As they passed Greenwich, two of Robert Dudley's attendants came on board and transported Arthur to Greenwich Palace. There, Arthur met Robert Dudley in person. Arthur reported that Robert had taken him to his rooms where he confirmed that he was, indeed, his father. He claimed that Robert had cried over him, and left Arthur to believe that he would do all he could for his beloved son.

The arrival of this mysterious youth, however, had not gone unmarked. Sir Francis Walsingham, the Queen's spymaster, had informants in the other ships in the convoy back to England, and Arthur's appearance was reported to him. Robert duly contacted Walsingham, stating that Arthur was a friend. Robert told his son, 'You are like a ship under full sail at sea, pretty to look upon but dangerous to deal with.'[3]

At first, Walsingham accepted the story and agreed to issue a licence to allow Arthur to travel freely without molestation. But when Robert took Arthur to meet Walsingham in person, once the spymaster had seen the young man, he began to drag his heels about the document. After their first meeting, he asked to see Arthur again. Frightened that he was about to be unmasked and fearing the consequences, Arthur went to the French Ambassador de la Mauvissière to ask for a passport for France. This was arranged; Arthur was to travel as the Ambassador's servant.

When they got to Gravesend the next morning, Arthur found his passport would only be validated if he presented it to William Brooke, 10th Baron Cobham, Lord Warden of the Port, who was presumably checking the papers of everyone using the port. However, fortune smiled on Arthur that day; he was able to leave the country after joining English soldiers on a troop transport sailing for Flanders; he landed with them at Bergen-op-Zoom.

It seems that, at this point, Arthur's allegiance to England and her Queen began to wane and he became involved in various plots to forward the Catholic cause. Englefield's report of his interview with Arthur relates 'Arthur's plot with one Seymour to deliver the town of Tele to the Spaniards, which plot was discovered ... He opened up communications with the elector of Cologne and the Pope ... After many wanderings about Germany he received a messenger from the Earl of Leicester at Sighen, but to what effect he does not say.'[4]

Had Robert become aware of his son's activities? Was he trying to bring him back to the English camp? Whatever the reason for that contact, Arthur went on a pilgrimage to Our Lady of Montserrat in Catalonia, visiting the shrine in October 1586. While in Spain in early 1587 he heard of the death of Mary, Queen of Scots and decided to go to France by ship. It was at this point that in June 1587 he was found off the Spanish coast and questioned. As he was an Englishman, Arthur's tale that he was a

Catholic and had just completed a pilgrimage was felt to be suspicious, so he was arrested and held in San Sebastian. When he asked to speak to Sir Francis Englefield, he must have decided that he risked being imprisoned or worse by the Spanish and so revealed his incredible story.

Arthur said he had decided to go to France because he was terrified that his fate would be the same as Mary, Queen of Scots, who had been executed. Robert Dudley, he believed, had plotted against Mary and this had contributed towards her death. He wrote in a letter to Englefield that he was worried that agents of the Queen would seek him out and arrange to have him murdered so that the secret of his birth would never be known.

He reminded his captors that there were other claimants to the throne of England apart from James VI of Scotland: he named Henry Hastings, 3rd Earl of Huntingdon (a descendant of the house of Plantagenet), and Edward Seymour, the eldest son of Catherine Grey. He added, presumably with himself in mind, '... both of them are descendants of Adam, and perhaps there is someone else who is their elder brother.'[5] If Philip II would protect him, he offered to write an account of the truth of his birth and life, which the Spanish could use as they liked. In the book he would reveal all, but show that he was '... everybody's friend and nobody's foe'.[6] He suggested that once this had been done, he could write to Robert, his father, so as to keep his good opinion.

Englefield did not know what to think of the young man's story. Arthur seemed to be as well educated and well travelled as he claimed to be, but there were many possibilities and Englefield certainly suspected that Elizabeth's Court 'may be making use of him for their iniquitous ends'.[7] Perhaps it was all a plot engineered by Elizabeth, to dupe the Spanish into acknowledging the young man as her son so that he could be offered as a possible heir to the throne, cutting James VI of Scotland out of the succession? Perhaps he was just a spy with a cover story so strange that he would either be believed or thought a lunatic; in either case, he would be released and allowed to go on his way?

Finally, Englefield came to the tentative conclusion that there was a good chance that Arthur was telling the truth:

> … it is also manifest that he has had much conference with the Earl of Leicester, upon whom he mainly depends for the fulfilment of his hopes. This and other things convince me that the queen of England is not ignorant of his pretensions; although, perhaps, she would be unwilling that they should be thus published to the world, for which reason she may wish to keep him [Arthur] in his low and obscure condition as a matter of policy, and also in order that her personal immorality might not be known (the bastards of princes not usually being acknowledged in the lifetime of their parents), and she has always considered that it would be dangerous to her for her heir to be nominated in her lifetime, although he alleges that she has provided for the Earl of Leicester and his faction to be able to elevate him (Arthur Dudley) to the throne when she dies, and perhaps marry him to Arabella (Stuart). For this and other reasons I am of opinion that he should not be allowed to get away, but should be kept very secure to prevent his escape.[8]

265

Although Arthur's claim was by no means proved, the Spanish Crown clearly felt it was sufficiently believable that it could cause political troublemakers to latch onto the story and create problems for them. As neither Englefield nor Philip II were willing to take any chances, it was ordered that Arthur be sent to a monastery for the time being. As his name does not occur again in Spanish or English records, it may be that he remained in the monastery until his death, or that he escaped and his elaborate cover story, no longer needed, was simply discarded.

So was Arthur Dudley, as he reported himself to be, the son of Elizabeth and Robert? His upbringing and experiences seem to make this unlikely. Firstly, it seems odd to go to the effort to bring up a child in secret only for the custodian to later tell him of his true parentage. The whole point of a secret child is that it remains secret. Also, a royal child would have been more likely to be placed in a household of minor nobility or gentry, rather than with an assistant estate manager who ended up as an innkeeper. Secondly, a potential, albeit illegitimate, heir to the throne would hardly have been allowed to roam around Europe unchaperoned for ten years. Countries hostile to England could have used him for their own ends or had him terminated if he had told his story to anyone. Thirdly, while Robert was apparently fond of Arthur, Elizabeth seems to have had no maternal feelings for the man. If she had felt her throne was threatened, she would have had no qualms about ordering his death for the good of the country.

What is more plausible is that part of the story is true. A child may have been handed over to Robert Southern at the palace in 1561. At this time, Robert Dudley was still courting Elizabeth, but perhaps had liaisons with other women as well. It is possible that Arthur was indeed the son of Robert, but by a lady at Court, not by the Queen. We know from the Queen's reaction to Robert's marriage to Lettice Knollys in 1578 that Elizabeth would have reacted badly to any lady who had an affair with her beloved Robert. She might expect, at the very least, to spend some time in the Tower and to be exiled from the Court, never to return. It was therefore exceedingly likely that such a baby would be born and smuggled out of the Court as soon as possible without any word of it getting back to the Queen.

Perhaps Arthur himself invented the story that Elizabeth was his mother, or may have come to this conclusion of his own accord since rumours about Robert and Elizabeth's relationship were rife. Or it is possible that Robert may have allowed this myth to take shape. In an attack on Robert Dudley published in 1584, *Leicester's Commonwealth*, the writer suggests that Robert would try to foist one of his illegitimate children on the throne by pretending that the child was Elizabeth's, and to this end the wording of the Act of Succession had been changed to allow the Queen's 'natural issue' as opposed to 'lawful issue'.

The book charged that Robert had 'contracted to her Majesty' that 'he might have entitled any one of his own brood (whereof he hath store in many places, as is known) to the lawful succession of the crown ... pretending the same to be by her Majesty' and that he was behind the decision to put 'words of Natural Issue' into the statute of succession for the crown, against all order and custom of our realm ... whereby he might be able after the death of her Majesty to make legitimate to the crown any one bastard of his own by any of so many hackneys as he keepeth, affirming it to be the natural issue of her Majesty by himself.'⁹

Another possibility is that Arthur's life history is more fiction than fact, and that Robert Dudley was not his father. Perhaps the exceptionally intelligent son of an estate manager was educated beyond his social class and invented a much grander parentage for himself than the dull and humble Mr and Mrs Southern. All the grand Court officials that intervened in his life may simply have been trying to straighten out the son of one of the Ashleys' servants who seemed to be set on creating chaos for his parents and himself. His rushing from one European Royal Court to another, involved in plots and chases, could just have been the fertile imagination of a young man who had to embroider an otherwise normal life. If this was the case, he must have loved his time at the Spanish Court, where he was the centre of attention. Philip II himself read Arthur's story and his future was discussed at the highest levels. He would live out the rest of his days in comfort, supported by the Spanish exchequer, perhaps in the calm and quiet of a monastery.

The last possibility, one that Englefield himself considered, is that Arthur was a spy. Here was a young Englishman who had travelled in France, Spain and the Netherlands, all political hotspots where English intelligence was needed. The story Arthur presented would explain why he might have been seen at places from Normandy to Paris, Flanders to Cologne, and why he moved so freely between England and Europe, returning home to renew his finances or meet with Robert Dudley. If a run-of-the-mill spy were to be apprehended, he might claim to be a sailor, a student, a merchant or a minor diplomat, trying to create some credible persona that would pass the scrutiny of the secret services springing up all over Europe.

Perhaps Arthur, justly concerned about ending up in prison or on the gallows, invented a magnificent, quite spectacularly original alibi that he was the illegitimate son of the Queen of England, wandering Europe trying to make sense of his life and avoiding the English agents sent after him. If his research was good and his story plausible, as it seems it was, then even a faint chance that he was telling the truth would be enough to save him. Perhaps the reason he is never again mentioned in the Spanish records is that, after a suitable period of grateful retreat paid for by the King of Spain, Arthur simply slipped away and came home, dropping the character of 'Arthur Dudley' that had so usefully served its turn, and reporting back to Robert Dudley and the spymaster Francis Walsingham all that he had learned during his travels.

12

The Case of
John Harington

✺

If Sir Francis Bacon and Arthur Dudley are to be discounted, then who could have been Robert and Elizabeth's son? John Harington is another possibility. Records show that he was born on 4 August 1560 in Kelston, Somerset (near Bath) to John Harington and his second wife, Isabella Markham, who were both in the service of Elizabeth I. Harington Senior was a poet and musician, a courtier and favourite of both Henry VIII and Elizabeth I. His first wife had been Etheldreda Malte, the illegitimate daughter of Henry VIII by Joanna Dingley. As discussed in a previous chapter, Harington Senior and his first wife, Etheldreda, had one child, a daughter, named Hester, who may have actually been the illegitimate child of Elizabeth and Thomas Seymour, 1st Baron Seymour of Sudeley. This would have made Etheldreda and her husband the foster parents of this royal child. Certainly Harington Senior was extremely loyal to Elizabeth and had served sentences in the Tower of London on two different occasions rather than betraying the princess when she was out of favour. Elizabeth would not forget his loyalty when she became Queen.

In the last days of Mary I's reign, in November 1556, Elizabeth met with the Spanish Ambassador de Feria to discuss which ministers she would keep and which she would remove when she acceded to the throne. Along with Robert Dudley and William Cecil, she also mentioned John Harington Senior.

After his first wife's death, John approached Isabella Markham, whom he had loved for many years, to ask for her hand. Isabella, the daughter of a knight, was by then a gentlewoman in the Queen's Privy Chambers. Unfortunately, Isabella's father did not give his approval in spite of intervention by the Queen in 1558, so it was not until his death in 1559 that the couple were able to marry. In June that year, before the marriage, records show that Elizabeth granted Harington Senior a life post 'for his service, to John Harington, the Queen's servant, of the office of receiver general of the revenues of lands in Nottinghamshire and Derbyshire'.[1]

After the marriage, a grant of land followed 'to John Harington [he and his male heirs], the queen's servant, and Isabel his wife, a gentlewoman of the privy chamber – of lands relating to Lenton and Radford, Nottinghamshire'.[2] In that same year, 1559, they had their first child, Elizabeth, and on 4 August 1560, their first son, John, was christened in the parish of Allhallows, London Wall.[3] Three other sons were to follow: Robert in about 1562, Francis in 1564 and James in 1565.

During these years, Harington Senior and Isabella were faithful members of the royal household. In 1562, they gave New Year gifts to the Queen, Mrs Harington giving a smock 'all over wrought with black silk', and Mr Harington offering 'a pair of sleeves and a partelett [the cloth that covered the upper chest and neck and supported the ruff], embroidered with gold and silver set with pearls'.[4]

If John was born in August 1560, that would mean he was conceived in December 1559, but if the Queen were his true mother, would this have been possible? As early as April 1559, foreign ambassadors to the Court were noting that Elizabeth allowed Robert Dudley unprecedented access to her. His

270

apartments at Court adjoined the Queen's. As Spanish Ambassador de Feria put it, '… her Majesty visits him in his chamber day and night'.[5]

At the time, Robert was granted honours by the Queen, being awarded the Order of the Garter in April. In May, the Venetian Ambassador remarked that 'My Lord Robert Dudley is in very great favour and very intimate with her Majesty.'[6] By late 1559, the ever-vigilant Kat Ashley, Elizabeth's companion and First Lady of the Bedchamber, was warning Elizabeth about her relations with Robert and how they were perceived by those who wished her mischief. In December, von Breuner, the Ambassador to the Holy Roman Emperor, wrote 'The Queen has more than once been addressed and entreated by various persons to exercise more prudence and not give people cause to suspect her in connection with this man …'[7]

Bearing all this in mind, it is, therefore, not impossible that Elizabeth fell pregnant over the Christmas and New Year festivities in 1559. It is often assumed, given that Arthur Dudley claimed to be born in 1561, the same year as Francis Bacon was born, that Elizabeth's alleged child was conceived during late 1560, but it could equally have been in late 1559. Elizabeth and Robert would have been 26 years old, she in the first flush of freedom as the new Queen, and he as her favoured courtier. It is known that their relationship was close, so it is not too hard to imagine that it was sexually intimate.

At the time, Robert's wife, Amy Robsart, was terminally ill. Elizabeth and Robert may have gone through a promissory form of marriage to allow themselves sexual relations until they could officially marry. If Elizabeth found herself pregnant, she would have had to conceal it to full term since Amy's death did not occur until September and the baby was born in August. In this case the bonny boy could have been handed over to two people who could be trusted absolutely to look after the child, nurture and protect him, and see him settled in adulthood. It was perhaps even the second time Harington Senior had fostered one of Elizabeth's children, if she was indeed Hester's mother.

Provision was made for the child in March 1563, when Elizabeth made a grant of the manor and ex-priory of Lenton in Nottinghamshire to Harington Senior, his wife Isabella and their male heir, their eldest son John. The Queen was his godmother (over the years she would end up with 102 godchildren), while his godfathers were Thomas Howard, 4th Duke of Norfolk, and William Herbert, 1st Earl of Pembroke, rather illustrious godparents for the son of a country gentleman from Somerset in the Queen's service.[8]

John was a clever child and went to Eton, like most young boys of a certain social standing at the time. By the age of 15, he was attending King's College, Cambridge, where he may have been quite surprised to receive a letter from his godmother, the Queen of England, containing a copy of a recent speech she had made to Parliament:

> Boy Jack, I have made a clerk write fair my poor words for thine use, as it cannot be such striplings have entrance into Parliament Assemblies as yet. Ponder them in thy hours of leisure and play with them till they enter thine understanding, so shalt thou hereafter perchance find some good fruits hereof when thy godmother is out of remembrance, and I do this because thy father was ready to serve us in trouble and thrall.[9]

Presumably the intelligent and enquiring mind of the young man had impressed Elizabeth, who seemed to take a discreet interest in

272

his intellectual development. From 1578, when John was 18 years old, his tutor was Dr John Still, whom he would later describe as:

> ... my reverent tutor in Cambridge ... who, when myself came to him to sue for my grace to a Bachelor [of Arts], first he examined me strictly, and after answered me kindly, that the grace he granted me was not of grace, but of merit, who was often content to grace my young exercises with his venerable preference, who, from that time to this, hath given me some helps, more hopes, all encouragement, in my best studies.[10]

John's tutor obviously made a deep impression on him with his kindness and support, and may have been a positive role model for this young man who would become an author and master of art. John would later help his former tutor reclaim some lands that had been claimed by Sir Thomas Heneage.

Shortly after his arrival at Cambridge, the Lord High Treasurer, William Cecil, his father's friend, wrote him a typical uncle's letter on the importance of study and learning, counselling, 'For at a good lecture you may learn more in an hour that a good teacher, perhaps, hath been studying for a day, and yourself by reading shall not find out in a month.'[11] He said that if John studied hard, he would become 'a great comfort to your father, and praise to your mother, an honour to the University that breeds you, a fit servant for the Queen and your country, for which you were born, and to which, next God, you are most bound; a good stay to your self, and no small joy to your friends, which I, that loves you, both wish and hope of.'[12]

In 1579, the Queen sent her godson a copy of her translation of one of Marcus Tullius Cicero's familiar epistles ('Tully to Curio').

She considered John would enjoy her work as he too had skill as a translator. Like her, he was a talented linguist, fluent in Latin, Greek, Spanish and Italian. He was also interested in mathematics and science, which were Robert Dudley's favoured subjects.

The lucky young man was not only in correspondence with the Queen and her chief minister, but also with one of Elizabeth's top advisers, the spymaster Sir Francis Walsingham. In 1580, he wrote the statesman a courtesy letter in Latin to inform him that he planned to study law on leaving Cambridge.

The letter also indicates that he was befriended by one of the Queen's favourites at the time, Robert Devereux, 2nd Earl of Essex. Translated, his letter finished, '… a young man of the highest nobility and remarkable virtue, the Earl of Essex, has treated me with great kindness. This he does, partly from the goodness of his nature, partly from consideration for my duties, but most of all because he regards me as numbered among those whose interests and welfare matter to you.'[13] Devereux was a skilled hand at ingratiating himself with promising young men who could be useful contacts at the Royal Court.

John left Cambridge in 1581 and, like many young noblemen, went to Lincoln's Inn to study law and associated subjects. Then in July 1582, when his father died, John returned to the family home to administer his estates, principally St Catherine's, Kelston and Batheaston around Bath.

He put his writing talent to use in a poem he penned about his city, which shows his penchant for risqué verse:

Of going to Bathe

A common phrase long used here hath been,
And by prescription now some credit hath:
That divers Ladies coming to the Bathe,

Come chiefly but to see, and to be seen.
But if I should declare my conscience briefly,
I cannot think that is their Arrant chiefly.
For as I hear that most of them have dealt,
They chiefly came to feel, and to be felt. [14]

Although he had studied the law, John was drawn by writing. Between 1582 and 1590, his great project was a translation into English of the Italian poet Ludovico Ariosto's epic romance poem *Orlando Furioso*. Apparently after translating a section dealing with the unfaithfulness of women, John, in a spirit of levity, had it circulated among the Queen's ladies-in-waiting, whom he felt must be fed up with their daily routine of needlework (they 'cannot always be pricking at clouts').

Elizabeth was apparently not amused, and ordered him to leave the Court until he had translated the whole text (over 33,000 lines of verse) to make amends for his insults to womankind. She may not have believed he would undertake such a challenge, but he completed it in 1591, as well as a biography of Ariosto, a commentary on the text and an index. It was published to great acclaim with a splendid frontispiece of a portrait of John and his favourite dog, Bungey. [15]

A support in this major task was John's wife, Mary Rogers (his 'sweet Mall'), whom he had married in 1583. It was a happy marriage, despite his wife hating his frequent absences at Court. [16] According to John, the Queen once jestingly asked his wife 'in merry sort' how she kept her husband's love, and Mary replied 'in wise and discreet manner' that she did 'persuade her husband of her own affections, and in so doing did command his.' [17]

John wrote a small, gentle verse on sweet Mall that shows his tenderness to Mary:

275

> *Your little dog that barked as I came by*
> *I struck by hap so hard, I made him cry;*
> *And straight you put your finger in your eye*
> *And lowering sat. I asked the reason why.*
> *'Love me and love my dog,' thou didst reply,*
> *'Love as both should be loved.' 'I will,' said I,*
> *And sealed it with a kiss ...*[18]

The couple had 15 children, many of whom died in infancy or childhood. The eldest, James, may have married and emigrated to America; the house and estates at Kelston were passed to another son, John, who married Dionysia Ley and established the English family line. (The Kelston Harington family should not be confused with that of a distant cousin, Sir John Harington, 1st Baron Harington of Exton, who became the guardian of James I's daughter, Elizabeth, and whose son, yet another John, became a close friend and servant to James I's son, Henry, Prince of Wales.)

Although John wrote on many light-hearted matters (he said of the Queen, 'Her Highness loveth merry tales'), he also had a more serious side. In 1590, he wrote the scholarly, religious work *A Discourse showing that Elyas must personally come, before the Day of Judgement*, and the unpublished, serious study *A Treatise on Play*, on how gambling (practiced by many nobles) might have ill effects on the young and vulnerable, and how this might be counteracted. He also supported the restoration of Bath Abbey, which had been stripped of its lead and allowed to fall into ruin, spending 20 years persuading sponsors and donors to help renovate the building.

The Queen had apparently forgiven John for the *Orlando Furioso* incident, since just after its publication she visited John at his principal residence at Kelston while on one of her progresses. The royal visit was a success, but painfully expensive, so much so that John was obliged to sell his house, St Catherine's Court in Batheaston, to pay all the bills. He thereafter lived at his house in Kelston (this Tudor house was destroyed in 1764).

John was running through his money faster than he could replenish it. His friend Devereux advised him to 'lay good hold on her Majesty's bounty and ask freely', so John penned a verse to this effect and bribed someone to place it behind the cushion of the Queen's chair of state. It read:

> *For ever dear, for ever dreaded prince,*
> *You read a verse of mine a little since;*
> *And so pronounced each word and every letter,*
> *Your gracious reading graced my verse the better:*
> *Since then your Highness doth by gift exceeding*
> *Make what you read the better for your reading;*
> *Let my poor muse your pains thus far importune,*
> *Like as you read my verse so – read my fortune*[19]

277

He signed the verse 'From your Highness's saucy Godson'.

Apart from his writing talents, John Harington is also credited with being the inventor of the flush toilet. This is not as incongruous as it first seems since the theory arises from a satirical book that John wrote in 1594 called *A New Discourse of a Stale Subject, called The Metamorphosis of Ajax* ('Ajax' referring to a toilet, in reference to the slang word 'jakes' for a privy). However, the historian Gerard Kilroy points out that the design of a water-closet shown in the middle of the book is actually by Thomas Combe, Harington's servant.[20]

According to John, the book used an earthy subject to broach more serious matters: '... may not I, as a sorry writer among the rest, in a merry matter, and in a harmless manner, professing purposely of vaults and privies ... draw the readers by some pretty draught to sink into a deep and necessary consideration, how to mend some of their privy faults?' Then, as now, it seems toilet humour worked as an effective means of attracting attention as the book was popular.[21] However, the Queen was not particularly amused by John's latest text, partly because it was thought to contain a ribald reference to the late Robert Dudley (who had died in 1588) and was also a coded political attack on certain instruments of state such as torture. John's cousin, Sir Robert Markham, reassured him that the Queen enjoyed his wit, but felt he sometimes took it too far, stating:

> Your book is almost forgiven, and I may say forgotten; but not for its lack of wit or satire ... and though her Highness signified displeasure in outward sort, yet did she like the marrow of your book ... The Queen is minded to take you to her favour, but she sweareth that she believes you will make epigrams and write micasmos ['Micasmus' was his penname for *The Metamorphosis of Ajax*] again on her and all the court; she hath been heard to say, 'that merry poet, her godson, must not come to Greenwich, till he hath grown sober, and leaveth the ladies sports and frolics'.[22]

Unfortunately John gained the Queen's disapproval again after taking part in Devereux's disastrous military expedition in Ireland in 1599 against the rebel Hugh O'Neill, Earl of Tyrone.

The campaign attracted a number of the younger gentlemen of the Court seeking fame and fortune. John was sent by the Queen as Captain of the Horse, partly to keep an eye on Devereux, as well as to keep a record of the activities of the expedition. John's cousin Sir Robert Markham wrote to him, 'You are to take account of all that passes in your expedition, and keep journal thereof, unknown to any in the company; this will be expected of you. I have reasons to give for this order.'[23]

Like many others on the campaign, John was knighted by Devereux, an honour the latter had been expressly forbidden to bestow and certainly not to all his cronies and supporters. However, the light-hearted John apparently did not take the knighthood too seriously: when the list of those receiving the honour was sent to London, he was listed as 'Sir Ajax Harington'.

At the end of September, John corresponded with his servant Thomas Combe, explaining that Devereux had divided his forces, and instead of going north had sent some to Munster in the south and some to Connaught in the west. John had gone to Connaught with four of his Markham cousins, and reported that they had some skirmishes, as had Devereux in Munster, 'without any great loss on either side'. The rebels harried them from the bogs, rocks and woods, and burned everything in their path – tenements, crops and livestock. Amidst the carnage, the pro-English Governor of Connaught took a force of 1,400 men into Sligo, where they were attacked and slaughtered by the rebels. John's cousin Griffin Markham took part in a cavalry charge to try and relieve the battered troops, but was shot and wounded and obliged to retreat. John ended his letter by asking Combe to relay to the Queen the wages that each man, from captain to footman, was receiving and what clothing they were given, for summer and winter. He showed his loyalty to her in the last lines, which read, 'Her Majesty, with wonted grace hath graced our bodies, and may heaven's grace cloth her in everlasting robes of righteousness, and on earth peace to her who always sheweth good will toward all men.'[24]

By late 1599, John wrote a perhaps misjudged report to Sir George Carey, Treasurer-at-war in Ireland and Lord Justice, describing a meeting with the rebel leader O'Neill. John was impressed with O'Neill and they talked about friends they had in common in England. John also enjoyed the company of O'Neill's sons, aged 13 and 15, and gave a copy of his English translation of *Orlando Furioso* to the boys. O'Neill was very pleased and drew John into the negotiations, sending a message via him to Devereux to say that it had been agreed to extend the current truce. O'Neill went on to praise Devereux for the honourable nature of the truce, which he hoped would eventually lead to peace.

Unfortunately, Elizabeth was furious with Devereux's unapproved truce and liberally granted knighthoods, and when John arrived back in England, it was, as he said, 'at the very heat and height of all displeasures'.[25] With Devereux under house arrest in Essex House, he sent John to the Queen to plead for him. John came to Court on December 1599 for this reason, but her Majesty wouldn't budge, thundering, 'By God's son, I am no Queen, that man is above me.'[26] She told John to make himself scarce, to which, he recalled, 'If all the Irish rebels had been at my heels, I should not have been better sped, for I did now flee from one whom I both loved and feared too.'[27]

Despite the dangerous position of being in the Queen's displeasure he retained his humour, writing to his friend, the diplomat Sir Anthony Standen, on 20 February 1560, 'I was threatened with the Fleet [prison]; I answered poetically, that, coming so late from the land-service [army] I hoped I should not be pressed to service in her Majesty's fleet in Fleet-Street.'[28] As a close supporter of Devereux who had spoken in person with O'Neill, he had stayed out of prison and he commented on his good fortune: 'After three days every man wondered to see me at liberty.'[29]

The Queen, loath to punish John unheard, at last granted him an audience at Whitehall, where in John's own words, as she was herself 'accuser, judge and witness, I was cleared and graciously dismissed'.[30] His friend Devereux would not be granted the same fate and was beheaded for treason on 25 February 1601.

During this episode, the statesman and patron of the arts (and incidentally Robert Dudley's nephew) Sir Robert Sidney wrote to let John know that some of his verses and prose writing had been happily received by the Queen. He was also pleased to say that the matter of Ireland, for the moment, was forgiven:

> Your Irish business is less talked of at her Highness's palace,
> for all agree, that you did go and do as you were bidden; and,
> if the great Commanders went not where they ought, how
> should the Captains do better without orders? ... The
> Queen hath tasted your dainties [John's writing] and saith
> you have marvellous skill in cooking good fruits.[31]

281

Sidney reminded John how important it was to retain the Queen's goodwill, she was now showing signs of her age, at 67 years. Elizabeth had stopped going for the long walks she loved and would sometimes be found in tears, remembering her friends and Councillors who had died. She would still dress in finery when required, and would take a little rich cake or wine, but now she walked with a stick and her temper was uncertain.

By 1601, even John was not always welcome at Court. The Queen had a long memory for a slight and her temper now was at its worst. She missed her former favourites and generally suffered from the strictures of old age.

In October, John went to see her to plead a case for one of Sir Hugh Portman's friends and left precipitously. He wrote in a letter to Portman, '... it is an ill hour for seeing the Queen ... I feared her Majesty more than the rebel Tyrone, and wished I had never received my Lord of Essex's honour of knighthood.'[32] He managed to get a short meeting with Elizabeth, but she was unsympathetic, saying, 'if ill council had brought me so far from home, she wished Heaven might mar that fortune which she had mended.'[33]

He went on to describe how she had lost interest in her clothes and now wore the same dress for days without changing her attire. When she ate, it was manchet (bread) and succory pottage (a thick soup of vegetables made with chicory). She kept to her Privy Chambers and was sharp and angry with her attendants. John asked to see the Queen again, but she sent a message back by the Lord Treasurer, Thomas Sackville, Baron Buckhurst, 'Go tell that witty fellow, my godson, to get home; it is no season now to fool it here.'[34] Although so many plots against her over the years had been foiled, she feared more were being prepared and arranged to have a sword kept by her to defend herself.

John was in London for Christmas 1602 and wrote to his wife that the Queen was slowly dying, which deeply saddened him. 'I cannot blot from my memory's table ... her watchings over my youth, her liking to my free speech and admiration of my little learning and poesie, which I did so much cultivate on her command.'[35] The Queen, slipping into forgetfulness, asked him if he had met with O'Neill, and when he replied that he and Devereux had done so, she wept for Devereux, her lost favourite.

John recited a few of his new verses, which made Elizabeth smile briefly, but she admitted, 'when thou dost feel creeping time at thy gate, these fooleries will please thee less. I am past my relish for such matters.'[36] He stayed with the Queen while she interviewed other courtiers, but it was obvious that she could not recall previous conversations, which made her angry. It was the last time John was to see her. He stayed in London during the last three months of her life, only returning to Kelston when she died on 24 March 1603.

John would go on to please Elizabeth's successor, James I of England (also James VI of Scotland). In 1602, John had written 'A Tract on the Succession', a dangerous text laying out the reasons that Mary, Queen of Scots should be the successor to Elizabeth as she had no direct heir. The text was never published, but a copy had been sent to James in Scotland. In the argument he used some of the material from the 1584 book Elizabeth had banned, *Leicester's Commonwealth*, which defamed Robert Dudley.[37]

In April 1603, the new King wrote to John from Holyrood Palace in Scotland:

> To our truly and well-beloved Sir John Harington, Knight, Right trusty and well beloved friend, we greet you heartily well. We have received your lantern [a piece of decorative metalwork in iron, brass, silver and gold, with a gold crown to hold perfume on top], with the poesie you sent us by our servant William Hunter, giving you hearty thanks, as likewise for your last letter, wherein we perceive the continuance of your loyal affection to us and your service: we shall not be unmindful to extend our princely favour hereafter to you and your particulars at all good occasions. We commit you to God, James R.[38]

283

In a letter to the Lord Chamberlain, Thomas Howard, John wrote that he would stay away from Court unless summoned, as the King was already surrounded by gentlemen and ladies keen to offer him their services. He would, he said, stay at Kelston with a saucy verse and a glass of good wine to offer any passing friend. He was still writing on 'matters both of merriment and discretion'; if he came to Court on the strength of his poems, he might find himself drawn into political intrigue. He finished his letter with a sound piece of advice: 'in these times discretion must stand at our doors, and even at our lips too; good caution never comes better, than when a man is climbing – it is a pitiful thing to set a wrong foot and, instead of raising one's head, to fall to the ground and show one's baser parts.'[39]

In May 1603, John corresponded with the Secretary of State, Robert Cecil, regarding a variety of subjects, including some notes on household rules and the care of servants that had been practiced by John's father (for example, a fine of 1d for swearing and 4d for teaching a swear word to a Harington child). Cecil wrote back, promising, 'I shall not fail to keep your grace and favour quick and lively in the King's breast.' He wrote to John about the perils at Court, his attempts to please his new master, and how much there was to be done in this time of transition when all the King's supporters wanted their loyalty to be rewarded. Somewhat indiscreetly, he even added that John was right to avoid the Court for awhile as 'Too much crowding doth not well for a cripple [John was ill, possibly with gout], and the King doth find scant room to fit himself, he hath so many friends as they choose to be called, and Heaven prove they lie not in the end.'[40]

John became embroiled in a series of problems, and the next time he wrote to Robert Cecil was from prison. He had tried to claim lands bequeathed to his father, Harington Senior, through a complicated line of succession. Lady Rogers, his mother-in-law, had also left lands to Mary and her brother Edward when she died in 1601. The contents of her house were bequeathed to the children of both Edward and Mary, but Edward claimed that John had broken into the house and looted it for his own benefit as Lady Rogers lay dying. John's cousin, Sir Griffin Markham, had also been part of the 'Bye Plot' to kidnap King James and force him to have a greater degree of religious toleration towards Catholics.

Although John was not in any way involved in the traitorous plot, he had agreed to stand surety for his cousin, who was now imprisoned with several of his co-conspirators, resulting in John being imprisonedfor non-payment of Sir Griffin's debts after his estateo had been seized by the Crown.

Robert Cecil was slow to save his friend, but luckily John had other contacts who could help him. He had become friendly with one of James I's gentlemen, Sir Thomas Erskine, later Earl of Kellie, Captain of the Guard and Groom of the Stool, who petitioned the King on his behalf. James agreed to arrange for the forfeited estates of Sir Griffin to go to John to settle the debts. This, however, took about a year, and in the meantime, John, fed up with his incarceration, simply escaped. He may have been helped by his wife Mary, who had come up to London, much against her better judgement, and lodged near the prison in Cannon Row. After John had fled, a Westminster bailiff broke into her house looking for him.

John then wrote to Cecil, explaining that Mary had had nothing to do with his escape and he thought it rather hard that she had to suffer the indignity of having her lodgings ransacked. He ended his letter by reminding Cecil that the debts he was imprisoned for were not his own and that Cecil had promised to help him. Cecil's reply was terse and tetchy. He had rather a lot on his plate at that time, he explained, running the country. He had done his best, but hardly needed to be lectured on compassion. He would also appreciate it if John would stop treating him as if he were his 'solicitor'. However, they had been close since childhood and Cecil ended the letter, 'as I have been, your loving friend'.[41]

John's friendship with Robert Cecil was somewhat unusual. Cecil was brilliant, small, very slightly hunchbacked and sensitive, and was possibly the most powerful man in the Council thanks to his father's instruction and guidance. He had a limited circle of friends, the best of whom seems to have been John. By the age of 28, he had been given his first title, knighted by Elizabeth, and made a Councillor. He was also a protégé of Sir Francis Walsingham, so that on his death, Cecil took over the running of the secret service. He served Elizabeth I and then James I as Secretary of State. It was largely down to Cecil's handling of the transition that led to James I assuming the throne so seamlessly, and he was duly rewarded. He was made Baron Cecil of Essendon in 1603, Viscount Cranborne the following year, and 1st Earl of Salisbury in 1605.

John's fortunes improved in 1604, when he was invited to a private meeting with the King. Unsure what to expect, he was relieved to find James most interested in an intellectual discussion: '... he [the King] enquired much of learning, and showed me his own in such sort, as made me remember my Examiners at Cambridge aforetyme. He sought much to know my advances in philosophy and uttered such profound sentences out of Aristotle, and such like writers, which I had never read, and which some are bold enough to say others do not understand.'[42]

The King then turned to his favourite subject of witchcraft, asking John's opinion of certain biblical references and telling him tales of Scottish witches. John, as ever, could not resist a touch of raunchy levity. When asked if he thought Satan favoured old women as his servants, he could 'not refrain from a scurvy jest' and riposted that 'the Devil walketh in dry places', a crude sexual reference to older women.[43]

The King enjoyed the joke, but when they moved on to more serious subjects, including the death of Mary, Queen of Scots, John was more uncomfortable. James told him that there had been a vision seen in Scotland of his mother's severed head before she was executed, and suggested John might like to study the subject of precognition, but that he should be careful which books he consulted as some were particularly evil. They finished their discussion with his Majesty asking John's 'opinion of the new weed Tobacco, and said it would, by its use, infuse ill qualities on the brain, and that no learned man ought to take it, and wished it forbidden.'[44]

John made a good impression on the King, as he did with almost everyone with whom he came into contact. In 1611, the Lord Chamberlain, Thomas Howard, wrote to invite John back to Court, if his health permitted. The King had been asking after the 'merry blade' who had so entertained him before. He required a good stimulating conversation, and the fact that John was a fine, handsome man was a bonus. James had lately taken against people he thought of as ugly and was demanding a better dress code so that those appearing before him looked their best. Lord Thomas did not think this would be a problem for John. He also informed him that any meeting with James I was preceded by one with his current favourite, Robert Carr, and that when speaking to the King, one should keep the conversation light and change subjects frequently. To stay on the King's good side, it was best to ask his opinion and discover that it is, by chance, exactly your own. Admire his favourite horse if you get the chance, and always remark in awe and amazement on any new items you notice about him.

However, John had had his fill of the Royal Court. His last visit had been in 1606, when James I's brother-in-law, Christian IV (King of Denmark and Norway 1588–1648), came on a state visit. There was heavy and indiscriminate drinking, so much so that during a masque the performers and audience were so drunk that the event petered out. The two Kings were escorted out as they could not stand, and a number of ladies were sick or rendered unconscious. John preferred to remain at home in Kelston, reading

287

his Bible and working to restore Bath Cathedral, surrounded by family and friends.

John did write to James I's eldest son, Prince Henry, giving details about John's early life. He described how, during the reign of Mary I, his father, John Harington Senior, was sent to the Tower for 11 months just for taking a letter to Princess Elizabeth and that his mother, Isabella Markham (his parents were not yet married at the time), was removed from the princess's service. His father's first wife, Etheldreda Malte, was one of the ladies who attended Elizabeth in the Tower.

In another rather more famous letter, dated June 1608, John wrote to Prince Henry (then aged 14) about the wit and wisdom of his dog Bungey. He reported that on one occasion, Bungey ran from Kelston to Greenwich Palace to deliver to the Queen a message placed in his collar. He lauded this rare messenger that never 'blabbed' a word about what he carried. On another delivery, he carried two bottles of wine strapped to his sides from Bath to Kelston. John was clearly very fond of Bungey. He had once almost lost him when he was dognapped by some duck hunters who sold him to the Spanish Ambassador. It took John some weeks to find his pet and arrange his return. Bungey had made himself quite at home with the Spaniards, and it was only when John coaxed the dog to do his tricks that they agreed to release him.

Despite their ups and downs, the friendship between John and Robert Cecil endured. One indication of that friendship may be seen in the aftermath of the Gunpowder Plot of 1605. Two of those involved, Henry Brooke, Lord Cobham, and his brother George Brooke, were Cecil's brothers-in-law. Both were found guilty, and although Henry Brooke was reprieved, George Brooke was executed. Another of the plotters, however, was John's eternally plotting cousin, Sir Griffin Markham, who was found guilty, but sent into exile, where he became an excellent spy for the King's secret service.

As with many men in a position of unassailable authority, Cecil was heartily disliked by many factions. He remained close to John, however. In 1612, Cecil, ill with advanced scurvy and skin cancer, came to Bath to take the waters that it was believed might help him, and to be near the one man he trusted. John, himself 'sick of a dead palsy', hurried to Bath to attend his friend. Theirs was a lifelong friendship that lightened the life of the shy and overworked Cecil, who died on 24 May 1612 at the age of 49, after returning home from Bath. John himself died at Kelston on 20 November at the age of 51.

If John was Elizabeth I and Robert Dudley's illegitimate son, there is no evidence that he knew this secret. If anyone other than his real and foster parents knew about his parentage, it would have been William Cecil, who may have passed the knowledge to his favourite and trusted son, requesting Robert to keep an eye on John. He certainly had a number of prominent well-wishers throughout his life, despite the vagaries of his fortunes.

Although some historians have identified Devereux as the Queen's illegitimate son, is it likely? Elizabeth, after all, ended up having him arrested, imprisoned and executed, hardly the kind of treatment one would expect a mother to give her son, even an unacknowledged one. Yet John, who was also involved in Devereux's Irish fiasco, was spared – against all expectations.

Granted, John's infractions were far less serious than his commander's, but it seems that Elizabeth had, in the end, more trust in John than in Devereux. Why though? The latter had spent many years in Elizabeth's favour, it is true, but he was self-centred, rude, arrogant and hot-headed, whereas John was loyal, apologetic, calm and funny. Is it more likely that John, rather than Devereux, was related to the Queen by blood? Perhaps tellingly, a portrait painted of Sir John Harington was thought to look so like Robert Dudley that it was mistakenly titled 'Portrait of Robert Dudley, Earl of Leicester'. But is this proof enough?

13

The Case of Robert Devereux

❧

And so to Robert Devereux. How likely is it that he was the reported child of Robert Dudley and Elizabeth? The birth of Robert Devereux was recorded as 10 November 1566 by his father, Walter Devereux, who would later become 1st Earl of Essex, and his mother Lettice Knollys. When his son was born, the father arranged to have horoscope charts made for the boy. The place of birth is thought to be Netherwood, Herefordshire, although one researcher, using the details on the horoscope chart, puts it in the southwest of London, possibly in the region of Nonsuch Palace.

Wherever the young Devereux put in his first appearance, Walter, an English nobleman serving under Elizabeth I, certainly acknowledged the new baby as his. In September 1576, as he lay dying in Dublin, where he had recently arrived as Earl Marshal of Ireland, Walter Devereux wrote a last letter to Elizabeth asking her to do what she could for the fortunes of his eldest son, then 10 years old, as he had no riches to pass to his children:

> Mine eldest son, upon whom the continuance of my house remaineth, shall lead a life far unworthy his calling and most obscurely, if it be not holpen [helped] by your Majesty's bounty ... I dare not wish him mine office of Earl Marshal

here, lest your Majesty should not think him worthy ... But he is my son, and may more fit in his life than his unfortunate father hath in his possession at his death.[1]

Elizabeth would help his son, who would, in turn, become a royal favourite.

The young Devereux was in fact a cousin of the Queen, by his maternal grandmother, who was Anne Boleyn's sister. When his father died, the boy took the title 2nd Earl of Essex and was made a ward of William Cecil, now 1st Baron Burghley. He was sent to Cambridge for his education, where the Queen sent him clothes and some silver plate. For Christmas and New Year 1577–78, the boy was invited to Court for the festivities. A report of the visit stated:

> On his coming, the Queen meeting with him, offered to kiss him, which he humbly altogether refused. Upon her Majesty bringing him through the Great Chamber into the Chamber of Presence, her Majesty would have him put on his hat, which no wise he would, offering himself in all things at her Majesty's commandment; she then replied that if he would be at her commandment, he should put on his hat.[2]

As no one but a fellow monarch should wear his hat in the presence of the Queen, yet any good subject should obey the Queen in all things, Elizabeth had presented the little chap with a knotty problem – he couldn't win either way. It may have been his refusal to allow her to kiss him that triggered Elizabeth's desire to tease and try to fluster him.

In September 1578, Devereux's mother secretly married his godfather, Robert Dudley, 1st Earl of Leicester. As Dudley had

had an affair with Lettice previously and her 35-year-old husband died rather abruptly, reportedly of dysentery, there were rumours that Robert Dudley had poisoned him. These appear to be unfounded, although Robert may have been instrumental in making sure Walter Devereux was out of the picture as he supported sending him to Ireland. Elizabeth was angry about the secret marriage and made both Robert and Lettice pay for it in many ways over the years, although she remained fond of her old favourite. Robert was very attached to his wife, and would be a devoted husband and father to his four stepchildren.

In 1581, aged around 14, Devereux took his degree and was permitted to go to the Netherlands with his stepfather, where he fought at the battles of Zutphen and Sluys and distinguished himself with his military service. On his return, he was rarely away from the Royal Court and began his rise as the Queen's favourite. The young man had a lively mind and was also a bit of a showman. When Robert Dudley died in September 1588, Devereux seemed to fill the space left in Elizabeth's emotional life by his death. He also took over some of his roles, replacing his stepfather as the Queen's Master of the Horse and receiving Robert's monopoly on sweet wines (he received a fee for all sweet wine imported into England for sale). Perhaps Devereux even looked a little like Robert Dudley, which may have accounted for why he found favour with Elizabeth. Unfortunately, Devereux lacked many of the characteristics that had made Robert so perfect a partner and foil to Elizabeth. He was somewhat arrogant and did not always show proper respect for the Queen.

Historian Lucy Aikin describes him as lacking '... the profound dissimulation, the exquisite address and especially the wary coolness, by which his predecessor [Robert Dudley] well knew how to accomplish his ends ... His character was impetuous, his natural disposition frank; and experience had not yet taught him to distrust either himself or others.'³

Francis Bacon also noted the young man's tendency towards self-destruction. He recorded a conversation between friends discussing Devereux: 'I know but one friend and one enemy my lord hath; and that one friend is the Queen, and that one enemy is himself.'⁴

Despite this, Elizabeth appeared to be besotted. Anthony Bagot, Devereux's steward remarked on how much time the couple spent together, writing: 'At night my lord is at cards, or one game and another with her, that he cometh not to his own lodgings until birds sing in the morning.'⁵

Rumours, of course, circulated that the pair got up to more than card games in those long nights, but the age difference between them was 33 years, and Devereux was still rather childish. He often acted more like a spoiled child than the Queen's lover. He was disdainful and insolent towards Elizabeth's most trusted and honoured courtiers. He even got into a fight with Sir Walter Raleigh, about which the Queen spoke sharply to him. Devereux tried to run off to join the army in the Netherlands, but Elizabeth ordered him back.

He was jealous of the Queen's attention of the young and good-looking Charles Blount, son of Lord Mountjoy, who fought well in the tiltyard. When Elizabeth gave Blount a gold chess queen as a reward, he wore it tied to his arm as a tilting favour. Devereux sniped at him 'every fool must have a favour'.⁶ Blount then challenged him to a duel and wounded Devereux in the leg, but Elizabeth was not overly worried: 'By God's death, it is fit that someone or other should take him down and teach him better manners, otherwise there would be no rule with him.'⁷ She sent the two away from Court until they made friends again, which they eventually did, though a few weeks later she had to stop a duel between Devereux and Raleigh.

In the meantime, the Anglo-Spanish War (1585–1604) had broken out. In 1589, Sir Francis Drake (a hero for his recent plundering of the Spanish treasure fleet and raid of Cadiz harbour, which destroyed some of the ships that would otherwise have swelled the Armada in 1588) was planning a force to invade Portugal, followed by a trip to the Azores to waylay another Spanish treasure fleet. Devereux, like many young noblemen who were short of money, yearned to go with Drake. The Queen told him not to go, but he and his followers slipped aboard the *Swiftsure* to follow Drake. He wrote to Thomas Heneage about his financial difficulties:

What my state now is I will tell you. My revenue is no greater than when I sued my livery, my debts at least two or three and twenty thousand pounds. Her Majesty's goodness has been so great I could not ask her for more; no way left to repair myself but mine own adventure, which I had much rather undertake than offend her Majesty with suits, as I have done. If I speed well, I will adventure to be rich; if not, I will not live to see the end of my poverty.[8]

The Queen, having previously invested in the enterprise, now refused to support the plan. She sent an angry peremptory note to Devereux, stating:

Your sudden and undutiful departure from our presence and your place of attendance, you may easily conceive how offensive it is, and ought to be unto us … We do therefore charge and command you forthwith … to make your present and immediate repair ... Whereof see you fail not, as you will be loth to incur our indignation, and will answer for the contrary at your uttermost peril.[9]

Devereux did not heed this warning, however, and only returned to England after the forces were overtaken with illness and defeat and failed to take Lisbon. Elizabeth, though displeased, did not follow through on her threats.

The following year, in 1590, Devereux secretly married Frances Walsingham, the only child of Francis Walsingham and his wife. She was the widow of the legendary, heroic soldier and poet Sir Philip Sidney, who had been killed in the Battle of Zutphen in the Netherlands in which Devereux himself had fought. Devereux did not reveal their marriage to the Queen until Frances became pregnant. Elizabeth was annoyed, but allowed Deverex to remain at Court with the proviso that his wife should retire to her mother's house in the country.

A year later, Devereux begged to be allowed to fight in France for Henri de Navarre at the siege of Rouen. France was split into factions; the Protestant Henri de Navarre, now Henri IV (King of France 1589–1610), was the uncrowned King, besieged by armies of Catholic loyalists supported by Spain. Elizabeth sent Devereux and his troops to support Henri IV. Devereux led a small force to attack an outer fort at Rouen, where his younger brother was killed in the fighting. When the Queen decided that Henri IV was mismanaging his armies, she ordered Devereux home. Henri IV would take the throne in July 1593 when he converted to Catholicism to win his country.

Back in England, Devereux continued his military career. In 1596, Elizabeth sent a fleet of 120 ships under the joint command of Devereux, Charles Howard (Lord Howard of Effingham) and

Sir Walter Raleigh, first to assist Henri IV in repulsing a Spanish naval assault on Calais, and then to move on to capture Cadiz. Elizabeth wrote to Devereux her wishes that he keep from harm and that God bless his journey and make it successful.[10]

On 15 April, Calais surrendered to the Spanish. When Henri IV refused England permission to try to retake the city, Devereux and Howard went on to their secondary target, destroyed the galleons guarding the harbour and captured Cadiz. Devereux was lauded for allowing the women and children to gather up their possessions and leave the town before it was sacked, a noble and unusual gesture. Elizabeth was pleased to write to her commanders, 'You have made me famous, dreadful and renowned not more for your Victory than for your Courage, nor more for either than for such plentiful life [there were minimal casualties], nor of mercy which may well match the better of the two.'[11]

Devereux wanted to hold Cadiz and wait for a treasure fleet due in from America, but he was overruled by Howard and Raleigh. The ships left for England about 48 hours before the treasure fleet arrived. Elizabeth wanted the war to end; Spain was in no position to mount a counteroffensive.

Flushed with his success, Devereux was enjoying his status with young adventurers who looked to him for danger, excitement and loot. On his return, he found himself very popular and imagined the Queen would reward him and his friends. He expected his supporters to receive posts from the Queen, but she did not comply. Elizabeth made Charles Howard 1st Earl of Nottingham in 1597, partly due to his service at Cadiz, which made the arrogant Devereux furious even though she made him Earl Marshal of England. When news filtered through that Philip II, up in arms over the last raid on Cadiz, was once again assembling a

297

fleet to attack England, Devereux was determined to force the Queen to give him command of the defence. According to a letter from Rowland Whyte, a postmaster of the Court and steward of Sir Robert Sidney, 'Her Majesty, as I heard, resolved to break [Devereux] of his will and to pull down his great heart; who found it a thing impossible and says he holds it from the mother's side; but all is well again, and no doubt he will grow a mighty man of our state.'[12]

Eventually, later in 1597, Devereux was given command of a small fleet with the mission of seeking out and destroying Spanish ships and then moving on to the Azores to try to intercept and capture a treasure fleet. Elizabeth's coffers, like Philip II's, were desperately short of money and both monarchs needed the arrival of such a vast fortune. However, the mission went wrong from the beginning, when bad weather kept the fleet in port, using up their supplies. They were finally able to sail in July, but due to adverse winds and wasted time, the ships headed straight for the Azores to try to intercept the treasure ships.

There was dissension on board from the start, with Devereux arguing with his deputies, Sir Walter Raleigh and Sir Thomas Howard. Through his lack of experience, Devereux fatally moved his ships at a critical moment and the Spanish fleet slipped into port behind them. He had missed his prize by only a couple of hours. The fleet was forced to return home.

Devereux's welcome consisted of a scolding; he had wasted the Queen's precious resources and had neither incapacitated the enemy nor provided the treasury with much-needed gold and silver. Elizabeth wrote him a letter, endorsed by William Cecil, that summed up his character faults, beginning, 'Eyes of youth have sharp sights, but commonly not so deep as those of elder age, which makes me marvel less at rash attempts and headstrong counsels which gives not leisure to judgement's warning, nor heeds advice, but makes a laughter of the one and despises with scorn the last ...'[13]

Devereux also drew the Queen's displeasure with his dalliances at Court. Although happily married, he was a remarkably handsome man and attracted the interest of certain ladies. He tried to keep his affairs secret, but rumours were hard to quell. In 1597, John Harington received a letter bringing him up to date with Court gossip, hinting at a flirtation between Devereux and one of the Queen's servants: '... [Elizabeth] swore she would no more show her [Lady Marie Howard] any more countenance, but out with all such ungracious flouting wenches; because, forsooth, she hath much favour and marks of love from the young earl [Devereux], which is not so pleasing to the Queen.'[14] The advice of Harington's correspondent was that someone should impress on the young lady the need for discretion, that she should carry out her duties modestly and not keep absenting herself, which in itself made the Queen suspicious. She should dress more circumspectly and, above all, she should keep well away from Devereux.

By the end of the 1590s, the Nine Years War (1595–1603) between Irish chieftains and English forces was at a bitter and bloody stalemate and Elizabeth and her ministers were discussing who to select as Lord Lieutenant of Ireland to try to get the upper hand. Devereux put forward Sir George Carew, but Elizabeth chose Sir William Knollys, Devereux's uncle. Devereux argued about the decision and turned his back on the Queen in a temper – a terrible insult. She smacked him round the ear and spat out, 'Go and be hanged,' at which he put his hand to his sword as if he would draw it. It was treason, punishable by death, to draw a weapon in the presence of the Queen. Charles Howard had to come between them, and Devereux stormed off. Elizabeth had had enough; he must apologize and learn to react with a cool head: 'he hath played long enough upon me and now I mean to play awhile with him and stand as much upon my greatness as he hath upon his stomach.'[15]

The Council was split on the Irish question. One group, led by Devereux, wanted war at any cost, and the other, led by William Cecil and his son Robert, favoured peace if it could be honourably achieved. By this time, William Cecil was terminally ill. Elizabeth came to the bedside of her 'Spirit' and fed him herself. Although he never played the lover with her, and had never fitted her picture of ideal male beauty, they were closer than most couples. He had always been honest with her and had been her chief adviser since she had assumed the throne – in turn, she had never betrayed him. Cecil had groomed his son, Robert, as his successor in the matters of gently and tactfully guiding the Queen. William Cecil died on 4 August 1598. Coincidentally, Philip II of Spain died a month later. Elizabeth had lost both her dearest Councillor and her dearest enemy.

With William Cecil gone, Devereux used his influence to gain the post of Lord Deputy of Ireland in 1599 and convinced the Council to let him lead a huge expeditionary force to put down the rebellion. A vast army of 16,000 troops and 1,000 horses was assembled to take down Hugh O'Neill, Earl of Tyrone, who had defeated the previous English forces sent against him. Devereux had a war chest in excess of £250,000 and a host of young Court gentlemen who wished to follow him to fame and glory and win wealth and position.

Not fully trusting Devereux after his debacle in the Azores, the Queen arranged for John Harington to go as Master of the Horse, telling him to report directly back to her about the campaign. Devereux, however, was confident of success, believing he had been given the power to make whatever commands he felt necessary and sure that he would win a great and unsurpassed victory for Elizabeth. As he put it in a letter to John Harington: 'I have beaten Knollys and Mountjoy in the Council, and by God I will beat Tyrone in the field; for nothing worthy her Majesty's honour hath yet been achieved.'[16]

But by July 1599, it seemed clear that Devereux was ignoring the list of instructions he had been given to pacify Ireland. Elizabeth wrote to him complaining that his letters were vague as to what he had actually achieved. He seemed to be spending a lot of money, but not one rebel had been challenged. Indeed, the rebels seemed to be enjoying the fact that they could abuse the Queen of England with impunity. She claimed that Devereux seemed to always lay the blame elsewhere, 'that you are deceived, that you are disgraced from hence in your friends' fortune, that poor Ireland suffers in you – still exclaiming against the effects of your own causes.'[17]

Devereux dissipated his troops' strength in campaigns in the south and west of Ireland, losing many to illness and disastrous engagements, and in the end he was forced to make a truce with the rebel O'Neill rather than beating him in battle. To make matters worse, he took the liberty of conferring a huge number of knighthoods to secure the loyalty of his soldiers, which he was expressly forbidden to do.

By September, the Queen had had enough. She wrote another letter; he had promised so much and done nothing, despite being granted all the men and provisions he requested. She demanded that he write to the Council giving 'a true declaration of the state to which you have brought our kingdom, and what be the effects which this your lordship's journey hath produced'.[18] The letter finished with a scathing criticism of his last report, in which he must have tried to defend his command: 'We have received a letter in form of a cautel [crafty trick], full of challenges [that are impertinent] and of comparisons that are needless, such as hath not been before this time presented to a state, except it hath been done with hope to terrify all men from censuring your proceedings.'[19]

Realizing he was on the verge of permanently alienating his greatest ally, Devereux left Ireland, against orders, to go back to London and make his case to the Queen in person. He arrived at Nonsuch Palace on 28 September. Fortunately he had been persuaded not to return with a large part of his army, which he had considered in order to intimidate his enemies. However, he did make the rash decision to go straight to Elizabeth's bedchamber, even though she had only just got out of bed, where he found her in a loose robe, without make-up or wig. She sent him off to gain the time to prepare herself. When he returned and tried to explain his Irish campaign, Elizabeth refused to be placated. He was put under arrest and sent to the Lord Keeper at York House.

As if to rub salt in his wounds, Devereux's previous rival (though now friend) and one of his junior officers, Charles Blount, was given the task of carrying out the campaign in Ireland. He proved astonishingly good at it, so that in December 1600, Elizabeth wrote him a jokey letter of appreciation. In a previous note, Blount had likened himself to a young servant girl trying to clean out a kitchen. Elizabeth carried on the theme, including a snide reference to Devereux: 'Mistress Kitchenmaid … with your frying pan and other kitchen stuff have brought to this last home [imprisonment or death] more rebels, and passed greater breakneck places than those that promised more and did less.'[20]

She went on to say that he had pleased her by following her orders to the letter. He proved himself worthy of her trust. In March 1603, just after the Queen's death, Blount, now 8th Baron

Mountjoy, finally defeated the Irish rebels and received the submission of O'Neill.

Meanwhile, Devereux, stuck in York House, belatedly realized that he had pushed the Queen too far and claimed he was ill. Elizabeth, as she had done with Robert Dudley when he had a diplomatic illness after they argued, sent doctors. A reconciliation seemed possible – Devereux wrote a grovelling letter of apology, which she accepted, but rather than being freed he was placed under house arrest at Essex House on the Strand. It was three months before he was allowed to move about freely, although he could still not come to Court.

Denied access to the Queen and stripped of his posts, Devereux faced financial ruin. He had lost his monopoly in sweet wines – Elizabeth decided to keep it for herself; if he deserved well of her, he might get it back. Devereux could not accept this. Her actions were, he said, 'as crooked as her carcase'.[21]

His friends, chiefly his sister, Penelope Devereux, Lady Rich (who, despite being married, was having an affair with Charles Blount), Henry Wriothesley, 3rd Earl of Southampton, and Sir Christopher Blount, his stepfather, encouraged him to plan a coup d'etat whereby he would seize the Queen, declare James VI of Scotland the official heir, dismiss and imprison all those advisers he believed were his enemies, place his own men as Elizabeth's Council, and rule as her chief minister and adviser – a sort of Lord Protector. As Devereux's supporters were all in debt, a successful coup would assure them of much-needed patronage.

In a Shakespearian show of hubris, on 7 September 1600, Devereux's supporters hired the Globe theatre and paid to have the Shakespeare play *Richard II* performed, with its message that a noble man might overthrow a weak and corrupt king. Elizabeth heard of this and on 8 February 1601 sent some of her Councillors to Essex House to try to ascertain Devereux's plans. In a moment of panic, he ordered that the delegation be locked in the library.

With Elizabeth at Whitehall, he then tried to start an uprising, riding through Temple Bar shouting that there was a plot against the Queen and him, and beseeching Londoners to rise and support him. Unfortunately for his plans, a royal herald rode after him, proclaiming him a traitor. No one rose in support of the usurper. He retreated to Essex House, where he was arrested that evening by Charles Howard (Lord Howard of Effingham).

On 19 February 1601, he was tried for treason in the Star Chamber, and despite Elizabeth's fluctuating fondness for him, the outcome was a foregone conclusion and he was condemned. Elizabeth signed his death warrant, and on 25 February 1601, Robert Devereux, 2nd Earl of Essex, was executed at the Tower at the age of 35. Devereux's death seemed to cause a change in the Queen. Although he had often been frustrating, foolhardy and pig-headed, Elizabeth never completely recovered from his loss. Now nearly at the end of her life, it was said she complained that she had no one she could trust. She lost interest in her clothes and began to lose weight, lose her temper over nothing and swear more frequently. A gentleman of the Court wrote, 'Her delight is to sit in the dark and, sometimes with shedding of tears, to bewail Essex.'[22]

Elizabeth and Devereux had a turbulent relationship, but he clearly had a special place in her heart. Given the events of his life, it seems unlikely that he was Elizabeth's child, but the timing of his birth does not exclude the idea. It is known that on 12 April 1566, seven months before Robert Devereux was born, Robert Dudley rode into London with 700 footmen wearing his livery and that of the Queen. He went to the house of Edward de Vere, 17th Earl of Oxford, opposite St Swithin's churchyard, where he waited. At the same time, Elizabeth left Greenwich by water in a small boat, attended by two of her ladies-in-waiting, and landed at the Three Cranes on the riverbank by St Paul's Cathedral. There a coach was waiting to take the Queen to St Swithin's.

Sadly, Robert Dudley and his entourage, having waited for her, had already gone. The Queen's carriage set off for Greenwich and passed Robert and his men waiting at the roadside. It was reported, '… she came out of her coach in the highway and she embraced the Earl and she kissed him three times.'[23] He got into the coach with her and they went to Greenwich together. One explanation for this odd outing to meet privately at a church could be that Elizabeth had found herself pregnant and they had agreed to enter into a form of marriage that would protect and legalize their child.

Whether or not Robert Devereux was the child of the Queen, it is quite plausible that his stepfather, Robert Dudley, was actually his father. His mother, Lettice Knollys, had an affair with Robert in 1566, which preceded their later affair in the 1570s. They later married after her first husband died. It may be notable that Walter Devereux called his eldest son Robert, which was not a family name, saving the name Walter for his second son. Robert Devereux's secretary, Henry Wotton, indicated not only that relations between Walter and Robert Devereux were not particularly warm, but that the son had been warned against Robert Dudley:

> I must not smother what I have received by constant information, that his [Robert Devereux's] own father died with a very cold conceit of him, some say through the affection to his second son, Walter Devereux … The said Earl of Leicester betrayed a meaning to plant him [Robert Devereux] in the Queen's favour; which was diversely

interpreted by such as thought that great Artisan of Court [Leicester] to do nothing by chance … Yet I am not ignorant there was some good while a very stiff aversion in my Lord of Essex from applying himself to the Earl of Leicester, for whatever conceit I know not, but howsoever that humour was mollified by time; and by his Mother, and to the Court he came under his lee.[24]

The young Devereux would have heard the whispers that Robert Dudley favoured him for a reason that slandered his mother's morals, but in time Lettice managed to win him round and he accepted Robert's patronage.

For his part, Robert did his best to promote Devereux during his life (he died when Devereux was 22 years old). The year before his death, Robert Dudley asked Elizabeth if his post of Master of the Horse could be given to Devereux. The Queen refused, as she said she had no greater post for Robert to take in exchange. He cheerfully told her that he desired no such post, just that his protégé should take his place (with the attendant £1,500 per year salary). When Robert died, Elizabeth followed his wishes and gave his stepson, or son, the post of Master of the Horse, with all its associations that were so dear to her heart.

Conclusion

Virgin Queen or Secret Mother?

୨୨

A
lthough in the later years of her rule and after her death
Elizabeth's virginity attained an almost mythical status,
contributing to an image of a pure queen devoted to her
people, evidence seems to support the fact that the Virgin Queen
image was a myth. In reality, Elizabeth may have enjoyed sexual
relations with at least one man out of wedlock. She may have flirted
with her numerous suitors, including Thomas Seymour at any early
age, but her extremely close relationship with Robert Dudley when
they were both in their twenties seems to point to something deeper
and more intimate between them.

Given the flurries of rumours, the fact that their rooms were
adjoining wherever they stayed and that they were often together
alone, it is hard to imagine that Robert and Elizabeth did not
consummate their relationship. It is, of course, a matter of
speculation as to what that exactly might have entailed – perhaps
they stopped short of vaginal intercourse. However, as certain
evidence also points to the existence of a secret child borne of their
relationship, it is likely that Elizabeth was not only sexually active,
but a mother as well.

In Hampton Court Palace hangs a portrait of a lady with long
auburn hair worn loose on her shoulders. She is dressed in Persian

costume, with a tall hat, a gold scarf and a full gown embroidered with fruits, flowers and birds. She is pregnant. Around her neck is a fine chain, from which hangs a ring. She stands in front of a tree with one hand resting on the crowned head of a weeping stag. On the tree trunk are the words *Iniusti justa querla* ('A just complaint to the unjust') and *Mea sic mihi* ('Mine thus to me'), and beside the head of the stag, *Dolor est medicina ad(ju)tori* ('Grief is the medicine for help'). The artist was Marcus Gheeraerts, court painter to Elizabeth from 1568 to 1577, or possibly his successor and son who bore the same name. At the bottom is a painted panel with a verse:

> *The restless swallow fits my restless mind / In still reviving, still renewing wrongs;*
> *Her just complaints of cruelly unkind / Are all the music that my life prolongs.*
> *With pensive thoughts my weeping Stag I crown / Whose melancholy tears my cares express;*
> *His tears in silence, and my sighs unknown / Are all the physic that my harms redress.*
> *My only hope was in this goodly tree / Which I did plant in love, bring up in care:*
> *But all in vain, for now too late I see / The shales [husks] be mine, the kernels others' are.*
> *My Music may be plaints, my physic tears / If this be all the fruit my love tree bears.*

308

There have been attempts to identify the lady as Elizabeth I on the grounds that the picture has been in the royal collection since certainly the time of Charles I and, more importantly, that it may have originally been titled 'Queen Elizabeth in Fancy Dress'. That the lady in the picture resembles some of the portraits of Elizabeth also seems to support this thesis. However, if that is the case, it seems to contradict Elizabeth's normal behaviour in every way – to commission a portrait while pregnant is hardly the act of a lady, moreover a member of royalty, desiring to keep that pregnancy a secret.

The imagery of the painting is typical of the Tudor period, when various elements of the picture had symbolic importance: the chosen costume, plants, animals and colours all had significance. Here one of the main items of interest is the verse. The speaker is deeply disturbed by something that has gone wrong in their life; the silent tears of a crowned and weeping stag mirror their sighs. They have not been able to place 'fruit' in the family tree, and will continue to mourn that '… this be all the fruit my love tree bears'.

Yet the woman in the portrait does not look particularly sad – and she is clearly well advanced in pregnancy. Unless the sitter chose to have a portrait made showing her in the late stages of an imagined pregnancy or one of a number of pregnancies that ended in the death of the child, there has to be another explanation.

The imagery and verse could work together if the author of the poem was a man, one who had been married several times, but who has failed to have any children by his first wife or wives. The crowned stag represents his manhood, silently weeping despite his rank (symbolized by the crown), and lacking an heir. Still he rails against his unjust fate. In his grief, he marries again to the lady in the portrait – the 'medicine'. In the tree, to the right of the woman's face, at least two fruits hang. In this interpretation, the portrait is a celebration of the wife who was able to give her husband an heir after many years of childlessness.

The portrait, which is almost certainly not of Elizabeth, typifies much of the kind of 'evidence' put forward to support the idea that Elizabeth bore an illegitimate child. However, this type of evidence neglects to bear in mind that Elizabeth would have strove hard to keep such a child's existence secret rather than draw attention to it.

In my opinion, the easiest to justify are the candidates for a child born in 1548 to Elizabeth and Thomas Seymour. The Bisham baby (or babies) died in infancy, while Hester Harington and Hugh Bethell lived and died away from the glaring public eye of the Court. If one of them really was Elizabeth's child, then they went to the grave with that secret.

The more usually touted candidates for a secret child, fathered by Robert Dudley, are far less 'secret'. These individuals lived more in the limelight: Francis Bacon and Robert Devereux were major figures in Elizabethan politics, and very much part of the comings and goings of the Court. Arthur Dudley was placed humbly, but was later brought to Court and then 'told' of his origins, which in itself is difficult to believe. Of all the four men discussed in the last section of this book, John Harington is the most likely to be the son of Robert and Elizabeth, raised, as he was, far from Court until his own ebullient charm and talent pushed him onto the royal stage.

But if there was an illegitimate child, would it be possible to recognize him or her from his or her resemblance to Elizabeth or the presumed father? Finding definite proof of a family resemblance in a portrait is extremely difficult. It is often impossible to determine how true a portrait may be to the person it represents. However, one portrait of Sir John Harington languished for some time mistitled as 'Robert Dudley, Earl of Leicester'. If only the lost portrait of Hester Harington could be found, perhaps it could be determined if they look like brother and sister, or even if their resemblance was based on Tudor or Harington blood.

From my research, my conclusion is that if Elizabeth did become pregnant and have a child, the period with the most conducive set of circumstances for this to have occurred was in 1548 when she was relatively unimportant, living in a private house surrounded by people devoted to her, and either passionately in love for the first time or the victim of Thomas Seymour's unwanted attentions. A second, but slightly less likely period occurs around 1560, when Elizabth had become Queen.

If a child had been born in either circumstance, the crucial issue would have been to place it surreptitiously so that no shred of scandal could ever be traced back to the Queen. Elizabeth and her inner circle knew that any proof of a bastard could potentially cost her the throne and perhaps her life.

In these circumstances, would she really have been foolish enough to place her son with such high officials as Walter Devereux, 1st Earl of Essex, or Sir Nicholas Bacon, just to fulfil a deep maternal need to keep her child close? And how likely was it that either Francis Bacon or Devereux was her son? The Queen certainly did not show much maternal affection to Francis Bacon during his life and even seemed to dislike him. She was much fonder of Devereux, but if she was his mother, it certainly did not stop her from signing his death warrant.

More importantly, if there was an heir, albeit an illegitimate one, why would Elizabeth have not put him forward as a candidate for the succession? By the 1570s, some elements of the English Court would have rejoiced if the Queen had admitted that she had borne an illegitimate child. It would not have been an unprecedented occurrence, and adroit political manoeuvring could have made it legally possible for the child to accede to the throne.

In my mind this makes it even more unlikely that the child was Francis Bacon, who was a self-proclaimed genius and certainly one of the finest minds of the day. Similarly, it takes Devereux out of the running: despite his braggadocio, he was a charismatic young man, a fine soldier and had the makings of a potentially competent leader. Even Arthur Dudley was a shrewd, quick-witted, handsome young man, who was good at languages, and was imaginative and resourceful. These candidates – a notable academic, a fine soldier or a resourceful spy – might have been welcomed by courtiers such as William Cecil and Francis Walsingham as a possible future King. Certainly, the people of England could have been persuaded to accept as King the illegitimate offspring of the Virgin Queen, since he carried the bloodlines not just of his popular mother, but of Henry VIII as well.

There is one candidate, however, who might not have been quite so welcomed as the future King of England. No one can deny the intellectual capacity of Sir John Harington; his serious works are on a par with much of the outstanding literature produced in the 16th and 17th centuries. However, his reputation at Court was that of a fool, a man who wrote ribald and nonsensical verses and irritated the Queen with his behaviour. John was also often in debt and never gained a position of real power. Of all the candidates likely to be Elizabeth's child, it is John Harington who would have had the most trouble gaining credibility and support as King of England. Thus, this man, impossible for the Queen to acknowledge for the aforementioned reasons, is, for me, the most likely candidate to be the son of Elizabeth I and Sir Robert Dudley, a couple, who, in the end, were an impossible match.

Endnotes

❧

Introduction
1. 'Queen Elizabeth – Volume 13: August 1560', *Calendar of State Papers Domestic: Edward, Mary and Elizabeth, 1547–80 (1856)*, pp. 157–158. No.21.
2. 'Queen Elizabeth – Volume 14V: March 1581', *Calendar of State Papers Domestic, Elizabeth, 1581–90 (1865)*, pp. 9–13. No.34.

Chapter One
1. 'Henry VIII: July 1527, 1–10', *Letters and Papers, Foreign and Domestic, Henry VIII, Volume 4: 1524–1530 (1875)*, pp. 1465–77. No.3218. Vatican Love Letters IV.
2. 'Henry VIII: September 1532, 16–30', *Letters and Papers, Foreign and Domestic, Henry VIII, Volume 5: 1531–1532 (1880)*, pp. 571–89. No. 1370, 1–3.
3. 'Henry VIII: September 1533, 1–10', *Letters and Papers, Foreign and Domestic, Henry VIII, Volume 6: 1533 (1882)*, pp. 449–66. No.1112.
4. 'Spain: December 1533, 16–25', *Calendar of State Papers, Spain, Volume 4 Part 2: 1531–1533 (1882)*, pp. 880–95. No.1164.
5. *The Young Elizabeth*, Alison Plowden, Sutton Publishing 1999, p.45.
6. 'Henry VIII: January 1536, 26–31', *Letters and Papers, Foreign and Domestic, Henry VIII, Volume 10: January–June 1536 (1887)*, pp. 64–81. No.199.
7. Ibid., pp. 349–71. No.876.7.
8. 'Spain: July 1536, 6–15', *Calendar of State Papers, Spain, Volume 5 Part 2: 1536–1538 (1888)*, pp. 187–205. No.71.
9. 'Spain: August 1536, 1–15', *Calendar of State Papers, Spain, Volume 5 Part 2: 1536–8 (1888)*, pp. 218–31. No.85.
10. 'Henry VIII: October 1536, 21–25', *Letters and Papers, Foreign and Domestic, Henry VIII, Volume 11: July–December 1536 (1888)*, pp. 315–49. No.860.
11. 'Henry VIII: July 1536, 21–25', op. cit., pp. 54–73. No.132.
12. 'Henry VIII: August 1536, 1–5', op. cit., pp. 90–103. No.203.
13. 'Henry VIII: August 1536, 16–20', op. cit., pp. 130–38. No.312.
14. 'Spain: January 1536, 21–31', *Calendar of State Papers, Spain, Volume 5 Part 2: 1536–1538 (1888)*, pp. 11–29. No.9.

15. 'Elizabeth: September 1559, 1–5', *Calendar of State Papers Foreign, Elizabeth, Volume 1: 1558–1559 (1863)*, pp. 524–42. No.1303, 16–17.
16. *Elizabeth the Great*, Elizabeth Jenkins, The Companion Book Club London, 1958, p.10.
17. Book of Broadsides, The Society of Antiquaries; 'Henry VIII: January 1541, 1–10', *Letters and Papers, Foreign and Domestic, Henry VIII, Volume 16: 1540–1541 (1898)*, pp. 211–19. No.433.4.
18. 'Spain: Appendix', *Calendar of State Papers, Spain, Volume 5 Part 2: 1536–1538 (1888)*, pp. 497–566. No.214.
19. 'Letters and Papers: December 1539, 16–20', *Letters and Papers, Foreign and Domestic, Henry VIII, Volume 14 Part 2: August–December 1539 (1895)*, pp. 255–62. No.697.
20. 'Henry VIII: December 1540, 1–10', *Letters and Papers, Foreign and Domestic, Henry VIII, Volume 16: 1540–1541 (1898)*, pp. 145–51. No.314.
21. Public Record Office, 31/3/26, fo.134.
22. *Chronicle of King Henry VIII of England: Being a Contemporary Record of Some of the Principal Events of the Reigns of Henry VIII and Edward VI. Written in Spanish by an Unknown Hand.* Martin Andrew Sharp Hume & George Bell (Eds). BiblioLife Reproduction Series.
23. 'Preface' to the *Gospel of St John*, partially translated by Princess Mary, *The First Tome or Volume of the Paraphrase of Erasmus upon the New Testament*, Nicholas Udall, 1548.
24. 'Henry VIII: July 1544, 26–31', *Letters and Papers, Foreign and Domestic, Henry VIII, Volume 19 Part 1: January–July 1544 (1903)*, pp. 596–651. No.1020.
25. 'Henry VIII: October 1545, 21–25', *Letters and Papers, Foreign and Domestic, Henry VIII, Volume 20 Part 2: August–December 1545 (1907)*, pp. 286–300. No.639.3.
26. British Library, MS Royal, 7.D.X, sigs. 2r–5r.
27. 'Henry VIII: December 1546, 1–5', *Letters and Papers, Foreign and Domestic, Henry VIII, Volume 21 Part 2: September 1546–January 1547 (1910)*, pp. 249–59. No.502.
28. *England Under the Reigns of Edward VI and Mary*, Patrick Fraser Tytler, 1839, p.17. *The Life and Reign*

of Edward VI, Sir John Hayward, published posthumously 1630.

Chapter 2
1. *Lives of the Queens of England from the Norman Conquest*, Agnes Strickland, 1864, Volume II, pp 445–6.
2. *The Chronicle of King Edward VI*, British Museum, Cotton MSS, Nero C, x.
3. 'Cecil Papers: 1549', *Calendar of the Cecil Papers in Hatfield House, Volume 1: 1306–1571 (1883)*, pp. 58–80. No.304.
4. Ibid.
5. Ibid.
6. Ibid. No no.
7. Ibid. No no.
8. Ibid. No no.
9. Ibid. No no.
10. *The Young Elizabeth*, op. cit., p.91.
11. 'Cecil Papers: 1549', *Calendar of the Cecil Papers in Hatfield House, Volume 1: 1306–1571 (1883)*, pp. 58–80. No.306.
12. Ibid.
13. 'Edward VI – Volume 2. December 1547', *Calendar of State Papers Domestic: Edward, Mary and Elizabeth, 1547–80 (1856)*, pp.... No.25.
14. MS *Rulers of England*, Box III (Elizabeth I), art.6, The Pierpont Morgan Library, New York
15. British Library, MS Cotton Otho. C.X., fol.236v.
16. *Collection of State Papers, relating to affairs in the reigns of King Henry VIII, King Edward VI, Queen Mary, and Queen Elizabeth, transcribed from original letters and other authentick memorials, left by William Cecill Lord Burghley, Vol. 1*, Samuel Haynes, London, 1740.
17. Ibid.
18. Ibid.
19. 'Edward VI – Volume 6: February 1549', *Calendar of State Papers Domestic: Edward, Mary and Elizabeth, 1547–80 (1856)*, pp. 13–14.
20. 'Edward VI – Volume 5: September 1548', op. cit., pp. 10–11. No.4.
21. Bodleian Library, University of Oxford, MS Smith 19, art.1, fol.1.
22. 'Edward VI – Volume 6: February 1549', op.cit., pp. 13–14.
23. 'Cecil Papers: 1549', *Calendar of the Cecil Papers in Hatfield House, Volume 1: 1306–1571 (1883)*, pp. 58–80. No.287.

24. *England Under the Reigns of Edward VI and Mary*, Patrick Fraser Tytler, op.cit.
25. Ibid.
26. Ibid.
27. Ibid.
28. Ibid.
29. *Collection of State Papers, relating to affairs in the reigns of King Henry VIII, King Edward VI, Queen Mary, and Queen Elizabeth*, op.cit.
30. Ibid.
31. Ibid.
32. 'Edward VI – Volume 6: February 1549', *Calendar of State Papers Domestic: Edward, Mary and Elizabeth, 1547–80 (1856)*, pp. 13–14. Nos.19–22.
33. Ibid.
34. *Collection of State Papers, relating to affairs in the reigns of King Henry VIII, King Edward VI, Queen Mary, and Queen Elizabeth*, op. cit.
35. Ibid.
36. Spain: January 1549', *Calendar of State Papers, Spain, Volume 9: 1547–1549 (1912)*, pp. 327–35, No.17. Also, including the quotation: *Collection of State Papers, relating to affairs in the reigns of King Henry VIII, King Edward VI, Queen Mary, and Queen Elizabeth*, op. cit., p.61–153.
37. 'Cecil Papers: 1549', *Calendar of the Cecil Papers in Hatfield House, Volume 1: 1306–1571 (1883)*, pp. 58–80. No.259.
38. Ibid. No.258.
39. Ibid. No.270.
40. Ibid. No.269.
41. Lansdown MSS, British Museum.
42. Ibid. Nos. 284–5.
43. Ibid. No.294.
44. Ibid.
45. *A History of the Reformation of the Church of England*, Gilbert Burnet, late Lord Bishop of Sarum, Volume 2, Part 2, Clarendon Press, Oxford, 1816, Article 19, p.223.
46. The fourth sermon before King Edward IV, 29 March 1549 in *Sermons by Hugh Latimer, sometime Bishop of Worcester*, J M Dent & Co, London, 1906.

Chapter 3
1. 'Cecil Papers: 1549', *Calendar of the Cecil Papers in Hatfield House, Volume 1: 1306–1571 (1883)*, pp. 58–80.
2. 'Royal Berkshire History', David Nash Ford; www.berkshire history.com/legends/elizab_babe01.
3. MSS, *The Life of Jane Dormer, Duchess of Feria*, Henry Clifford (fl.

1610); transcribed by Cannon E E Estcourt and edited by Rev. Joseph Stevenson, published by Burns & Oates Ltd, London, 1887.
4. 'Royal Berkshire History', David Nash Ford; www.berkshire history.com/legends/elizab_babe02.
5. Ibid.
6. *Mistress Blanche: Queen Elizabeth I's Confidante*, Ruth Elizabeth Richardson, Logaston Press, 2007, p.97.
7. www.wargs.com/royal/camilla.

Chapter 4
1. British Library, MSS Lansdowne 1236, fol.35.
2. Cecil Papers: 1549', *Calendar of the Cecil Papers in Hatfield House, Volume 1: 1306–1571 (1883)*, pp. 58–80.
3. *The Whole Works of Roger Ascham*, Rev. Dr. J A Giles, Vol. 1, Pt 1 (Ed), R. J. Smith, London, 1865.
4. Ibid.
5. *The Whole Works of Roger Ascham*, Rev. Dr. J A Giles, op. cit.
6. *The Norton Anthology of English Literature*, 6th ed., Vol. 1, W. W. Norton & Company, New York, 1993, p.991.
7. *An harborowe for faithful and trewe subiectes*, ['A harbour for faithful and true subjects'] Dr John Aylmer, 1559.
8. Ibid.
9. British Library, MS Cotton Vespasian, F.III, fol.48
10. 'Spain: November 1550', *Calendar of State Papers, Spain, Volume 10: 1550–1552 (1914)*, pp. 184–192.
11. 'Spain: November 1551', *Calendar of State Papers, Spain, Volume 10: 1550–1552 (1914)*, pp. 391–399.
12. 'Spain: January 1551, 26–31', *Calendar of State Papers, Spain, Volume 10: 1550–1552 (1914)*, pp. 203–219.
13. 'Spain: May 1553', *Calendar of State Papers, Spain, Volume 11: 1553 (1916)*, pp. 37–48.
14. *Leicester's Commonwealth: The Copy of a Letter Written by a Master of Art of Cambridge (1584) and Related Documents*, D. C. Peck (Ed), Ohio University Press, Athens, Ohio and London, 1985, p.132–3.
15. From the transcript of Ralph Starkey in the MS. Harl. 35, f. 364.
16. British Library, MS Harley, 6986, art.16, fol.23.
17. British Library, MS Lansdowne, 1236, fol.39.
18. 'Spain: September 1553, 6–10', *Calendar of State Papers, Spain, Volume 11: 1553 (1916)*, pp. 211–229.
19. *Narratio Historici Vicissitudinis*

Rerum quae in inclyto Britanniae Regno acciderunt, Petrus Vincentius, Wittenburg, 1553.
20. 'Spain: September 1553, 6–10', *Calendar of State Papers, Spain, Volume 11: 1553 (1916)*, pp. 211–229.
21. *The Girlhood of Queen Elizabeth: A Narrative in Contemporary Letters*, Frank A. Mumby, Constable & Co, London, 1909, p.83.
'**22.** Spain: November 1553, 26–30', *Calendar of State Papers, Spain, Volume 11: 1553 (1916)*, pp. 387–407.
21. *The Girlhood of Queen Elizabeth: A Narrative in Contemporary Letters*, op. cit., p.143.
24. Ibid.
25. *Lives of the Queens of England*, op. cit., Volume III, p. 78.
26. *England under the Reigns of Edward VI and Mary, from original letters*, Patrick Fraser Tytler, op. cit., Volume 2.
27. *Elizabeth Tudor: The Lonely Queen*, Sir Arthur Salusbury MacNulty, Christopher Johnson Publishers, 1954.
28. 'Spain: February 1554, 16–20', *Calendar of State Papers, Spain, Volume 12: 1554 (1949)*, pp. 100–23.
29. *Archives du ministère des Affaires étrangères , Correspondance politique, Angleterre*, Volumes IX–XX.
30. 'Queen Mary – Volume 4: March 1554', *Calendar of State Papers Domestic: Edward, Mary and Elizabeth, 1547–80 (1856)*, pp. 62.
31. 'Spain: April 1554, 1–5', *Calendar of State Papers, Spain, Volume 12: 1554 (1949)*, pp. 181–206.
32. *Acts and Monuments*, John Foxe, Volume II, 1583, pp.2091–7.
33. 'Spain: April 1554, 21–30', *Calendar of State Papers, Spain, Volume 12: 1554 (1949)*, pp. 220–230.
34. *Acts and Monuments*, op. cit.
35. *The Diary of Baron Waldstein: A Traveler in Elizabethan England*, G. W. Groos (Translator), Thames & Hudson, London, 1981, p.117–119.
36. The Bedingfield Papers: 'State Papers relating to the Custody of the Princess Elizabeth at Woodstock, 1554', C.R. Manning, *Norfolk Archaeology*, Vol. IV, 1855, p.166 onwards.
37. Ibid.
38. *Queen Elizabeth*, Mandell Creighton, The Crowell Historical Classics Series, Thomas E. Crowell Co, New York, 1899.
39. *Acts and Monuments*, op. cit.
40. 'Venice: May 1557, 11–15', *Calendar of State Papers Relating to English Affairs in the Archives of*

Endnotes

Venice, Volume 6: 1555–1558 (1877),
pp. 1041–95.

41. *Queen Elizabeth: Various Scenes and Events in the Life of Her Majesty,* Gladys E. Locke, Sherman, French & Co., Boston, 1913, pp.52–3.

42. *Acts and Monuments,* op. cit.

43. Queen Mary – Volume 8. May 1556, *Calendar of State Papers Domestic: Edward, Mary and Elizabeth, 1547–80 (1856),* pp. 82–4.

44. 'Venice. May 1557, 11–15', *Calendar of State Papers Relating to English Affairs in the Archives of Venice, Volume 6: 1555–1558 (1877),* pp. 1041–95.

45. 'Venice: June 1556, 1–15', *Calendar of State Papers Relating to English Affairs in the Archives of Venice, Volume 6: 1555–1558 (1877),* pp. 472–84.

46. *History of England,* John Lingard, Vol. V, Charles Dolman, London, 1854, p.246.

47. British Library, MS Lansdowne 1236, Fol.37.

48. 'Venice: December 1556, 1–10', *Calendar of State Papers Relating to English Affairs in the Archives of Venice, Volume 6: 1555–1558 (1877),* pp. 831–50.

49. *The Virgin Queen: The Personal History of Elizabeth I,* Christopher Hibbert, Penguin Books, London, 1992, p.58.

50. *Lives of the Queens of England from the Norman Conquest,* op. cit., p.115.

51. 'Venice: May 1557, 11–15', *Calendar of State Papers Relating to English Affairs in the Archives of Venice, Volume 6: 1555–1558 (1877),* pp. 1041–95.

Chapter 5

1. The Distresses of the Commonwealth, with Means to Remedy Them, Armagil Waad/Wade (Clerk to the Privy Council), 1558, in 'Queen Elizabeth – Volume 1: December 1558', *Calendar of State Papers Domestic: Edward, Mary and Elizabeth, 1547–80 (1856),* pp. 116–9.

2. British Museum, MS Reg.17.C.iii.f.2.b.

3. *Fragmenta Regalia, or Observations on the late Queen Elizabeth, her Times and Favourites,* Sir Robert Naunton, 1641.

4. *Annals of the First Four Years of the Reign of Queen Elizabeth,* Sir John Hayward, 1612, p.6–7.

5. *His Booke – Most Approved and Long experienced Water–Works containing the manner of Winter and Summer drowning of Meadow and Pasture…, etc.,* Rowland Vaughan, 1610.

6. *Annales Rerum Gestarum Angliae et Hiberniae Regnante Elizabetha,* William Camden, 2 Vols., 1615 and 1625.

7. *Memoirs of the Court of Queen Elizabeth,* Lucy Aikin, Vol. 1, 1818.

8. *England under the Reigns of Edward VI and Mary,* Patrick Fraser Tytler, op. cit., Vol. 2, 1839, p.23.

9. *The Great Lord Burghley. A study in Elizabethan Statecraft,* Martin A. S. Hume, James Nisbet & Co., London, 1898, p.49.

10. 'Simancas: March 1559', *Calendar of State Papers, Spain (Simancas), Volume 1: 1558–1567 (1892),* pp. 37–46.

11. Public Record Office, State Papers, Domestic, Elizabeth, 12/1/7.

12. Bodleian Library, MSS 'Brief Lives', notes, John Aubrey; first published in full as *Brief Lives chiefly of Contemporaries set down by John Aubrey between the years 1669–96,* Rev. Andrew Clark (Ed.), Clarendon Press, 1898.

13. *The Queen's Conjuror: The Science and Magic of Dr Dee,* Benjamin Woolley, Harper Collins, London, 2001.

14. 'Simancas: December 1558', op. cit., pp. 7–21.

15. *Illustrations of British History, Biography and Manners in the Reigns of Henry VIII, Edward VI, Mary, Elizabeth and James I,* Edmund Lodge, Vol. 1, John Chidley, London, 1838.

16. *Queen Elizabeth and Some Foreigners: being a series of hitherto unpublished letters from the archives of the Hapsburg family,* Victor von Klarwill (Ed.) & Prof. Thomas H. Nash (Translator), Bodley Head, London, 1928, p.94.

17. *Sir Humphrey Gilbert, Elizabeth's Racketeer,* Donald Barr Chidsey, Harper & Brothers, New York, 1932, p.20.

18. *Queen Elizabeth,* Mandell Creighton, Thomas E Cromwell, New York, 1966, p.34.

19. *Memoirs of the Court of Queen Elizabeth,* op. cit., p.320–1.

20. Ibid.

21. 'Simancas: January 1559', op. cit., pp. 21–6.

22. 'Venice: November 1558, 16–30', *Calendar of State Papers Relating to English Affairs in the Archives of Venice, Volume 6: 1555–1558 (1877),* pp. 1547–1562.

23. 'Simancas: April 1559', op. cit., pp. 46–64.

24. 'Elizabeth: June 1559, 1–10', *Calendar of State Papers Foreign, Elizabeth, Volume 1: 1558–1559 (1863),* pp. 298–308.

25. 'Elizabeth: July 1559', *Calendar of State Papers Foreign, Elizabeth, Volume 1: 1558–1559 (1863),* pp. 98–112.

26. *Queen Elizabeth and Some Foreigners,* Victor von Klarwill, op. cit., p.31–45.

27. 'Simancas: May 1559', op. cit., 64–78.

28. 'Elizabeth: June 1559, 26–30', *Calendar of State Papers Foreign, Elizabeth, Volume 1: 1558–1559 (1863),* pp. 337–346.

29. 'Cecil Papers: 1559', *Calendar of the Cecil Papers in Hatfield House, Volume 1: 1306–1571 (1883),* pp. 150–165.

30. 'Simancas: December 1558', op. cit., 7–21.

31. 'Simancas: December 1559', op. cit., pp. 117–120.

32. 'Elizabeth: August 1560, 21–25', *Calendar of State Papers Foreign, Elizabeth, Volume 3: 1560–1561 (1865),* pp. 246–260.

33. 'Elizabeth: October 1559, 11–20', *Calendar of State Papers Foreign, Elizabeth, Volume 2: 1559–1560 (1865),* pp. 31–44.

34. 'Elizabeth: February 1560, 21–25', *Calendar of State Papers Foreign, Elizabeth, Volume 2: 1559–1560 (1865),* pp. 394–403.

35. *The Lives of the Queens of England from the Norman Conquest,* op. cit., p.164–5.

36. *A Collection of State Papers, relating to the affairs in the Reigns of King Henry VIII, King Edward VI, Queen Mary and Queen Elizabeth,* op. cit., p.368.

37. *Memoirs of the Court of Queen Elizabeth,* op. cit., p.347.

38. 'Elizabeth: June 1559', Calendar of State Papers, Scotland: volume 1: 1547–63 (1898), pp. 215–219.

39. *The Life of Queen Elizabeth,* Agnes Strickland, J. M. Dent & Co, London, 1840–48, p.154–5.

40. 'Simancas: May 1559', op. cit., pp. 64–78.

41. *Annales Rerum Gestarum Angliae et Hiberniae Regnante Elizabetha,* William Camden, 1615 & 1625.

42. 'Simancas: October 1559', op. cit., pp. 97–109.

43. British Library, MS Lansdowne 94, art.14, fol.29, copy.

44. Ibid.

45. 'First Prayer as a Creature of God', *Christian Prayers and Meditations in English, French, Italian, Spanish, Greek and Latin*, J. Day, London, 1569.

46. 'Elizabeth: June 1559, 26–30', *Calendar of State Papers Foreign, Elizabeth, Volume 1: 1558–1559 (1863)*, pp. 337–346.

47. 'Elizabeth: October 1559, 11–20', *Calendar of State Papers Foreign, Elizabeth, Volume 2: 1559–1560 (1865)*, pp. 31–44.

Chapter 6

1. *History of the Church of England from the Abolition of the Roman Jurisdiction*, Richard Watson Dixon, Volume 3: 'Edward VI AD 1549–53', George Routledge & Sons, London, 1885, p.301.

2. *Annales Rerum Gestarum Angliae et Hiberniae Regnante Elizabetha*, op. cit., p.419.

3. *Elizabeth and Leycester*, Frederick Chamberlin, Dodd, Mead & Co., 1939, p.55.

4. 'Cecil Papers: 1566', *Calendar of the Cecil Papers in Hatfield House, Volume 1: 1306–1571 (1883)*, pp. 324–342.

5. Elizabeth and Leycester, op. cit., p.85–6.

6. 'Elizabeth: August 1562, 6–10', *Calendar of State Papers Foreign, Elizabeth, Volume 5: 1562 (1867)*, pp. 215–240.

7. *The Progresses and Public Processions of Queen Elizabeth I*, John Nichols, London, 1788.

8. *Household Accounts and Disbursement Books of Robert Dudley Earl of Leicester, 1558–1561, 1584–1586*, Simon Adams (Ed), Camden Fifth series Vol. 6, CUP for the Royal Historical Society, 1995, p.155.

9. 'Venice: February 1559', *Calendar of State Papers Relating to English Affairs in the Archives of Venice, Volume 7: 1558–1580 (1890)*, pp. 24–41.

10. 'Simancas: April 1559', op. cit., pp. 46–64.

11. 'Venice: May 1559', *Calendar of State Papers Relating to English Affairs in the Archives of Venice, Volume 7: 1558–1580 (1890)*, pp. 79–94.

12. 'Simancas: April 1559', op. cit., pp. 46–64.

13. 'Venice: June 1559', *Calendar of State Papers Relating to English Affairs in the Archives of Venice, Volume 7: 1558–1580 (1890)*, pp. 94–105.

14. *Memoirs of the Court of Queen Elizabeth*, op. cit., p.281.

15. 'Venice: May 1559', *Calendar of State Papers Relating to English Affairs in the Archives of Venice, Volume 7: 1558–1580 (1890)*, pp. 79–94.

16. *Queen Elizabeth and Some Foreigners*, Victor von Klarwill, op. cit.

17. 'Elizabeth: December 1559, 6–10', *Calendar of State Papers Foreign, Elizabeth, Volume 2: 1559–1560 (1865)*, pp. 164–179.

18. 'Simancas: October 1559', op. cit., pp. 97–109.

19. Ibid.

20. 'Simancas: November 1559', op. cit., pp. 109–117.

21. *Wiltshire Archaeology and Natural History Magazine*, May, 1877.

22. 'Simancas: November 1559', op. cit., pp. 109–117.

23. Ibid.

24. 'Cecil Papers: July–December 1560', *Calendar of the Cecil Papers in Hatfield House, Volume 1: 1306–1571 (1883)*, pp. 243–256.

25. *Household Accounts and Disbursement Books of Robert Dudley, Earl of Leicester*, op. cit., p.151.

26. *Queen Elizabeth and Some Foreigners*, Victor von Klarwill, op. cit.

27. Ibid.

28. *Memoirs of the Court of Queen Elizabeth*, op. cit., p.100–1.

29. 'Elizabeth: June 1560, 16–20', *Calendar of State Papers Foreign, Elizabeth, Volume 3: 1560–1561 (1865)*, pp. 118–134.

30. *Queen Elizabeth and Her Times: A series of original letters, selected from unedited private correspondence*, Thomas Wright, Volume 1, Henry Colburn, London, 1838, p.30.

31. 'Queen Elizabeth – Volume 13: August 1560', *Calendar of State Papers Domestic: Edward, Mary and Elizabeth, 1547–80 (1856)*, pp. 157–158.

Chapter 7

1 *Household Accounts and Disbursement Books of Robert Dudley Earl of Leicester*, op. cit., p.40.

2. Ibid., p.94.

3. British Library, Harleian MS, No.4712.

4. Ibid.

5. Ibid.

6. 'Venice: May 1559', *Calendar of State Papers Relating to English Affairs in the Archives of Venice, Volume 7: 1558–1580 (1890)*, pp. 79–94.

7. 'Simancas: November 1559', op. cit., pp. 109–117.

8. *Household Accounts and Disbursement Books of Robert Dudley*

Earl of Leicester, op. cit., p.421.

9. 'Amye Robsart,' Canon J E Jackson, *Wiltshire Archaeological and Natural History Magazine*, Vol. XVII, 1878; Longleat House, Wiltshire, Dudley MS.

10. Historical Manuscripts Commission, *Diary & Correspondence of Samuel Pepys*, Volume II, 705.

11. Ibid., 703.

12. Ibid.

13. Ibid.

14. Ibid.

15. Ibid., 711.

16. 'The Death of Amy Robsart', *The English Historical Review*, Professor Ian Aird, Longman Green & Co, London, Volume LXXI, 1956, p.69.

17. *Amye Robsart and the Earl of Leycester*, George Adlard, J. R. Smith, London, 1870, p.40.

18. Historical Manuscripts Commission, *Diary & Correspondence of Samuel Pepys*, op. cit.

19. 'Simancas: September 1560', op. cit., pp. 174–176.

20. Ibid.

21. Longleat House, Wiltshire, Dudley MS, IV, 23.

22. Ibid.

23. 'Amye Robsart,' Canon J. E. Jackson, op. cit.

24. Historical Manuscripts Commission, Hatfield MSS I, 252.

25. *Amye Robsart and the Earl of Leycester*, op. cit., p.59.

26. 'Elizabeth: October 1560, 6–10', *Calendar of State Papers Foreign, Elizabeth, Volume 3: 1560–1561 (1865)*, pp. 334–352.

27. Ibid.

28. *Lord Hardwicke's State Papers*, London, 1778.

29. Ibid.

30. 'Elizabeth: December 1560, 26–31', *Calendar of State Papers Foreign, Elizabeth, Volume 3: 1560–1561 (1865)*, pp. 463–480.

31. Historical Manuscripts Commission, Salisbury MSS. 1:345046, 349–52.

32. Cambridge University Library, 'The copie of a leter wryten by a Master of Arte of Cambrige to his friend in London, concerning some talke past of late between two worshipfull and grave men, about the present state, and some procedinges of the Erle of Leycester and his friendes in England...', Paris, 1584.

33. *Queen Elizabeth and Some Foreigners*, Victor von Klarwill, op. cit.

34. British Museum, Add. MSS, 35834–6, 35841, I, 168.

Endnotes

35. 'Elizabeth: December 1560', *Calendar of State Papers, Scotland: Volume 1: 1547–63 (1898)*, pp. 495–503.

36. British Library, Hardwick Papers, I, 14 July 1561, 72.

37. *Elizabeth and Leicester*, Elizabeth Jenkins, Victor Gollancz Ltd, London, 1961, p.77.

38. 'Simancas: January 1561', op. cit., pp. 178–180.

39. Ibid.

40. Ibid., pp. 184–191.

41. 'Cecil Papers: 1561', *Calendar of the Cecil Papers in Hatfield House, Volume 1: 1306–1571 (1883)*, pp. 257–263.

42. 'Simancas: June 1561', op. cit., pp. 205–209.

43. British Library, Harleian MSS, No.6286.

44. 'Elizabeth: July 1562, 26–31', *Calendar of State Papers Foreign, Elizabeth, Volume 5: 1562 (1867)*, pp. 182–197.

45. British Museum, Add. MSS, 35830, f.212.

46. 'Elizabeth: June 1562, 1–5', *Calendar of State Papers Foreign, Elizabeth, Volume 5: 1562 (1867)*, pp. 65–74.

47. 'Simancas: June 1562', op. cit., pp. 237–249.

48. Ibid.

49. British Museum, Harleian MSS, 6990, fol.43.

50. 'Simancas: October 1562', op. cit., pp. 261–265.

51. 'Elizabeth: November 1561, 21–30', *Calendar of State Papers Foreign, Elizabeth, Volume 4: 1561–1562 (1866)*, pp. 410–423.

52. British Library, Additional MS, 32379, 'Discourses of Sir N Bacon', fol.21.

53. *A catechism written in Latin by Alexander Nowell. Together with same catechism translated into English by Thomas Norton.* Appended is a sermon preached by Dean Nowell before Queen Elizabeth at the opening of Parliament which met January 11, 1563, G. E. Corrie (Ed), Cambridge University Press 1853.

54. *Queen Elizabeth and her Times, a series of original letters*, op. cit., p.121.

55. British Library, Additional MS, 32379, 'Discourses of Sir N Bacon', fol.21.

56. *Tractatus et Literae Regum Scotiae 1448–571*, British Library, Royal MS 18, B, VI.

57. Ibid.

58. British Library, Lansdowne MS

94, art.14, fol.29.

59. 'Simancas: February 1563', op. cit. pp. 295–305.

60. *Tractatus et Literae Regum Scotiae 1448–571*, op. cit.

61. 'Addenda, Elizabeth – Volume 11: February 1563', *Calendar of State Papers Foreign, Elizabeth, 1547–65 (1870)*, pp. 535–538.

62. *Queen Elizabeth and her Times, a series of original letters*, op. cit., p.171–3.

63. Ibid., p.174–6.

64. 'Simancas: March 1563', op. cit., pp. 305–316.

65. *Memoirs of the Court of Queen Elizabeth*, op. cit., p.379–80.

66. *Robert Dudley Earl of Leicester*, Alan Kendall, Cassell, London, 1980, p.49

Chapter 8

1. *Correspondance de Bertrand de Salignac de la Mothe Fénelon*, Charles Putzon Cooper (Ed), Paris & London, 1838, Volume 5, pp.118–9.

2. 'Elizabeth: April 1565, 1–15', *Calendar of State Papers Foreign, Elizabeth, Volume 7: 1564–1565 (1870)*, pp. 326–337.

3. *History of England from the Fall of Wolsey to the Death of Elizabeth: Reign of Elizabeth*, James Anthony Froude, Volume 2, Longman, Green & Roberts, London, 1863, p 175

4. *The Life of Queen Elizabeth*, op. cit., p.208–9.

5. *Queen Elizabeth and Her Times: A series of original letters*, op. cit., pp.175–6

6. 'Cecil Papers: 1564', *Calendar of the Cecil Papers in Hatfield House, Volume 1: 1306–1571 (1883)*, pp. 288–315.

7. *The Life and Times of Elizabeth I*, Neville Williams, George Weidenfeld & Nicolson/Book Club Associates, London 1972, p.69.

8. *Fragmenta Regalia*, Sir Robert Naunton, 1641, p.9.

9. Windsor Castle, Royal; Library, Queen Elizabeth's French Psalter, last leaf.

10. *Queen Elizabeth and Her Times: A series of original letters*, op. cit., pp.208–9.

11. *The Memoirs of Sir James Melville of Halhill, containing an impartial account of the most remarkable Affairs of State during the Sixteenth Century...*, Sir James Melville, London, 1683, 97.

12. Ibid., p.101.

13. Ibid.

14. Ibid.

15. *Elizabeth and Mary Stewart*, Frederic von Raumer, London, 1836.

16. *The Memoirs of Sir James Melville of Halhill*, op. cit.

17. *Elizabeth and Leicester*, op. cit., p.124.

18. *History of England from the Fall of Wolsey to the death of Elizabeth*, James Anthony Froude, 1856–70, viii, 246.

19. 'Simancas: November 1566', op. cit., pp. 591–598.

20. The Syndics of Cambridge University Library, MS Gg.III.34, fols.208–12.

21. Ibid.

22. 'Cecil Papers: 1567', *Calendar of the Cecil Papers in Hatfield House, Volume 1: 1306–1571 (1883)*, pp. 342–352.

23. Ibid.

24. 'Simancas: August 1565', op. cit., pp. 458–470.

25. *Correspondance de Bertrand de Salignac de la Mothe Fénelon*, op. cit., Volume 1.

26. Ibid.

27. 'Cecil Papers: July–December 1570', *Calendar of the Cecil Papers in Hatfield House, Volume 1: 1306–1571 (1883)*.

28. *Correspondance de Bertrand de Salignac de la Mothe Fénelon*, op. cit.

29. Ibid.

30. *Catherine de Medici*, Leonie Frieda, HarperCollins, 2003, pp 179–80

31. *Correspondance de Bertrand de Salignac de la Mothe Fénelon*, op. cit.

32. 'Cecil Papers: January 1572', *Calendar of the Cecil Papers in Hatfield House, Volume 2: 1572–1582. (1888)*, pp. 1–10.

33. *The Lives of the Lord and Keepers of the Great Seal from the earliest times to the reign of King George IV*, John Lord Campbell, Volume 2, Lanchard & Lea, Philadelphia, 1851, p.140.

34. Two separate letters:
  * Ibid., pp.134–5.
  ** Ibid., p.135.

35. Ibid., p.142.

36. *Annals of the Reformation and Establishment of Religion and other various occurrences in the Church of England during Queen Elizabeth's Happy Reign*, John Strype, 1728, Volume 3, Chapter 30.

37. *Oxford, Son of Queen Elizabeth I*, Paul Streitz, Oxford Inst. Press, 2008

38. *The Life Story of Edward de Vere as 'William Shakespeare'*, Percy Allen, Cecil Palmer, London, 1932; *The Seventeenth Earl of Oxford, 1550–1604*, B M Ward, John Murray,

London, 1928; *This Star of England*, Charlton & Dorothy Ogburn, Coward–McCann, New York, 1952; *Shakespeare and the Tudor Rose*, Elisabeth Sears, Meadow Geese Press, Marshal Hills, MA, 2002; *The Monument*, Hank Whittemore, Meadow Geese Press, Marshal Hills, MA, 2005.

39. The Syndics of Cambridge University Library, MS Dd.V.75, fols.28r.

40. *Memoirs of the Life and Times of Sir Christopher Hatton*, Harris Nicholas, Richard Bentley, London, 1847, p.106; *Annales Rerum Gestarum Angliae et Hiberniae Regnate Elizabetha*, William Camden, op. cit.

41. 'Cecil Papers: March 1579', *Calendar of the Cecil Papers in Hatfield House, Volume 2: 1572–1582. (1888)*, pp. 234–245.

42. *Projets du Mariage de la Reine Elizabeth*, Artaud De La Ferrière, 1882.

43. *Memoires de Michel de Castelnau Seigneur de Mauvissiere et de Concressaut*, Michel de Castelnau Sieur de Mauvissière, Paris, 1621.

44. 'Cecil Papers: December 1579', *Calendar of the Cecil Papers in Hatfield House, Volume 2: 1572–1582. (1888)*, pp. 280–303.

45. *Original Letters illustrative of English History: including numerous royal letters...*, Sir Henry Ellis, Volume 2, London, 1825.

46. *The Courtships of Queen Elizabeth*, Martin Hume, McClure, Phillips & Co, New York, 1904, pp.211–2.

47. From a letter from the Duc d'Alençon to Elizabeth, which may be one of those in *Calendar of the Cecil Papers in Hatfield House, Volume 2, 1572–82*.

48. From a letter from Francis Anthony of Sousa to Diego Botelho in Antwerp in 'Elizabeth: January 1582, 21–31', *Calendar of State Papers, Foreign, Elizabeth, Vol.15, 1581–2*, pp.459–478.

49. 'Simancas: November 1581, 16–30', *Calendar of State Papers, Spain (Simancas)*, Volume 3: 1580–1586 (1896), pp. 219–229.

50. Bodleian Library, University of Oxford, MS Tanner 76, fol.94r.

Chapter 9

1. *The History of the Worthies of England*, Sir Thomas Fuller, 1662

2. *Elizabeth I: Collected Works*, Leah S Marcus, Janel Mueller, Mary Bath Rose, University of Chicago Press,

2000, p.307–8 [the original source is 'by permission of' – British Library, MS Additional 63742, fol.116r]

3. *Queen Elizabeth and Some Foreigners*, Victor von Klarwill, op. cit., pp.353–6.

4. British Library, MS Cotton Galba C.VIII, fol.27v.

5. 'Queen Elizabeth – Volume 213: July 22–31, 1588', *Calendar of State Papers Domestic: Elizabeth, 1581–90 (1865)*, pp. 508–520.

6. British Library, MS Harley 6798, art.18, fol.87.

7. 'Queen Elizabeth – Volume 215: August 12–31, 1588', *Calendar of State Papers Domestic: Elizabeth, 1581–90 (1865)*, pp. 529–541.

8. *Memoirs of Robert Carey, Earl of Monmouth*, John Boyle, Earl of Cork and Orerry (Ed), 1759.

9. Ibid.

10. *Diary of John Manningham*, British Library, MS Harleian Collection, 5353.

Chapter 10

1. 'Aphorisms', *Book One, No.XC, Novum Organon: True Directions concerning the Interpretation of Nature*, Francis Bacon, 1620.

2. '*L'Histoire Naturelle de Francois Bacon*', Pierre Amboise (translator), Sylva Sylvarum: L'Atlas Nouveau, Sir Francis Bacon, Antoine de Sommaville & Andre Soubron, Paris, 1631

3. *In Praise of Knowledge*, Francis Bacon, 1592; Discourse in Praise of his Sovereign, Francis Bacon, 1592. Possibly both were intended to be part of a masque.

4. *The works of Francis Bacon, Baron of Verulam, Viscount St Alban and Lord High Chancellor of England*, Francis Bacon, P Johnson, London, 1803, Volume 5, pp.206–8.

5. 'Journal of the House of Commons: March 1593', *The Journals of all the Parliaments during the reign of Queen Elizabeth* (1682), pp. 479–513.

6. British Museum, Additional MS 5503, fol.1.

7. Ibid.

8. Lambeth Palace Library MSS 649, fol.315.

9. Lambeth Palace Library MSS 650, fol.90.

10. Lambeth Palace Library MSS 653, fol.175.

11. *Elizabeth and Essex: A Tragic History*, Lytton Strachey, Curtis Publishing, York, 1928, p.62.

12. Lambeth Palace Library MSS

650, fol.31.

13. *Resuscitation: or bringing into public light several pieces of the works, civil, historical, philosophical and theological, hitherto sleeping, of the Right Honourable Francis Bacon, Baron of Verulam, Viscount St Alban, according to the best corrected copies*, William Rawley, 1657, p.89.

14. 'Sir Francis Bacon His Apologie', *The Works, the Letters and the Life of Francis Bacon*, James Spedding, Longmans, Volume 10, 1858–74, pp.143–4.

15. *Resuscitation*, op, cit., Supplement, p.106 ff.

16. 'Sir Francis Bacon His Apologie', op. cit.

17. Ibid., pp.149–50.

18. Ibid., p.154.

19. Ibid.

20. British Museum, Additional MSS 5503, fol.19b.

21. Ibid. fol.25b.

22. British Museum, Lansdowne MSS, XCL, fol.183.

23. *Novum Organum*, op. cit.

24. *The Temple*, George Herbert, Nicholas Ferrar, 1633.

25. *Essays*, Sir Francis Bacon, 1625, chapter 7, 'Of Parents and Children'.

26. Ibid. chapter 10, 'Of Love'.

Chapter 11

1. *Calendar of State Papers, Spain (Simancas)*, Volume 4: 1587–1603 (1899), pp. 101–118, June 1587, 16–30.

2. Ibid.

3. Ibid.

4. Ibid.

5. Ibid.

6. Ibid.

7. Ibid.

8. Ibid.

9. *The Copy of a Letter Written by a Master of Art of Cambridge*, Rouen(?), 1584 [from 1586 a.k.a. Leicester's Common Wealth].

Chapter 12

1. *Calendar of Patent Rolls, Elizabeth, Vol. 1*, p.90

2. *Calendar of Patent Rolls, Elizabeth, Vol. 2*, p.910–1

3. *Registers of Christenings, Marriages and Burials of the parish of Allhallows*, London Wall, Edward Basil Jupp & Robert Hovenden (Eds), Chiswick Press, London, 1878.

4. *The Progresses and Public Processions of Queen Elizabeth*, op. cit., Volume 1, p.116.

5. 'Simancas: April 1559', *Calendar of*

State Papers, Spain (Simancas), Volume 1, op. cit., pp. 46–64.

6. 'Venice: May 1559', *Calendar of State Papers Relating to English Affairs in the Archives of Venice, Volume 7: 1558–1580 (1890)*, pp. 79–94.

7. *Queen Elizabeth and Some Foreigners*, Victor von Klarwill, op. cit.

8. *The Queen was godmother, a) Calendar of Patent Rolls 1560–3*, pp.155–6 & 510–11; the godfathers, b) *Memoranda, historical and genealogical, relating to the parish of Kelston*, Francis J. Poynton, c.1879.

9. *Nugae Antiquae*, Dr Henry Harington, Volume 2, London, 1769, p.154.

10. *Nugae Antiquae*, Dr Henry Harington, Volume 1, London, 1769, p.22–4

11. *Nugae Antiquae*, Volume 2, op. cit., p.238–40

12. Ibid.

13. 'Queen Elizabeth – Volume 144: November 1580', *Calendar of State Papers Domestic: Edward, Mary and Elizabeth, 1547–80 (1856)*, pp. 685–689.

14. 'Sir John Harington: A Protesting, Catholique Puryton', *The Proceedings of the Bath Literary and Scientific Institution*, Gerard Harington, Volume 8, 2004.

15. *Orlando Furioso in English Heroical Verse*, John Harington, 1591.

16. *The Harington Family*, Ian Grimble, Jonathan Cape, London, 1957, pp.115–8.

17. Ibid., p.115.

18. Ibid., p.115–6.

19. *Memoirs of the Court of Queen Elizabeth*, op. cit., p.423.

20. *The Epigrams of Sir John Harington*, Gerard Kilroy, Ashgate, 2009.

21. *A New Discourse of a Stale Subject called The Metamorphosis of Ajax*, Sir John Harington, 1596.

22. *Nugae Antiquae*, Volume 2, op. cit., p.241.

23. Ibid., p.242.

24. *Nugae Antiquae*, Volume 1, op. cit., pp.32–9.

25. Ibid., p.40.

26. *Nugae Antiquae*, Volume 1, op. cit., pp.216.

27. Ibid., pp.216–7.

28. Ibid., p.40.

29. Ibid.

30. Ibid.

31. Ibid., pp.1–4–5

32. Ibid., pp.46–7.

33. Ibid.

34. Ibid.

35. *The Harington Family*, Ian Grimble, op. cit., pp.134–5.

36. Ibid.

37. a) *Tract on the Succession to the Crown*, Sir John Harington, 1602; b) *The Copy of a Letter Written by a Master of Art of Cambridge*, op. cit.

38. *Nugae Antiquae*, Volume 1, op. cit., p.48.

39. *Nugae Antiquae*, Volume 2, op. cit., pp.101–3.

40. Ibid., pp.84–5.

41. *The Harington Family*, Ian Grimble, Jonathan Cape, London, 1957, pp.141–2.

42. *Nugae Antiquae*, Volume 2, op. cit., pp.104–7.

43. Ibid.

44. Ibid.

Chapter 13

1. British Museum, Harleian 6455, 1633, f.38.

2. *Elizabeth and Sixtus: A Seventeenth Century Sidelight on the Spanish Armada*, H Kendra Baker, The C. W. Daniel Company, London, 1938, p.19.

3. *Memoirs of the Court of Queen Elizabeth*, op. cit., p.238–40.

4. 'Spurious Apophthegms No.12', *A Collection of Apothegms New and Old, by the Right Honourable Francis Bacon, Baron of Verulam, Viscount St Alban*, London 1661.

5. *The Life and Times of Elizabeth I*, Neville Williams, George Weidenfeld & Nicolson, London 1972, p.192.

6. 'Essex', *Fragmenta Regalia, or Observations on the late Queen Elizabeth, her Times and Favourites*, Sir Robert Naunton, 1641.

7. Ibid.

8. Hatfield Papers, Part 3, 966.

9. *Queen Elizabeth: Various Scenes and Events in the Life of Her Majesty*, Gladys Edson Locke, Sherman French, Boston, 1913, pp.251–2.

10. *Lives and Letters of the Earls of Essex*, W. B. Devereux, London, 1853, I:345.

11. *Elizabeth I: The Word of a Prince*, Maria Perry, The Folio Society, London, 1990, p.299

12. *Memoirs of the Court of Queen Elizabeth*, op. cit., p.393

13. 'Queen Elizabeth – Volume 264: July 1597', *Calendar of State Papers Domestic: Elizabeth, 1595–97 (1869)*, pp. 447–484.

14. *Nugae Antiquae*, Volume 1, op. cit., pp.75–7.

15. *The Life and Times of Elizabeth I*, Neville Williams, George Weidenfeld & Nicolson, London 1972, p.200

16. *Nugae Antiquae*, Volume 2, op. cit., p.124.

17. 'Elizabeth I: Volume 205: July 1599', *Calendar of State Papers, Ireland, 1599–1600 (1899)*, pp. 76–111.

18. 'Elizabeth I: Volume 205: September 1599', *Calendar of State Papers, Ireland, 1599–1600 (1899)*, pp. 142–169.

19. Ibid.

20. Lambeth Palace Library, Carew Papers MS 601, f.142 10.

21. *Prerogative of Parliaments in England*, Sir Walter Ralegh, London, 1661

22. *Tudor Problems, being Essays on the Historical and Literary Claims, Ciphered and Otherwise indicated by Francis Bacon, William Rawley, Sir William Dugdale and Others, in Certain Printed Books during the Sixteenth and Seventeenth Centuries*, Parker Woodward, Gay & Hancock, London, 1912.

23. 'Historical Memoranda of John Stowe: General, 1564–7', *Three fifteenth-century chronicles: With historical memoranda by John Stowe* (1880), pp. 128–147.

24. *Reliquiae Wottonianae*, Sir Henry Wotton, 1615, p.173.

ELIZABETH I

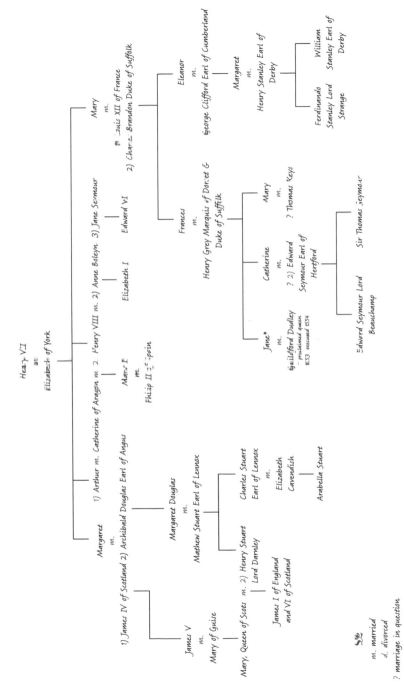

Henry VII
m.
Elizabeth of York

Margaret   1) Arthur m. Catherine of Aragon m. 2 Henry VIII m. 2) Anne Boleyn 3) Jane Seymour   Mary
m.   m.
1) James IV of Scotland 2) Archibald Douglas Earl of Angus   1) Louis XII of France
                                              Mary I   Elizabeth I   Edward VI   2) Charles Brandon, Duke of Suffolk
James V   m.
m.   Margaret Douglas   Philip II of Spain
Mary of Guise   m.   Frances   Eleanor
               Mathew Stuart Earl of Lennox   m.   m.
                                                                          Henry Grey Marquis of Dorset &   George Clifford Earl of Cumberland
Mary, Queen of Scots m. 2) Henry Stuart   Charles Stuart   Duke of Suffolk   Margaret
                         Lord Darnley   Earl of Lennox   m.
                                                 m.   Henry Stanley Earl of
James I of England   Elizabeth   Jane*   Catherine   Mary   Derby
and VI of Scotland   Cavendish   m.   m.   m.
                                                                 Guildford Dudley ? 2) Edward   ? Thomas Keys   Ferdinando   William
                                            Arabella Stuart   – proclaimed queen Seymour Earl of   Stanley Lord   Stanley Earl of
                                                                 1553 executed 1554   Hertford   Strange   Derby

                                                                          Edward Seymour Lord   Sir Thomas Seymour
                                                                              Beauchamp

𝕾

m.. married
d.. divorced
? marriage in question

THE DUDLEYS

Sir Edmund Dudley
m.
1) Anne sister of Andrew Windsor Baron Windsor 2) Elizabeth, daughter of Edward Grey Viscount Lisle

- **Elizabeth**
  m.
  William Staurton Baron Staurton
  |
  Issue

- **John Dudley Duke of Northumberland**
  m.
  Jane daughter of Sir Edward Guildford

  - **Henry**
    m.
    Winifred daughter of Richard Rich Baron Rich

  - **John**
    m.
    Anne daughter of Edward Seymour Duke of Somerset

  - **Ambrose**
    m.
    1) Anne Whorwood, 2) Elizabeth Tallboys 3) Anne Russell

  - **Mary**
    m.
    Sir Henry Sidney
    |
    Issue

  - **Robert**
    m.
    1) Amy Robsart 2) ? Douglas Sheffield 3) Lettice Knollys

    - Sir Robert Dudley
      |
      Issue

    - Robert Dudley Earl of Denbigh

  - **Henry**
    m.
    Margaret Audley

  - **Guildford**
    m.
    Jane Grey

  - **Catherine**
    m.
    Henry Hastings Earl of Huntingdon

  - **Others died in infancy**

- **Sir Andrew Dudley**

- **Jerome Dudley**

- **Simon Dudley**

- **Elizabeth Dudley**

🜍

m. married
d. divorced
? marriage in question

THE ROBSARTS

Robert Baron of Cannon, in Heinalt

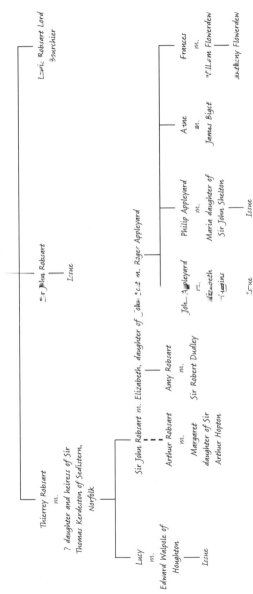

Thierrey Robsart
m.
? daughter and heiress of Sir
Thomas Kerdeston of Sedistern,
Norfolk

Sir John Robsart
Issue

Lewis Robsart Lord
Bourchier

Sir John Robsart m. Elizabeth, daughter of _dau...t... m. Roger Appleyard

Lucy
m.
Edward Walpole of
Houghton

Issue

Arthur Robsart
m.
Margaret
daughter of Sir
Arthur Hopton

Amy Robsart
m.
Sir Robert Dudley

John Appleyard
m.
Elizabeth
Twins

Issue

Philip Appleyard
m.
Maria daughter of
Sir John Shelton

Issue

Anne
m.
James Bigot

Frances
m.
William Flowerdew

Anthony Flowerdew

m. married
d. divorced
- - - illegitimate

Index

𝕾

325